ANATOMY OF A MONSTROSITY

TRUMP
ANATOMY OF A MONSTROSITY

By NATHAN J. ROBINSON

Published by:
CURRENT AFFAIRS PRESS
P.O. Box 441394
W. Somerville, MA 02144
currentaffairs.org

First U.S. Edition

Distributed on the West Coast by
WATERS & SMITH, LTD
MONSTER CITY, CA

ISBN 978-0997844771

LIBRARY OF CONGRESS CATALOG-IN-PUBLICATION DATA
Robinson, Nathan J.
Trump:
Anatomy of a Monstrosity / Nathan J. Robinson
p. cm
Includes bibliographical references and index
ISBN 978-0997844771
1. Trump, Donald J. 2. Political science 3. Elections
4. Social Philosophy 1. Title

*To all those who have had the misfortune
of sharing a planet with Donald J. Trump, and to
those who shall someday get rid of him
and everything for which he stands.*

*"We are here to help each other
through this thing,
whatever it is."*
—KURT VONNEGUT

"What kind of son have I created?"
—MARY TRUMP, mother of Donald Trump[1]

CONTENTS

TRUMP

ANATOMY OF A MONSTROSITY

How This Happened,

What It Means, and

What To Do About It

By NATHAN J. ROBINSON

CURRENT
AFFAIRS
currentaffairs.org

PREFACE

THIS IS NOT REALLY A BOOK ABOUT DONALD TRUMP AS A HUMAN
being. It is about Donald Trump as a phenomenon. It is not centrally concerned with his family history, real estate deals, or marital follies (although these receive a mention or two). Instead, it is about how Donald Trump was elected President of the United States. I am not especially interested to figure out "who Donald Trump really is," since nobody really knows. Instead, I am interested in *how Donald Trump happened*. While the first section of the book covers Trump's backstory, much of the text is concerned with analyzing the two years during which Trump navigated himself successfully to the White House, with special emphasis on how Democrats failed to stop him. I will mostly be interested in understanding how Trump managed to do what he did, and (even more importantly) figuring out what comes next.

Essays and articles about Donald Trump can be deeply tiresome and repetitive. It is frequently unclear what purpose writing about Trump actually serves. After all, political journalists and jabberers have emitted millions upon millions of words about Trump in the last two years. They have said everything that could conceivably be said, about six times over. Trump has been the subject of at least eight full-length biographies,[2] and there is an entire class of pundits who make prosperous livings issuing daily denunciations of Trump. It would seem unnecessary to add further material to the pile. What, after all, can be said about this man that isn't said constantly, and to little effect?

Actually, I *don't* think there is very much of worth left to write about Trump himself. Most of what I might seek to prove about Trump is already self-evident in this book's cover photograph: he is a raving, blustering, showboating flim-flam artist, who makes persistent loud noises and sports a risible hairdo. These facts can be proven readily, and do not require several hundred pages of meticulously-footnoted argumentation. Trump is Trump, and little more need be said.

There's a bit of a paradox here, though. Trump is simultaneously extremely easy to understand *and* rather difficult. Because Trump is a bullshit artist of the highest order, it is almost impossible to access his "true" intentions or real feelings. Any attempt to understand Trump will inevitably suffer from the problem that much about Trump is simply *unknowable.* We do not know how much he means the things he says. We do not know what he intends to do, or how he would react in particular situations. All of this will be uncovered only through our experience of his presidency.

It is tempting, then, to psychoanalyze Trump. Did his run for the presidency stem, as some have speculated,[3] from a deep desire for revenge after his humiliation by Barack Obama at the 2011 White House Correspondents' Dinner? Is his ruthlessness and ambition the product of his unrequited adoration of his father,[4] who was never impressed by even Donald's loftiest business accomplishments?

But psychoanalysis is necessarily speculative and inconclusive. Who knows what goes on within the Trump-brain? Thus instead of trying to penetrate the inner core of Trump's being, one's time is probably better spent figuring out the causes of his extraordinary rise to power. "What" and "how" questions are more fruitful than "why" questions, since "why" questions are without answer in an absurd and meaning-less universe. Why must there be a Donald Trump? God only knows. But *how can we rid the world of its Trumps?* That is a line of inquiry that may actually be useful to pursue.

In this book, I want to answer three fundamental questions: *How did it happen? What does it mean?* And *What do we do now?* The election of Trump as President left media commentators shell-shocked. Very few of them had truly appreciated that such a thing could actually happen. Many had seen 2016 as the year in which Hillary Clinton would stroll casually and confidently into the White House. When she did not, many comfortable certitudes evaporated, and American political life was thrown into utter disarray. While spending more of one's breath criticizing Trump may be senseless, there is still much more work left to do in trying to figure out *what is going on.*

Some may object to, or be disappointed by, the amount of time I spend in this book discussing the Democratic Party. But I do not feel as if it is possible to answer the question of why Donald Trump won without discussing the question of why Hillary Clinton lost. I am concerned to understand a particular political *moment* in addition to understanding a single man, and that moment was shaped just as much by the collapse of Democratic political fortunes as the ascent of Republican ones. I don't think an analysis of Trump can be useful or accurate without addressing what he is responding to and why it has worked for him. This is not, I stress, a biography of Donald Trump, but a guide to understanding the causes and meaning of his election as President of the United States.

◆　　◆　　◆　　◆

IN CONDUCTING THIS INQUIRY, I WILL ATTEMPT TO BALANCE MY OWN SET of moral and political convictions with the dispassion necessary for useful and fair-minded analysis. I will confess up front that my studies of Trump have left me with a distinctive (and unfavorable) impression, one which I can't hope to conceal. From my own perspective, Trump displays nearly all of the most odious tendencies in the human character. Making him the most powerful individual in the world seems, to understate things somewhat, a decision of dubious advisability. I cannot think it will go well. I suspect a lot of people will be hurt by his presidency, and I do not like that it is happening.[5] Yet even though I feel this way, I am nevertheless capable of examining Trump analytically, and understanding his appeal. Explanation is not justification, nor does maintaining a critical perspective necessarily make one biased and unreliable.

In fact, I think I take Trump far more seriously than many of his most partisan critics. I emphasize, despite the opinions I have formed on him, the importance of not falling into the fatal trap of writing off Trump as merely stupid and laughable. Trump is a serious political figure and examinations of him should be careful. Sloppy Trump criticism only helps Trump, a point I shall return to later on.[6]

One thing it is important for Trump's detractors to realize is just how powerful Trump's personal attraction can be. He is, in some ways, mesmerizing. He is simultaneously deeply grotesque and oddly charming. He is *singular* and *compelling* even as he is being cruel and scary. If there is such a thing as "charisma," Trump assuredly possesses it. It is worth understanding these traits, and how Trump has managed to be one of the few American businesspeople to successfully convert spectacular wealth into spectacular celebrity and political power.

But let me emphasize also that while I do think some analysis of Trump can be helpful, I believe that time is better apportioned building *one's own* set of principles, and developing a compelling political *alternative* to Trump. Whatever we may *not* know about Trump, one of the things we *do* know is that negative attention is insufficient to undermine his political power. This was a lesson that should have been learned in the Bush years. It was not enough to mock and criticize Bush. One needed to destroy him. And the best way to develop a strong political opposition is to have a positive agenda that can attract broad support.

At the same time, it is important to go back over the origins of the Trump phenomenon, so that one can understand it. It is especially important to answer the question of whether Trump was *inevitable*, or whether mistakes were made by those who opposed him that enabled his rise. I am of the firm belief that his presidency was indeed preventable, and that if Democrats and leftists do certain things differently in the future, it is possible to both defeat Trumpism and make sure that it never again recurs.

This is not to say that defeating Trump is an easy business. His power is immense, and he is a far more cunning and formidable political opponent than he is usually treated as being. But anyone horrified by Trump must think seriously about what works and what doesn't, and not succumb to resignation. The only thing that makes defeat certain is a confidence in its inevitability. Whether or not optimism is warranted by the facts, it is warranted by necessity.

The future is a mysterious place. Things happen in it that nobody ever thought remotely plausible. Tell anyone in 2003, before Barack Obama's name was known outside Chicago, that within half a decade there would be a black president, and you would have been laughed at. Tell anyone in 2006, during the third season of *The Apprentice*, that within 10 years Donald Trump would be elected president, and you might have been laughed at even harder. The arc of history doesn't bend toward anything except the unexpected.

This gives strong grounds for fear and despair, but also for hope. Anything can happen, and what happens may be better or worse than anything remotely imaginable. At the height of the AIDS epidemic in the 1980s, it would have seemed extraordinary to dream of a world of antiretroviral drugs, in which HIV-positive people live long and prosperous lives. Similarly, though, in 1928, when the Nazis were still an amusing and powerless bunch of pompous street thugs, the full nightmare of the Holocaust might have seemed improbably dystopian.

History takes extraordinary turns. Which turns it takes depends on the actions and choices of human beings. Fight for a world worth living in, and one may quickly produce something extraordinarily beautiful and just. Allow hatred and violence to gestate, and one may find oneself in a world of death camps and firing squads, more desolate and inhumane than all of one's nightmares combined.

For those of us who believe in the eradication of selfishness, violence, and cruelty, the election of Donald Trump to the presidency has been unfortunate news. He is, after all, a spectacularly venal man, one who has gotten very far in life by caring about nobody but himself. His seems a strong signal that nice guys do, in fact, finish last, and that assholes get everything they want.

But assuming Trump doesn't press the nuclear button on his first few days in office, and eradicate the entire species (which is possible[7]), there's still a bit of time to put the wheels of history in reverse. Assuming people don't succumb to apocalyptic thinking, they may yet be able to undo Trump. But doing so will require some strategic thinking, some quick acting, and a greater amount of both self-criticism and solidarity than many progressives have previously shown ourselves capable of. Above all, it will require a commitment both to realizing the objective of stopping Trump, and to establishing a set of values that offers people a meaningful and constructive alternative to Trump.

I don't have any especially astounding insights into the questions I pose, about how Trump showed up and what to do about him. One of the most important lessons of the 2016 election, to me, was that people should be skeptical of claims to superior expertise and knowingness. Attempts to explain society must necessarily work from very limited data. We know so little about what kind of creatures we are and what we will do next. It's crucial, above all, to display humility in our attempts to understand and predict the direction of social and political life.

This doesn't, however, diminish the importance of *trying* to figure things out. However flawed and futile our attempts may be, they are all we have. It will never be possible to fully make sense of a seemingly senseless world. All we can do is fumble our way together in the darkness, and try our best to help each other reach the light.

INTRODUCTION:
TRUMP U

THE THEME SONG TO THE APPRENTICE, THE O'JAYS' 1973 SOUL-FUNK single "For the Love of Money," takes a cynical view of the acquisition of wealth. The title line is taken from 1 Timothy 6:10: "For the love of money is the root of all evil: which while some coveted after, they have erred from the faith, and pierced themselves through with many sorrows." The O'Jays expand on the principle, listing the various sins toward which the pursuit of financial gain may lead a person:

> For the love of money
> People will steal from their mother
> For the love of money
> People will rob their own brother
> For the love of money
> People can't even walk the street
> Because they never know
> Who in the world they're gonna beat
> For that lean, mean, mean green
> Almighty dollar, money [8]

When students arrived for their first day at Trump University, instructors were required to ensure that "For The Love of Money" would be playing in the background. It was a thoroughly fitting song. [9]

The O'Jays did not include "starting a fraudulent university to siphon elderly people's savings" on their list of things people would do for the love of money. But the story of Trump University could well have made for an extra verse.

"Trump U" (as its internal instructional manual calls it[10]) portrayed itself as a legitimate institution like any other. It boasted of its "graduate programs, post graduate programs, doctorate programs."[11] It promised students that they would learn the secrets of Donald Trump's success, and acquire the skills they needed to dominate the field of real estate. The instructors would be "hand-picked" by Donald Trump himself,[12] who was known to "drop by."[13]

But Trump University was never really about teaching students anything. Its internal manual, obtained by *Politico*, revealed that "Trump University" was an elaborate scheme designed to identify potential students' net worth and relentlessly pressure them to sign up for high-priced memberships of dubious value. Former Trump University salesman Ronald Schnackenberg said in sworn testimony that:

> *While Trump University claimed it wanted to help consumers make money in real estate, in fact Trump University was only interested in selling every person the most expensive seminars they possibly could... Based upon my personal experience and employment, I believe that Trump University was a fraudulent scheme, and that it preyed upon the elderly and uneducated to separate them from their money.*[14]

The rates charged by Trump U were extraordinary, ranging from several thousand dollars for the basic program to $35,000 for the "Gold Elite" offering.[15] Students were constantly subjected to upselling, encouraged to purchase more and more Trump University materials and packages.

In return, according to the investigations of journalist David Cay Johnston, students got almost nothing of any value, just a "scam in which the desperate and the gullible paid Trump about $40 million for what turned out to be high-pressure salesmanship."[16] The "University" was nothing of the sort. There was no campus, just a New York City address that served as the place of registration for countless "stock market swindlers, boiler room operators, and penny stock cons."[17] There were no professors; its instructors had no qualifications to speak of. One of them was a manager at a fast food joint, and two others were in personal bankruptcy.[18] As one legal complaint against the school documented, while promotional materials "portrayed Trump University as a University with an admissions process and 'Ivy League quality' rivaling Wharton Business School, Trump University was unaccredited and unlicensed to operate as an institution of higher learning."[19] It "provided no degrees, no credits, no licenses, nor anything else of marketable value to student-victims."[20]

Not only was Trump University not a university, but it had hardly anything to do with Trump, except to line his pockets. The idea that Trump "hand-picked" the instructors was a total fabrication; all of the instruction was outsourced to a third-party training company. Trump himself definitely never "dropped by." Instead, students were encouraged to have their photographs taken next to a cardboard cutout of Donald Trump.[21] It would be the closest they got to him.

To the extent that the university actually offered programming, it dispensed boilerplate advice with little actual value. Sometimes, the financial suggestions it gave students were downright dangerous. One Trump program promised to identify "five money sources and strategies that have helped thousands of students invest in real estate."[22] One of these five strategies is "credit cards." As the material says, "if a seller will take $10,000 down on a fixer-upper that you expect to make $20,000 on, why not use credit cards?"[23] Another encourages students to "borrow from your own retirement account" in order to fund their real-estate dreams.[24] Some of the advice given was downright illegal. Texas consumer protection investigators concluded that "the so-called strategies that are taught are highly speculative and may be tantamount to encouraging attendees to sell real estate without a license."[25]

One might expect students to have quickly identified Trump University as a scam. But the truly shocking aspect of the enterprise is just how systematically the company used psychologically manipulative tactics in order to convince vulnerable people to part with their money and continue signing up for courses. The Trump University "playbook" describes various ways of identifying exactly how much money people have, and figuring out how to get past their "excuses" for not spending it on Trump courses, including convincing them to take on huge amounts of debt.[26] Throughout the playbook, salespeople are encouraged to tell people, over and over, that they are failing to live their dreams, and can only achieve their dreams by handing Trump University their savings. For example, if a student objects by saying "I don't like using credit cards" or "I just paid my credit cards off," a salesperson is told to give the following reply:

> *I see, do you like living paycheck to paycheck? Do you like just getting by in life? Do you enjoy seeing everyone else but yourself in their dream houses and driving their dream cars with huge checking accounts? Those people saw an opportunity, and didn't make excuses, like what you're doing now...*[27]

If a person voiced fear of taking thousands of dollars in additional debt, salespeople were to reassure them that debt was a necessary precondition of success, then present a vision for the beautiful life people would have with the secrets Trump University would give them access to:

> *Every single company goes into debt when they are first starting out, EVERY SINGLE BUSINESS! The prof-*

its pay off the debt and before you know it, your new real-estate business will start making amazing returns. Is it worth a small investment to own your own company, finally be your own boss, and keep all the profits that you make! … Imagine having the freedom to pick up kids from school, never miss another recital or sports game again because you made the decision to not allow fear and comfort zones to hold you back anymore in life.[28]

The playbook tells instructors and salespeople that "We want to dictate what they do…Therefore, if you move quickly and give students a sense of urgency to register, they will move quickly."[29] This is called "negotiating student resistance,"[30] and it often involved a combination of bullying people about their failures and making impossible promises of the wealth and happiness that would come from partnering with Trump. Salespeople told students that they "needed to be part of the Trump family to succeed,"[31] and told them that the more money they spent, the bigger their payoffs would be. "Money is never a reason for not enrolling in Trump University," salespeople were told. "If they really believe in you and your product, they will find the money."[32] And "if they complain about the price, remind them that Trump is the BEST!! This is the last real estate investment they will ever need to make."[33]

Everything about Trump University was carefully arranged to manipulate people into parting with as much money as possible. The playbook suggests various ways of subconsciously influencing people's decision-making, including keeping the room temperature under 68 degrees and continuously congratulating people every time they take a step toward paying the university more money. People needed to be made uncomfortable, the playbook said, and "you must be very aggressive during these conversations in order to push them out of their comfort zones."[34] Part of this aggression involved telling reluctant customers that Mr. Trump would not accept their "excuses":

> *You will never get ahead in life with excuses. Mr. Trump won't listen to excuses and neither will we. Excuses will never make you more money; they will just continue to cost you more missed opportunities in life.*[35]

Thus Trump University attempted to make people feel like "losers" if they didn't take on debt, telling them that they were foolish and would never be successful. The irony, of course, is that the people with the soundest financial judgment were being treated as having the worst judgment, and Trump University was portraying the worst possible advice as the only sensible course of action. But the pitch was effective; faced with a psychologically shrewd pitch mixing carrots and sticks (promises of riches and warnings about failure), participants signed up to "create the life you've dreamed of."[36]

Furthermore, the operation deliberately preyed on the vulnerable. Salesman Ronald Schnackenberg was pressured to get people to purchase products he knew they couldn't afford:

> *Recounting his experience with one couple, which included a man who was on disability, [Schnackenberg] said, "After the hard-sell sales presentation, they were considering purchasing the $35,000 Elite program. I did not feel it was an appropriate program for them because of their precarious financial condition." Far from being commended by his bosses for his honesty, Schnackenberg said that he was reprimanded. Another salesperson then "talked them into buying the $35,000 program after I refused to sell this program to them," he testified. "I was disgusted by this conduct and decided to resign."*[37]

The Trump University operators appeared to have known that the operation would attract the attention of the authorities. "If a district attorney arrives on the scene," the playbook says, "contact the appropriate media spokesperson immediately."[38] (Staff were also warned of the dangers of prying reporters.) Indeed, the states of Texas and New York began investigating the school. In New York, the Attorney General concluded that the University had "engaged in a methodical, Systematic Series of misrepresentations."[39] The Texas Attorney General came to a similar conclusion, saying that the university implausibly promised "to teach these novices everything they need to know to be a successful residential real estate broker — in 3 days," even though "the course materials in a number of respects are simply wrong under Texas law."[40]

Angry students who had been scammed by Trump University ultimately sued the school, reaching a settlement of $25 million at the end of 2016.[41] Sherri Simpson, a single mother who paid $35,000, recalled that "All of it was just a fake."[42] Simpson said "the three-day workshop was pretty much useless" and the "mentor" she was assigned "disappeared." She went on "I'm aggravated that I lost all that money... He promised to hire the best, to hand-pick the instructors, make sure everyone affiliated with the program was the best. But he didn't do that."[43] Simpson went public to warn the country of her experience with Trump: "America, do not make the same mistake that I did with Donald Trump. I got hurt badly..."[44]

Ex-Marine Ryan Maddings had the same experience. "It was a con," Maddings told *The Daily Beast*. "I'm 25-years-old, barely making $3,000 a month and they told me to increase my credit limit. I just maxed out three credit cards and I'm supposed to be able to qualify for loans to buy real estate?"[45] Goaded by Trump's salespeople, Maddings ended up taking around $45,000 in credit card debt to purchase Trump products and seminars, later borrowing even more to finance the real estate investments he was told would make him rich. Maddings ended up in bankruptcy, and continues to pay off the debt he amassed by following the University's dubious advice.

In response to the lawsuit, Donald Trump cited the high marks the university had received in student evaluations.[46] But a *New York Times* investigation revealed that Trump U instructors had put students under intense pressure to give positive evaluations.[47] The surveys were not anonymous and the university "asked students to submit the surveys in exchange for their graduation certificates."[48] The company made it clear to instructors that they needed to obtain all "5" ratings or suffer consequences, and one student reported being told by his instructor "I won't leave until you give me all 5s."[49] Another Trump U alumnus "tried to give his Trump University teacher a poor review — but said he was talked out of it by employees of the program, who called him three times, hounding him to raise his original scores."[50] The university "applied pressure on students to offer favorable reviews... and ignored standard practices used to ensure that the surveys were filled out objectively."[51] Bob Guillo, who spent $36,000 on a Trump course, said that it was "absolutely a con," and that "the role of the evaluations was a defense against legal actions."[52]

Thus the university, while ostensibly a series of prestigious business instruction courses, was little more than theft, fleecing tens of thousands of dollars out of desperate people, giving them little in return but a piece of paper with the word "Trump" on it (plus a photo with the cutout). It promised people that it would make them great, but instead just took their money and ran. It was a story that offered telling lessons on the Trump *modus operandi...*

◆   ◆   ◆   ◆

ON THE MORNING OF NOV. 9, 2016, THE PEOPLE OF EARTH AWOKE TO a bizarre and sobering new reality. Donald J. Trump, reality television star and unconvicted sex criminal,[53] had been elected President of the United States. The fate of human civilization was now in the hands of the star of *The Apprentice,* who had been granted access to the nuclear codes.

This was, to somewhat understate things, both unexpected and concerning. Unexpected because experts and pundits had confidently predicted that Hillary Clinton would resoundingly defeat Trump on Election Day. Concerning because Trump's personality seems to define the term "unfit for office."[54] With zero experience in government, and a career in diplomacy consisting entirely of expletive-laden feuds with other celebrities, Trump was the most unusual presidential candidate in the modern history of the office. Most politicians are dull and restrained. They meticulously groom their images, making sure never to say anything that might alienate core constituencies. Trump certainly grooms his image as much as anyone else. But "alienating core constituencies" is, for Trump, almost a daily ritual. No matter what else one may think of him, he *is* a kind of anti-politician, willing to shamelessly flout the conventions of Washington decorum. Trump speaks in colorful, schoolyard language; things are "sad!" a "disaster," and "boring." People are lowlifes, crooked, losers, failures.[55]

To his supporters, this makes him a man of the people, willing to stick it to the stuffy, complacent Establishment. To his opponents, it makes him stupid and a boor, a man with the mind of a sixth-grader, the last person who should be entrusted with the formidable responsibilities of elected office. Depending on whom you ask, Trump is either a refreshing truth-teller, hated for his willingness to be honest and politically incorrect, or a crude and vulgar child, a stubby-fingered bigot who has an opinion on everything and understands nothing.

Yet Trump could be something somewhat different: neither a fool nor an honest man, but a manipulative and resourceful con artist, a person adept at tricking people into letting him have his way. Seen like this, Trump is not "telling it like it is," since he is attempting to manipulate people rather than enlighten them. But he also isn't *stupid* or *childish*. Instead, he's a cruel and deceitful man playing a stupid and childish character. If Trump is a *con man*, rather than simply a fool, he should be feared rather than simply mocked. This perspective on Trump does not mean that under all of the Twitter-insults is a brilliant, soulful, literate man. Con men are smarter than they look, but only when it comes to conning people. They're not necessarily book-smart. They just know how to get their way.

The saga of Trump University provides support for the "manipulative con man" view of Trump, rather than the "truth-telling businessman" or the "greedy idiot with a bad haircut" view. The Trump University strategy of extracting wealth was very carefully thought-out. The advice it offered may have been *bad* or *dumb* for the people receiving it, but those running the program were no dupes themselves. They knew sales, they knew manipulation. They knew, in other words, the art of the deal.

This is what Donald Trump is: a shrewd showman, who knows how to turn people's aspirations into profit. He has managed, better than anyone else, to monetize the American Dream: to reap personal benefit from people's inner desire for prosperity and power. Everyone wants to be the boss, and Donald Trump has packaged and sold the "boss" image for years. He has made his name synonymous with *being so rich you don't have to care what anybody else thinks*. And he sells ways (from neckties to diplomas) for you to make yourself feel as if you are living the same life as he is. But Trump also exposes a certain deception at the heart of the American Dream itself: when there is gross inequality, its promises are entirely illusory. You can buy knockoff Trump products that will make you feel like Trump, but you will never actually be Trump. Instead, all you're likely to end up with is debt.

Trump's own life story shows how misleading it is to think success comes largely from *merit* or *hard work*. Despite styling himself as a self-made man, he was earning a fortune from a trust fund when he was still in diapers.[56] Despite promising people that coming to his courses and putting in the work would lead to good fortune, he left them with nothing but a credit card bill. Success, it seems, depends largely on how many people you can convince to part with their savings. And *that* depends on how ruthless you're willing to be in lying to them about their chances of reaping great rewards.

This phenomenon is not confined to Trump. People all across the United States are captivated by the dream of wealth and prosperity, only to find themselves drowning in debt despite their effort and sincerity. They do everything they were told they ought to do, and yet somehow they still don't succeed. And Trump can help us understand why this is the case. He shows that there is money to be made in *convincing people* that they can make it to the top, without actually delivering on the promise. People are desperate for something to believe in, and Trump is happy to oblige them by indulging their fantasies. Trump University *explicitly* used the language of the American Dream to defraud people. Trump's salespeople would paint a picture of the wonderful lives people could have if they handed over their credit cards; they would be rich, they would be free of burdens, they would have better relationships with their kids. All they needed to do was give over everything they had.

It is fitting that one of Trump's primary investments has been in casinos. After all, casinos are the perfect embodiment of the warped Trumpian version of the Dream: they will offer you a fantastical vision of your own success, taking advantage of your hopelessness or anxiety, before leaving you with nothing. They will tantalize and betray you.

The more economically unequal the world becomes, the closer it gets to offering people this kind of cruel and hollow false promise. People are told they can succeed, if they just put in a life of hard work. But they don't succeed. Instead, they just make a small class of very wealthy people even wealthier. Thus there become two classes of people: the small group of billionaires at the top, and everyone else. And the small group of billionaires keeps telling people that if they just work harder and keep handing over their earnings, perhaps they, too, can join the billionaires.

A photograph taken in 2014 shows this contrast well.[57] It depicts a street in Mumbai, in which the emaciated and impoverished live in squalor beneath an enormous billboard advertising a new Trump Tower. On the billboard, a grinning Trump sits in an elegant wingback chair, in his gilded penthouse. The caption beneath Trump reads: "There is only one way to live—The Trump Way." Of course, the photograph demonstrates that there are, in fact, at least two ways to live: the Trump Way, and the way street children in Mumbai must live. But Trump offers people a cruel false hope, with no acknowledgment of the reality of their conditions.

Trump surely does not see his Mumbai billboard as taunting the poor, but offering them a vision of the lives they could have. We know that he has little sympathy for people who remain impoverished. As Trump says of people who experience multi-generational poverty:

> I've watched politicians bragging about how poor they are, how they came from nothing, how poor their parents and grandparents were. And I said to myself, if they can stay so poor for so many generations, maybe this isn't the kind of person we want to be electing to higher office... How smart can they be? They're morons.[58]

To Trump, then, the suffering of the poor is just a sign that they're not very smart, or haven't tried very hard. Show Trump a photo of his billboard in Mumbai, and he won't see rich and poor, he'll see a winner and a bunch of losers.

If we had to isolate the quality about Donald Trump that is most disturbing, this might be it. He appears to have very little sympathy for people who suffer misfortune. You get what you can take in this life, and if you don't end up with much, tough luck. Trump appears to believe very little in charity. Despite his prodigious wealth, his record of charitable giving is downright miserly; he has been called the "world's least charitable billionaire."[59] Tony Schwartz, who wrote *The Art of the Deal* for Trump, says that this is because Trump is so self-absorbed that he is incapable of imagining a cause beyond himself: "If your worldview is only you — if all you're seeing is a mirror — then there's nobody to give money to... Except yourself."[60]

Indeed, the Trump Foundation, to which Trump has given only sporadically over the years, has been subject to heavy criticism for making its charitable donations to... Donald Trump himself. The Foundation once spent money buying "two large portraits of [Trump], including one that wound up hanging on the wall of the sports bar at a Trump-owned golf resort."[61] And the foundation used $258,000 "to settle lawsuits that involved the billionaire's for-profit businesses."[62] The Foundation's largest-ever gift, $264,631, "was used to renovate a fountain outside the windows of Trump's Plaza Hotel."[63] (Its smallest gift ever, $7, was to the Boy Scouts, "at a time when it cost $7 to register a new Scout."[64] Trump did not reply to the *Washington Post*'s inquiry as to whether the money went to register his 11-year-old son as a Scout.)

Trump enjoys the adulation that comes with appearing charitable, however. In 1996, according to the *Post*, a charity called the Association to Benefit Children held a ribbon-cutting ceremony for the opening of a nursery school for children with AIDS. Chairs were set up on the stage for the foundation's major donors. But when the ceremony began, one of the donors' chairs was occupied by an unexpected gate-crasher: Donald Trump. As the charity's president recalled: "Trump was not a major donor. He was not a donor, period. He'd never given a dollar to the nursery or the Association to Benefit Children."[65] Yet Trump sat through the ceremony having his photograph taken, "looking for all the world like an honored donor to the cause."[66] At the end, Trump "left without offering an explanation. Or a donation."[67] The heads of the charity were baffled by Trump's act: he had showed up, taking the place of a donor and pretending to be one (and forcing the actual donor, who had given a substantial portion of the money to build the nursery, to sit in the audience), without offering a cent to their cause.

But according to the *Washington Post*'s investigation of Trump's charitable work, this is consistent with Trump's general approach. He has spent "years constructing an image as a philanthropist by appearing at charity events and by making very public — even nationally televised — promises to give his own money away," but the promises frequently go unfulfilled, and he has "sought credit for charity he had not given — or had claimed other people's giving as his own."[68] The *Post* found numerous examples of Trump vowing to give money away, including the proceeds of Trump University and his salary from *The Apprentice*, with no evidence that he had actually followed through. Furthermore, the small amount of charitable giving Trump did do "has almost disappeared entirely in recent years."[69]

Trump's combination of miserliness and self-inflation is on full display in an unusual anecdote uncovered by the *Post*, about a time when Trump dangled the promise of helping a group of schoolchildren fund a trip before ditching them and riding away in his limo:

> *[In 1997, Trump] was "principal for a day" at a public school in an impoverished area of the Bronx. The chess team was holding a bake sale... They were $5,000 short of what they needed to travel to a tournament. Trump had brought something to wow them. "He handed them a fake million-dollar bill," said David MacEnulty, a teacher and the chess team's coach. The team's parent volunteers were thrilled. Then disappointment. Trump*

then gave them $200 in real money and drove away in a limousine. Why just $200? "I have no idea," MacEnulty said. "He was about the most clueless person I've ever seen in that regard. The happy ending, he said, was that a woman read about Trump's gift in the New York Times, called the school and donated the $5,000. "I am ashamed to be the same species as this man," MacEnulty recalled her saying.[70]

In Trump's history with philanthropy, we can see the general Trump-tendencies at work: empty promises, showmanship, and the ostentatious display of riches. The Trump Foundation, Trump University, and Trump's America each display a common trait: the appearance of caring, with the reality of self-enrichment. Trump does as much as possible to convince people he is helping them out, and as little as possible to actually do so. In every single respect, Trump has perfected the art of the con.

PART ONE

Who He Is

"How can you say you love us? You don't love us!
You don't even love yourself. You just love your money."[71]
– Trump's son, DONALD JR., age 12, to his father

THE LIFE OF
TRUMP

DONALD J. TRUMP IS AN EASY MAN TO UNDERESTIMATE. HIS attention span maxes out at about twenty-six seconds,[72] and he has almost certainly never read a book in his adult life.[73] Liberals thoroughly enjoy mocking his perceived lack of intellect. *New York* magazine scoffs at him for being "stupid, lazy, and childlike,"[74] and *Salon* calls him an "idiot."[75] The common descriptors of Trump are repeated *ad nauseum:* boorish,[76] obnoxious,[77] egotistical,[78] crude,[79] bullying,[80] greedy,[81] megalomaniacal,[82] arrogant,[83] etc. He is treated as a self-evidently ridiculous figure, one whose unapologetic embrace of his own massive personal failings makes him impossible to take seriously. Trump has been the butt of thousands upon thousands of jokes, mocked widely for his ignorance, crassness, and vanity.

Since his early rise to fame in the 1980's, Trump's name has been synonymous with gaudiness and greed. Trump is the very definition of *ugly rich*, the sort of man who believes that gold-plating something increases its tastefulness, and who installs a 12-foot waterfall in his 80-foot living room (Trump does, in fact, have a 12-foot waterfall in his 80-foot living room.[84]) He is a man whose knowledge of art is limited to its value at auction, and who judges the quality of books by whether they are leather-bound. As journalist Timothy O'Brien says, he has a "lottery winners' sense of what you do when you're wealthy. You have a huge marble apartment with giant old pictures…"[85] Because Trump is "uncultured," because his idea of a "tasteful family photo-graph" is to have his wife draped sensually over a grand piano with as much leg showing as possible,[86] he is held in contempt by elites. They associate a lack of taste and formal learning with a lack of intelligence.

This may be a serious mistake. You don't get to Donald Trump's position without a certain amount of savvy. Trump may not have read a book since grade school, but he is unmatched in wiliness. It is easy to believe that Trump does not know what he is doing, simply because he seems so much like a man who does not know what he is doing. But Trump may well know more than he lets on. At the very least, he is happy to embrace his own caricature. When Trump says things like "I'm like a smart guy"[87] and speaks about his "super genius stuff,"[88] it's easy for people to mock him as woefully ignorant of his own ignorance. A certain portion of this is clearly calculated, though. Trump realizes that the more ludicrous he seems, the less his opponents think he can best them. Thus it is in his interest to appear as ludicrous as possible, thereby catching his enemies off guard. There is a certain genius to Trump's apparent madness. To a certain extent, the trick worked for George W. Bush too, a Connecticut son of Yale and Harvard who built a successful political career impersonating a Texas Good ol' Boy. There, too, the press were perfectly willing to play along, delighting in mocking Bush's intelligence without realizing they were playing his game.

It's impossible to actually figure out the answer to the question of how much "Donald Trump" is an act versus an accident. The inner workings of Donald Trump's mind remain a mystery even to veteran biographers. But we can debate how best to conceive of him, in order to take the most productive approach in dealing with him. And the right approach may well be to think of him less as a clown, and more as a bully and thief. The story of Trump is not the story of a dumb man, but the story of a merciless, mean, and conniving one.

◆   ◆   ◆   ◆

"When that kid was 10, even then he was a little shit."[89]
— CHARLES WALKER,
Donald Trump's second-grade teacher,
on his deathbed

DONALD TRUMP WAS, BY THE ACCOUNTS WE HAVE AVAILABLE, an unpleasant child. He passed his days getting into fights and throwing rocks at toddlers in playpens.[90] (One woman recalled entering her backyard to find Donald using her young son as "target practice" with stones.[91]) According to his brother Robert, "Donald was the child who would throw the cake at the birthday parties... If I built the bricks up, Donald would come along and glue them all together, and that would be the end of my bricks."[92] Neighboring children were warned to stay away from Donald,[93] because of his reputation as a bully who carried a switchblade.[94] "He was a pretty rough fellow when he was small," recalled his father.[95] Indeed, little Donald even gave his music teacher a black eye.[96] Trump was soon packed away to military school in an effort to rein him in.

A military education did not do much to alter Trump. According to his coach, Trump was "a real pain in the ass."[97] Donald "mercilessly bullied" his roommate Ted Levine, the smallest kid in the class.[98] When Levine fought back, Donald tried to throw him out a second-floor window.[99] Levine remembers that at one point, when he was attacked by Donald, "it took three people to get him off me."[100] One might consider Trump's childhood irrelevant to an assessment of Trump's present character, were it not for Trump's own declaration that "when I look at myself in the first grade and I look at myself now, I'm basically the same."[101] (Few who knew him at the time appear to dispute this.)

Trump's father Fred was infamously stern. "The old man was like a terror," recalls one of Trump's biographers. "Really tough, really demanding and cold."[102] Fred Trump's real estate business was highly successful, though he was "known neither for quality buildings nor for being a good landlord."[103] A journalist recalls telling the elder Trump that Donald was currently on a flight. "I hope his plane crashes,"[104] Trump Sr. replied bitterly.

Still, little Donny Trump was a child of privilege and comfort, inhabiting a 23-room house with nine bathrooms.[105] He had a paper route, but when it rained he would deliver the papers in a chauffeured limousine.[106] Other children who visited the Trump home were impressed by the fact that they had "a cook, a chauffeur, and an intercom system," as well as a (then-rare) color television.[107] Donny's expensive train set, with all manner of special gadgets and switches, was the envy of his neighbors.[108] "Everyone talked about the Trumps because of the house and the cars," recalls Ann Rudovsky, who lived nearby.[109]

Donald's elder brother, Fred Jr. ("Freddy"), had a difficult life. Freddy never cared for the family business, and dreamed of being a commercial airline pilot. After attending Lehigh University, Freddy joined TWA, a decision for which he incurred the relentless hectoring of his father and younger brother, who "often belittled Fred junior for [his] career choice."[110] "What is the difference between what you do and driving a bus?" Donald would ask him.[111] After years of being "bullied and bested" by Donald,[112] "emotionally crucified" for not joining the family business,[113] Fred, Jr. became an alcoholic and died at the age of forty-three. Ivana Trump believed that Freddy's early death was hastened by the cruelty of Donald and Fred, Sr.[114] For his part, according to Wayne Barrett, Donald concluded that "Fred was his example of what not to be, because Fred was too open and generous with people."[115] "Freddy just wasn't a killer," Trump said.[116]

Donald quickly distinguished himself in the family business. In 1974, alongside his father, he earned his first headline in *The New York Times* ("Major Landlord Accused of Anti-Black Bias in City"[117]). Donald took seriously his father's encouragement to be a "killer" and a "king."[118] Combining predatory ruthlessness, media-savvy bluster, and excellent market timing, Trump spent the late 70's and early 80's building an impressive roster of properties in Manhattan.

The growth of Donald Trump's reputation in New York City was stunningly rapid. By his early 30's, he was known throughout the city. Trump was charismatic, smart, flamboyant, and ambitious, and his signature hyperbolic puffery was present in his speech from his earliest days as a dealmaker in the city. As the counsel to New York's City Planning Chairman said at the time, Donald was "an incredible self-promoter... He talks, talks, talks. He makes you feel like he's making you part of the greatest deal mankind has ever had the privilege to develop and if you don't jump in with him, there's a line waiting to."[119] The attorney also noted Donald's reputation for bullshitting, politely noting that "We have a healthy sense of reserve when we approach Donald."[120]

Trump's rise was aided to a significant extent by his father's preexisting wealth. Though Trump often speaks of the "small loan" from his father (actually about $14 million[121]) with which he started his operations in Manhattan, Fred Sr. was an important source of political connections as well as cash. The elder Trump had spent decades cultivating close relationships with city officials,[122] a network of influence that Donald took full advantage of as he embarked on his own empire-building project. Trump biographer Timothy O'Brien says the idea that Fred's assistance was limited to a single million-dollar loan is "pure hokum," and that Donald's father "kept him supported" throughout his early career.[123] When the Trump Castle casino was on the brink of going under, for example, Fred stepped in and bought $3.5 million worth of chips in order to keep the business running.[124]

(This was a violation of gaming commission rules that later led to Trump being fined.[125]) O'Brien says Trump "inherited, probably conservatively, over $150 million from Fred."[126]

In the early years of Donald Trump's involvement with his father's empire, the Trump family's rental practices became notorious. Trump's father Fred even became the subject of a short poem by the folk singer Woody Guthrie, who rented from Fred, Sr. and condemned "Old Man Trump" for "stirring up" "racial hate" and "draw[ing] that color line here at his Beach Haven family project." "Beach Haven is Trump's Tower/Where no black folks come to roam," Guthrie wrote.[127] Indeed, the racial renting practices of the Trump family quickly attracted the scrutiny of the federal government, and Richard Nixon's Justice Department built a case that the Trumps were deliberately excluding blacks from their units. As Nicholas Kristof reports:

> Blacks were repeatedly dispatched as testers to Trump apartment buildings to inquire about vacancies, and white testers were sent soon after. Repeatedly, the black person was told that nothing was available, while the white tester was shown apartments for immediate rental.[128]

A former building superintendent said that "he was told to code any application by a black person with the letter C, for colored, apparently so the office would know to reject it,"[129] and the government compiled "overwhelming evidence that the company had a policy of discriminating against blacks."[130] Eventually, the Trumps were forced to settle and change their policies.

Donald was a notorious enough landlord in his own right. He "complained about having to rent properties to welfare recipients,"[131] and was ruthless in trying to get rid of rent-controlled tenants. When Trump took over 100 Central Park South, a building he intended to demolish in order to build new luxury condos, he waged a vicious war in an effort to get rid of the tenants. He sent eviction notices to everyone, battling them in court. He initiated what tenants alleged were "drastic decreases in essential services," and "persistent delay[s] in repairing defective conditions with life-threatening potential," while "instructing employees to obtain information about the private lives [and] sex habits of the tenants."[132] According to tenants, "leaks went unfixed... and broken appliances went unrepaired."[133] Trump attempted to house homeless people in vacant units, in an effort to get neighbors to leave. Trump publicly lambasted his tenants, calling them "millionaires in mink coats, driving Rolls-Royces,"[134] parasites exploiting him through rent control.

The tenants fought back for years, and eventually managed to win, remaining in their units and preventing Trump from demolishing the building. In so doing, said Tony Schwartz, they "managed to do what city agencies, colleagues, competitors, preservationists, politicians, architecture critics, and the National Football League have never managed to do: successfully stand in the way of something Donald Trump wants."[135] But while the tenants ultimately prevailed, their lawyer was impressed with Trump's tenacity in trying to drive them out, observing that "He knows how to negotiate, he knows how to use leverage and he's very perceptive about his opponent's vulnerabilities."[136] Or, as one of the tenants put it: "He has such an ego... He wants to be Jesus. He wants to be Hitler. He wants to be the most powerful thing in the world."[137]

◆   ◆   ◆   ◆

DONALD TRUMP HAS ALWAYS BEEN DISTINCT FROM OTHER REAL estate moguls, insofar as he is just as much a showman as a developer. He reminded some of "a carnival barker trying to fill his tent"[138] and Trump's ambitions were directed just as much toward the acquisition of fame as the acquisition of real estate. Part of this involved emblazoning the Trump name on every last square inch of façade. As one person who dealt with Trump recalled: "Having his name on the building was one the things Donald wanted very badly… we were able to use that to our advantage in our negotiations with him."[139] (Trump has always insisted that he does not plaster his buildings with enormous golden "Trump" letters for reasons of ego, but because doing so boosts the market value.)

Trump's pursuit of celebrity was highly successful. In 1983, he was featured on the first episode of *Lifestyles of the Rich and Famous* alongside Cher and Princess Diana.[140] The goings-on of Donald and his wife Ivana filled the tabloid press, and Trump was regularly the subject of profiles in newspapers and financial magazines. Trump launched splashy building project after splashy building project, all the while "sucking up to politicians, manipulating public opinion, [and] bullying opponents."[141]

In the process, Trump engaged in some highly questionable practices, cutting corners when necessary. In the building of Trump Tower, Trump illegally employed unauthorized Polish workers, underpaying them and forcing them to work in dangerous conditions. "We worked in horrid, terrible conditions," recalled construction worker Wojciech Kozak. "We were frightened illegal immigrants and did not know enough about our rights."[142] (They were, reports *Vanity Fair*'s Marie Brenner, "astonishingly exploited on the job."[143]) He gave false financial statements to banks to whom he was pitching projects, a deception for which he could have been prosecuted.[144] Perhaps unavoidably for a developer at the time, he did dealings with Mob affiliates.[145]

Trump was also predictably ruthless with employees:

> *He would talk to maybe fifty people, from the guy running the vacuum cleaners to the top manager, and just harass them all. He'd tell them how bad the place looked, what he thought they were doing wrong. He would call*

them all stupid and dumb. Because he terrorized and intimidated, people would go the other way when Donald Trump was on the property.[146] (Ivana Trump's reputation was similar: "Screaming at her employees" was "part of her hallmark."[147])

Mark Bowden of *Vanity Fair* confirms that when he visited with Trump, "It was hard to watch the way he treated those around him, issuing peremptory orders."[148]

Still, in his pre-*Apprentice* years, while Trump was known for arrogance and flamboyance of personality, he was not necessarily competence. Trump's time in the Atlantic City casino business was a disaster, and resulted in the repeated bankruptcy of his companies. Trump adjusted his business model over time. Timothy O'Brien notes that Trump "was a joke in between 1993 and 2003, putting his name "on mattresses and underwear and vodka and buildings" in an effort to recover from the total collapse of his empire in the early 1990's.[149] After the 1980's, Trump essentially ceased building projects of his own. Instead, Trump simply managed his brand, licensing the Trump name to skyscrapers that he has nothing to do with. He cashed in as much as possible on his name, hence the development of *Trump* magazine,[150] Trump Vodka,[151] Trump Ice Spring Water,[152] etc. Trump even sold his own line of frozen meat products through the Sharper Image, the infamous "Trump Steaks." (The steaks did not take off. Sharper Image CEO Jerry Levin calls the idea of selling steak at The Sharper Image "truly a non sequitur" to begin with, and admits that "we literally sold almost no steaks."[153])

In fact, Trump's projects may have been far more about pursuing the appearance of success than success itself. As Timothy O'Brien notes, "he's been a horrible deal-maker. His career is littered with bad deals."[154] Trump couldn't even make money in the casino business,[155] even though casinos are literally just buildings to which people come in order to fling their money into a hole.[156] More than one observer has enjoyed pointing out that Trump's endless "deals" probably cost him more money than they ever made him, and that "if Trump had just put his father's money in a mutual fund that tracked the S&P 500 and spent his career finger-painting, he'd have $8 billion."[157]

Yet while it's true that Trump has always portrayed himself as far more successful than he actually is, this is somewhat unfair to Trump. If we conclude from this that Trump is an idiot, we may misunderstand his goal. If Trump were attempting to make money, then he certainly hasn't done so in a particularly impressive or efficient way, considering the sum of his father's wealth with which he started his business life. But Trump is not necessarily pursuing money alone: he is also pursuing influence, celebrity, and power. And there have been times when Trump has made decisions that, while they do not necessarily aid him financially, certainly contribute toward the expansion of "Trump" as an international phenomenon. Trump is widely assumed to be driven by the pursuit of larger and larger gobs of money. The truth, however, may be closer to what Trump himself says at the opening of *The Art of the Deal:* "I don't do it for the money… I do it to do it."[158] Trump likes *making deals,* not running business, and frequently seems more motivated by the pursuit of *glory* than the pursuit of money. As Trump himself says, he likes *winning*, and money is just "a convenient way of keeping score."[159] Trump is certainly not frugal, but he also appears far more concerned with appearing rich than being rich. He is "the reality TV version of a successful businessman"[160] and the role seems to suit him fine.

One should perhaps not be too critical of this practice. It takes impressive skill to build up a name with such significance that people are willing to pay for the privilege of putting it on buildings. Far from representing simple desperation or laziness, Trump's licensing empire is a testament to his highly astute self-cultivation. We can laugh at Trump as a financial failure, forced to exaggerate his net worth and put his name on buildings he doesn't actually own or run. But in doing so we misunderstand his intent: Trump hasn't been seriously trying to make as much money as possible. He has been trying to become Donald Trump, the world's best-known "billionaire," America's boss. And at this, he has succeeded phenomenally.

◆   ◆   ◆   ◆

THERE IS, PERHAPS, LITTLE ELSE WORTH SAYING ABOUT TRUMP'S biography. Though the tabloid press have been obsessed with its every detail, Trump's life has not, in fact, been terribly interesting. His trajectory is by now well-known. As Carlos Lozada summarizes, Trump "came of age with the narcissism of the 1970s and made his name and fortune during the 'greed is good' 1980s. He endured a tabloid sex scandal in the 1990s and morphed into a reality-TV star in the 2000s."[161] He was born a rich person, became a richer person, lost a lot of wealth to become a somewhat less rich person, and is now an extremely rich person who will remain extremely rich for the foreseeable future. He likes golf, limos, penthouse apartments, and his Palm Beach mansion. He believes that his success is the product of his own initiative and hard work, despite inheriting a small fortune from his father. Compared with a thousand other multi-millionaires, the only thing more interesting about Trump is his unusually-shaped hair. In every other respect, he is a run-of-the-mill exemplar of the "wealth-made man," a person whose entire personality and life history have been determined by his pursuit of financial gain and social status.

A few moments in recent Trump history are nevertheless worthy of note. In 2012, Trump became a highly active user of Twitter, where he developed a reputation for being both completely bizarre and completely unfiltered. He engaged in what *The New York Times* characterized as a stream of "endless feuds, ego stroking and casual cruelty."[162] Some representative early Trump-tweets include: "Everyone knows I am right that Robert Pattinson should dump Kristen Stewart. In a couple of years, he will thank me. Be smart, Robert."[163] And: "26,000 unreported sexual assaults in the military-only 238 convictions. What did these geniuses expect when they put men & women together?"[164] Plus: "It's freezing and snowing in New York – we need global warming."[165]

Trump's Twitter account also served as a venue for his heckles and jibes at various public figures. Long before he was tweeting abuse at "Lyin' Ted" Cruz, or putting down Jeb Bush ("Jeb Bush just got contact lenses and got rid of the glasses. He wants to look cool, but it's far too late. 1% in Nevada!"[166]), Trump was perfecting the art of the 140-character insult. Of Arianna Huffington: "@ariannahuff is unattractive both inside and out. I fully understand why her former husband left her for a man- he made a good decision."[167] And to Cher, after she mentioned his "rug": "@cher—I don't wear a "rug"—it's mine. And I promise not to talk about your massive plastic surgeries that didn't work."[168]

Trump's tendency toward cruelty occasionally caused real personal pain, as when he made a nasty crack about 81-year-old actress Kim Novak:

> [Novak] was a near-recluse when friends urged her to take a chance and appear at the Academy Awards last year. Sitting at home, Donald J. Trump spotted Ms. Novak, then 81, on his television screen and recoiled at her appearance. He tapped out a message on Twitter. "I'm having a real hard time watching… Kim should sue her plastic surgeon!" To Ms. Novak, who read the message after the show, it was a devastating setback in her return to public life: She retreated to Oregon, fell into what she called "a tailspin" and refused to leave her house for days. In an open letter to her fans a few weeks later, Ms. Novak denounced Mr. Trump's tweet as bullying.[169]

Trump said he enjoyed the Twitter platform because by using it "I can let people know that they were a fraud...I can let people know that they have no talent, that they didn't know what they're doing."[170] Many of Trump's tweets were used to taunt the so-called "haters and losers" of the world, as in: *"Sorry losers and haters, but my I.Q. is one of the highest -and you all know it! Please don't feel so stupid or insecure, it's not your fault."*[171] (In fairness, Trump was always magnanimous to the haters and losers. After all, he would be generous enough to Tweet: "best wishes to all, even the haters and losers, on this special date, September 11th."[172] And as he clarified: "Every time I speak of the haters and losers I do so with great love and affection. They cannot help the fact that they were born fucked up!"[173])

◆   ◆   ◆   ◆

BUT ANY ATTEMPT TO CHART TRUMP'S LIFE TRAJECTORY CANNOT leave out the series of events that began his serious entry into United States politics: Trump's embrace of "birtherism." In 2011, Trump began to drop hints that he believed Barack Obama had not been born in the United States. "I'm starting to think that he was not born here," he said.[174] Trump relentlessly pressed the issue, suggesting that Obama was hiding something. Obama had already released his "short-form" certificate in 2008; nevertheless, Trump suggested that "he doesn't have a birth certificate, or if he does, there's something on that certificate that is very bad for him."[175] Trump gave one idea for what this might be, saying that perhaps, "where it says 'religion,' it might have 'Muslim.'"[176] Trump told Americans that if Obama "wasn't born in this country, which is a real possibility ... then he has pulled one of the great cons in the history of politics."[177]

An exasperated Obama caved to Trump later in 2011, releasing his full long-form birth certificate, which unsurprisingly showed nothing of particular interest. But Trump, after declaring victory, and even with two forms of Obama's birth certificate available, continued to bring up Obama's place of birth. In 2012, he said that an "extremely credible source" had told him that Obama's birth certificate was "a fraud."[178] He cast doubt on whether the birth certificate was really a birth certificate: "Was it a birth certificate? You tell me. Some people say that was not his birth certificate. Maybe it was, maybe it wasn't. I'm saying I don't know. Nobody knows."[179] He even dabbled in the completely conspiratorial, at one point tweeting: "How amazing, the State Health Director who verified copies of Obama's 'birth certificate' died in plane crash today. All others lived."[180]

Trump also developed an obsession with Obama's college records. He had already publicly called for hackers to "please hack Obama's college records" in order to determine whether they said he was born in the United States, or qualified for some form of international scholarship.[181] But Trump went further, and implied that Obama might not have actually qualified for admission to the Ivy League schools he attended. Trump suggested that Obama had been a "terrible student" whose grades weren't good enough to get him into Columbia and Harvard. "Let him show his records," Trump said.[182] Trump had also alleged that none of Obama's classmates could remember who he was, saying "the people that went to school with him, they never saw him, they don't know who he is. It's crazy."[183] (Scores of people who went to school with Obama begged to differ on the subject.)

Trump's campaign against Obama was unusual, even for Trump. It was Trump's first sustained political activity of any kind, and he even indicated that it was part of the reason he was considering running for president. It was unclear why Trump chose this particular issue on which to take a major stand, considering that it was largely the stuff of the conspiratorial fringe, and there was no evidence at all to support any of Trump's suspicions. One can speculate, as many have, that the issue of race hovered in the background. Trump implied that Obama was admitted to Harvard only due to affirmative action policies, that he was both unqualified and somehow undeserving. The only thing that could warrant such a suspicion was Obama's race.

Trump may have had entirely cynical motives, however. One suspects that he did not necessarily actually care particularly much about the issue, but saw it as a convenient opportunity to position himself in noisy public opposition to Obama. The embrace of birtherism could have come from a genuine concern over the veracity of Obama's claims to U.S. birth. But perhaps it is more likely that Trump recognized the possibility of advancing himself through grandstanding. After all, no amount of evidence seemed to satisfy him; Trump was determined to continue his public quest to throw the president's legitimacy into doubt, no matter what. In was only during the 2016 campaign that Trump finally admitted that Obama had been born in the United States.[184] But his 2011-2012 blitz seems to have served its purpose: it drew attention to Trump, "involving" him in politics and setting up his run for office. It also established a pattern that would continue up to his winning of the White House: no matter how many times political and media elites condemned Trump, or pointed out the offensiveness or stupidity of what he said, Trump would refuse to back down. Trump knew that the people he was speaking to, the people whose anger he was whipping up, were elsewhere. He knew that the birth certificate controversy was not a live political issue in D.C. But he also knew that there were plenty of places where it could be made into a live issue. And the people in those places get to vote, too...

"You've got to treat them like shit." [185]
—DONALD J. TRUMP, on women

TRUMP & WOMEN

I N 1989, DONALD TRUMP WAS GOING BALD. THIS TERRIFIED HIM.*
Trump has insisted that a man should never, ever go bald, and should
do everything possible to keep his hair. For Trump, this meant opting
for a "scalp reduction" surgery designed to remove the expanding hair-
less area on the back of his head. For the operation, Trump went to
Dr. Steven Hoefflin, the L.A.-based plastic surgeon who had recently
performed over $25,000 worth of cosmetic work on Ivana.

The results were not initially to Trump's satisfaction. The tight-
ening of Trump's scalp was giving him terrible headaches. Further,
Hoefflin disguised the area of the surgery by tattooing the underlying
skin to match Trump's hair color. But Trump felt as if the color was a
poor match, and believed Hoefflin had erred. "I'm going to kill you!"
Trump shouted at Hoefflin over the phone. "I'm going to sue you. I'm
going to cost you so much money. I'm going to destroy your practice."
Trump declared that he would not be paying the surgeon's bill.

But just as much as he blamed Hoefflin, Trump blamed Ivana.
Hoefflin had, after all, been her doctor, and Trump was furious at her

*NOTE: all factual statements in this passage are taken directly from Harry Hurt III, *The Lost Tycoon: The Many Lives of Donald Trump* (Echo Point Books, 2016). Hurt draws his facts about the alleged rape from Ivana's sworn deposition.

for recommending the doctor in the first place. What happened next, as described by reporter Harry Hurt III, makes for disturbing reading:

Ivana Trump has been relaxing in the master bedroom of the Trump Tower triplex thinking about the trip she will be going to take to Tahiti… Ivana has been hoping the trip will help them get over the tragedy of the helicopter crash. Suddenly, according to Ivana, The Donald storms into the room. He is looking very angry, and he is cursing out loud. "Your fucking doctor has ruined me!" he screams. The Donald flings Ivana down onto the bed. Then he pins back her arms and grabs her by the hair. The part of her head he is grabbing corresponds to the spot on his head where the scalp reduction operation has been done. The Donald starts ripping out Ivana's hair by the handful, as if he is trying to make her feel the same kind of pain he is feeling.   Ivana starts crying and screaming. The entire bed is being covered with strands of her golden locks. But The Donald is not finished. He rips off her clothes and unzips his pants. Then he jams his penis inside her for the first time in more than sixteen months. Ivana is terrified. This is not love-making. This is not romantic sex. It is a violent assault. She later describes what The Donald is doing to her in no uncertain terms. According to the versions she repeats to some of her closest confidantes, "He raped me." When The Donald finally pulls out, Ivana jumps up from the bed. Then she runs upstairs to her mother's room. She locks the door and stays there crying for the rest of the night. The next morning Ivana musters up the courage to return to the master bedroom. The Donald is there waiting for her. He leaves no doubt that he knows exactly what he did to her the night before. As she looks in horror at the ripped-out hair scattered all over the bed, he glares at her and asks with menacing casualness: "Does it hurt?"

Four years later, as Hurt prepared to publish his account, Donald Trump's lawyers would release a statement by Ivana about the incident. It read as follows:

> *During a deposition given by me in connection with my matrimonial case, I stated that my husband had raped me... O]n one occasion during 1989, Mr. Trump and I had marital relations in which he behaved very differently toward me than he had during our marriage. As a woman, I felt violated, as the love and tenderness, which he normally exhibited towards me, was absent. I referred to this as a 'rape,' but I do not want my words to be interpreted in a literal or criminal sense.*

Ivana's "disavowal," and her endorsement of her ex-husband's presidential campaign, helped keep the story from becoming a major issue during the 2016 race. But Ivana's statement from the time should be read carefully. She did not deny the specific facts that Hurt relates. In fact, she affirmed that something *did* happen, something that made her feel "violated." But she said that she did not *want* her words to be interpreted "literally" or "criminally." Keep in mind that this statement was sent by Donald Trump's lawyers. Its words are therefore very carefully chosen. Ivana could have said that none of the *facts* are correct. But instead, she said that she didn't want these to be taken as an allegation of a crime.

The story is given even further credence by the Trump Organization's comments on the matter. When *The Daily Beast* sought comment on the rape story, Trump lawyer Michael Cohen said the following:

> *You're talking about the frontrunner for the GOP, presidential candidate, as well as a private individual who never raped anybody. And, of course, understand that by*

the very definition, you can't rape your spouse... There's very clear case law.[186]

Thus when Trump's lawyer insisted that Trump never raped Ivana, he did not deny the alleged *facts*. He did not insist that Trump did not tear Ivana's hair out, or that he did not force his penis into her against her will while she sobbed. Instead, he denies that any such an act would *legally constitute rape*. (Incidentally, this is false. New York law at the time did indeed prohibit raping a spouse.[187]) Cohen said that "[s]he was not referring to it [as] a criminal matter, and not in its literal sense, though there's many literal senses to the word." But Cohen's defense was an attempt to redefine the word "rape" so as not to cover the alleged facts, instead of a denial of the facts.

Cohen's statement to *The Daily Beast* contained further attempts at deflection:

> *I will make sure that you and I meet one day while we're in the courthouse. And I will take you for every penny you still don't have. And I will come after your Daily Beast and everybody else that you possibly know... So I'm warning you, tread very fucking lightly, because what I'm going to do to you is going to be fucking disgusting. You understand me? You write a story that has Mr. Trump's name in it, with the word 'rape,' and I'm going to mess your life up... for as long as you're on this frickin' planet... I think you should go ahead and you should write the story that you plan on writing. I think you should do it. Because I think you're an idiot. And I think your paper's a joke.*

Again, Cohen did not address whether Hurt's underlying facts were correct or incorrect. The lawyer did not provide any alternate story, or contradictory claim. Instead, he simply issued a torrent of curses and threats. The public statements of both Ivana in 1993 and Trump's lawyers in 2015 therefore seemed to acknowledge that the story was, in its fundamentals, true. During Trump's presidential campaign, when the story emerged again, Ivana insisted to the press that she and Donald were now "the best of friends" and there was "no truth" to the story.[188] But the character of her original denials, and her admission that *something* did happen that felt, to her, like rape, suggest the story should be taken far more seriously than it has been. It would not be unreasonable to conclude, based on what we do know, that Trump did brutally rape his wife, out of enraged embarrassment over his botched hair loss reduction surgery.

◆   ◆   ◆   ◆

TRUMP WAS NO MORE RESPECTFUL IN THE REST OF HIS MARITAL LIFE. The alleged rape of Ivana was one part of an ongoing pattern of cruel behavior. According to Ivana, Trump "increasingly verbally abused and demeaned [her] so as to obtain her submission to his wishes and desires" as well as "humiliated and verbally assaulted" her.[189] Trump demanded submission and subservience, saying that "when I come home and dinner's not ready, I go through the roof."[190] Trump said in an interview that this was part of his philosophy, that while "psychologists" say women want to be "treated with respect," Trump himself had "friends who treat their wives magnificently, and get treated like crap in return."[191] "Be rougher," Trump told his friends, and "you'll see a different relationship."[192]

As a result, Ivana was apparently "terrified of her husband."[193] Donald belittled and berated Ivana with remarks like: "You're showing too much cleavage" and "Who would touch those plastic breasts?"[194] Trump also went out of his way to humiliate Ivana in public. "I would never buy Ivana any decent jewels or pictures," Trump said. "Why give her negotiable assets?"[195]

Trump's treatment of his wife fit with his usual pattern of behavior toward women. Trump has been overheard declaring that "you've got to treat [women] like shit,"[196] and a trail of accusers can confirm that he means what he says. Long before Trump was exposed for bragging on tape that he grabs women "by the pussy" without their consent,[197] he had been notorious for sexist and abusive behavior.

Many women have alleged outright sexual assault. Jill Harth sued Trump in 1997 for having repeatedly tried to force himself on her. When Harth and her boyfriend met Trump for dinner to talk about holding an event at a Trump hotel, Trump sent his hand crawling up her skirt and between her legs. "He was relentless," Harth recalled "I didn't know how to handle it. I would go away from him and say I have to go to the restroom. It was the escape route."[198] During the time Harth spent at the table, Trump, "spent a majority of his time talking about the breasts he sees in beauty contests."[199] Later, Harth and her boyfriend met Trump at Mar-a-Lago to sign a contract for their event. While alone with Harth, Trump, "allegedly grabbed [her] and pulled her into his daughter's empty bedroom." As she recalled, "I was admiring the decoration, and next thing I know he's pushing me against a wall and has his hands all over me… He was trying to kiss me. I was freaking out."[200] According to Harth: "I remember yelling, 'I didn't come here for this,' He'd say, 'Just calm down.'"[201] Trump later paid Harth an undisclosed sum of money as part of a lawsuit settlement in a different case, leading Harth to drop her remaining legal claims against him.[202] (She has not, however, wavered on her story.)

A seemingly endless list of other women have reported similar accusations against Trump. In the 1980s, Jessica Leeds found herself sitting next to Trump on a plane, and remembers him spending the flight trying to grope her. ("His hands were everywhere. It was an assault."[203]) Cathy Heller attended a Mother's Day brunch at Mar-a-Lago in 1997, and remembers Trump becoming angry when she would not let him kiss her on the mouth, grabbing her and forcing a kiss on the side of her face.[204] Temple Taggart McDowell, a Miss Utah USA (and registered Republican), refused to be left alone in a room with Trump after his repeated unwanted kisses and embraces.[205] Yoga instructor Karena Virginia remembers Trump grabbing her breast unprompted. When she flinched, he repeated "Don't you know who I am? Don't you know who I am?"[206]

There are more. Rachel Crooks, a receptionist in Trump Tower, was appalled when Trump approached her and kissed her directly on the mouth. ("I was so upset that he thought I was so insignificant that he could do that.") Kristin Anderson says that while sitting next to Trump on a sofa in a New York nightclub, he suddenly moved his hand up her dress and touched her vagina, leaving her "very grossed out and weirded out."[207] Mindy McGillivray told the *Palm Beach Post* that when she was 23, Trump "grabbed her ass" even as Melania Trump stood a few feet away.[208] *People* magazine reporter Natasha Stoynoff recalled that in December 2005, Trump pushed her against a wall and began "forcing his tongue down my throat."[209] (Six corroborating witnesses affirmed that Stoynoff told them about the incident at the time.[210]) Ninni Laaksonen, Miss Finland 2006, says that Trump grabbed her buttocks immediately as they waited to go on stage for *The Late Show with David Letterman*.[211] Former Miss Washington USA Cassandra Searles says Trump "grabbed her ass," and is a "misogynist" who treats women like "cattle."[212]

This is not an exhaustive list. Yet it is somewhat extraordinary that so many women have come forward to accuse Trump, particularly since Trump has threatened to sue each and every individual who goes public with a claim of sexual assault. Trump biographer Timothy O'Brien says that his reporting revealed a pattern of "violent sexual behavior" by Trump but, generally speaking, that women are "afraid to go on the record."[213] Given the sort of threats issued by Trump lawyers against *The Daily Beast*, it is no surprise that a victim might hesitate. Trump's lawyer has bragged about "destroying" the life of a young beauty queen,[214] and Trump has said he goes out of his way to make his enemies' lives miserable.[215]

Trump has insisted that every single one of these women is lying for self-interested reasons (even though many are not seeking any financial compensation) and pledged to sue them all.[216] (He has also suggested that they might be too unattractive for him to have wanted to grope.[217]) But the accounts of Trump's victims were given a significant credibility boost in October 2016, by none other than Trump himself. Caught on a hot microphone in 2005 (while his wife Melania was pregnant) chatting with *Access Hollywood* host Billy Bush,[218] Trump admitted that questions of consent matter little to him. Bush and Trump were speaking about actress Arianne Zucker, as they awaited Trump's arrival. Trump explained to Bush that his fame allowed him to do "anything" to women:

> *I better use some Tic Tacs just in case I start kissing her. I'm automatically attracted to beautiful — I just start kissing them. It's like a magnet. Just kiss. I don't even wait. And when you're a star, they let you do it. You can do anything. Grab 'em by the pussy. You can do anything.*[219]

Trump confirms the *modus operandi* reported by his accusers: he doesn't wait, he just starts grabbing and kissing. Their stories line up perfectly with his own: they say he touches women without their consent, and gets away with it because of his fame and power. He says he touches women without their consent, and gets away with it because of his fame and power.[220] Thus there should be no remaining doubt over the veracity of the allegations. Trump is an unrepentant serial sex criminal, who has been able to avoid charges thanks to his extraordinary power and his reputation as a litigious bully.

◆   ◆   ◆   ◆

IN ADDITION TO THE PHYSICAL ACTS OF AGGRESSION, AN EXTRAORDINARY torrent of verbal sexism pours forth from Trump. There is, of course, the usual patronizing stuff, such as calling every woman "hon" and "dear."[221] But this is just the beginning. When *Vanity Fair* editor Graydon Carter sat Swedish model Vendela Kirsebom next to Trump at a party, Kirsebom came to Carter after 45 minutes "almost in tears" and begging to be moved, saying "she [couldn't] handle sitting next to Trump any longer because of all of his lewd behavior."[222] According to Carter, "[i]t seems that Trump had spent his entire time with her assaying the 'tits' and legs of the other female guests and asking how they measured up to those of other women, including his wife." Kirsebom said Trump was "the most vulgar man I have ever met."[223]

Trump gave full voice to his vulgarity during a series of opinions on *The Howard Stern Show.* Of Lindsay Lohan, he says "she's probably deeply troubled, and therefore great in bed."[224] Of Kim Kardashian: "Does she have a good body? No. Does she have a fat ass? Absolutely."[225] He speculates about whether he could have "nailed" the late Princess Diana, concluding that he could have.[226] When asked if he would stay with Melania if she were disfigured in a car accident, Trump asks: "How do the breasts look?"[227]

Other public Trump remarks show the same conception of women as little more than fleshy matter to be groped and discarded. "Nice tits, no brains," he said of ex-wife Marla Maples.[228] Of his primary opponent Carly Fiorina: "Look at that face! Would anyone vote for that? Can you imagine that, the face of our next president?!"[229] Speaking about a female physician who worked at Mar-a-Lago, and asked where she had done her medical training, Trump indicated he judged her entirely by her looks:

I'm not sure... Baywatch Medical School? Does that sound right? I'll tell you the truth. Once I saw Dr.

Ginger's photograph, I didn't really need to look at her resume or anyone else's. Are you asking 'Did we hire her because she'd trained at Mount Sinai for fifteen years?' The answer is no. And I'll tell you why: because by the time she's spent fifteen years at Mount Sinai, we don't want to look at her. [230]

Some comments strayed into creepier territory, including those pondering the sexual futures of preteen girls. Of a 10-year-old girl, Trump said: "I am going to be dating her in 10 years. Can you believe it?"[231] To two 14-year-olds, Trump said: "Just think—in a couple of years I'll be dating you."[232] Trump has also imagined dating his daughter Ivanka, and openly thinks about her sexually. A former Miss Universe, Brook Lee, recalls Trump asking her: "Don't you think my daughter's hot? She's hot, right?" Lee remembers thinking: "'Really?' That's just weird. She was 16. That's creepy."[233] On other occasions, Trump has said of his daughter that she has "got the best body," and mused that "if Ivanka weren't my daughter, perhaps I'd be dating her."[234] When Ivanka was just 13 years old, Trump also reportedly asked a friend "Is it wrong to be more sexually attracted to your own daughter than your wife?"[235]

According to ex-employees on *The Apprentice*, Trump's sexism did not let up on the set of his television show, where Trump "lavishe[d] attention on the women contestants he finds attractive, makes sexist remarks, and asks the male contestants to rate the women."[236] The Associated Press interviewed 20 former employees of the show about his habitual commentary on women. As one employee recalled:

We were in the boardroom one time figuring out who to blame for the task, and he just stopped in the middle and pointed to someone and said, 'You'd f... her, wouldn't you? I'd f... her. C'mon, wouldn't you?'...

Everyone is trying to make him stop talking, and the woman is shrinking in her seat...[237]

Another remembered:

If there was a break in the conversation, he would then look at one of the female cast members, saying 'you're looking kind of hot today, I love that dress on you,' then he would turn to one of the male cast members and say 'wouldn't you sleep with her?' and then everyone would laugh... There would be about 10 or 12 cameras rolling and getting that footage, which is why everybody was like, this guy just doesn't care.[238]

Yet another:

He was always very open about describing women by their breast size. Any time I see people in the Trump organization say how nice he is, I want to throw up. He's been a nasty person to women for a long time...[239]

And a midlevel *Apprentice* producer:

He would talk about the female contestants' bodies a lot from the control room... He walked in one day and was talking about a contestant, saying, 'Her breasts were so much bigger at the casting. Maybe she had her period then.[240]

According to a former contestant:

So much of the boardroom discussion concerned the appearance of the female contestants - discussing the female contestants' looks - who he found to be hot. He asked the men to rate the women - he went down the line and asked the guys, 'Who's the most beautiful on the women's team?'[241]

A male contestant confirmed the story, telling the media that "I think it was most uncomfortable when he had one [female] contestant come around the board table and twirl around."[242] Penn Jillette, who was on the *Celebrity Apprentice*, says he "found some of the ways [Trump] used his power in sexual discussions to be a little bit distasteful to me…"[243]

Trump appears to believe that some of the women wanted this, having said that "all of the women on *The Apprentice* flirted with me - consciously or unconsciously."[244] Yet those on the show say that his behavior made people deeply uncomfortable, but that Trump's power made it impossible to stop him: "In all jobs, people have to sign sexual harassment paperwork, but Mr. Trump was putting on a TV show so he got to do it."[245]

◆   ◆   ◆   ◆

TRUMP'S BEHAVIOR WAS NO DIFFERENT WHEN HE WAS RUNNING BEAUTY pageants. When he bought the Miss Universe franchise, Trump was able to give full expression to his sentiments regarding the opposite sex. "They had a person that was extremely proud that a number of the women had become doctors," Trump said. "And I wasn't interested."[246] Instead, Trump was proud of having "made the heels higher and the bathing suits smaller."[247] (As Trump promoted his incarnation of the contest: "If you're looking for a rocket scientist, don't tune in tonight, but if you're looking for a really beautiful woman, you should watch."[248])

Notoriously, Trump made a habit of entering the contestants' changing areas while they were getting ready, in order to help himself to eyefuls of their nude and semi-nude bodies. As one remembered:

> *The black curtains opened and in walks Mr. Trump smiling. He wished us all good luck, did not stay very long*

and left. As teenagers, it no doubt caught us off guard, as the timing of the entrance could've been better and less awkward for us all.[249]

One contestant said that Trump's sudden entry was "shocking" and "creepy."[250] Trump apparently entered when "we were all naked," saying "Don't worry, ladies, I've seen it all before."[251] Looking back, a contestant found Trump's behavior "absolutely inappropriate."[252] When another contestant asked Ivanka Trump about her father's behavior, she says Ivanka replied: "Yeah, he does that."[253]

Trump did not deny entering beauty contestants' dressing rooms without their consent. In fact, he boasted about the practice on the *Howard Stern Show*:

> *I'll go backstage before a show, and everyone's getting dressed and ready and everything else... You know, no men are anywhere. And I'm allowed to go in because I'm the owner of the pageant. And therefore I'm inspecting it... Is everyone OK? You know, they're standing there with no clothes. And you see these incredible-looking women. And so I sort of get away with things like that.*[254]

Thus Trump apparently knew the women did not want him to see them naked, but knew that he could "get away with" it since he had extraordinary power as the owner of the pageant. Furthermore, he admits to doing it specifically for the purpose of staring at their bodies, even though the girls ranged in age from 15 to 19.[255]

Trump did not just ogle his contestants in states of undress, but frequently went out of his way to humiliate them. As one contestant recalled, Trump demanded that she let press photographers observe her exercising, something that made her uncomfortable: "I was about to cry in that moment with all the cameras there. I said, 'I don't want to do this, Mr. Trump.' He said, 'I don't care.'"²⁵⁶ (Trump later referred to the same contestant as "Miss Housekeeping" for being Latina, and as "Miss Piggy" when she gained weight.²⁵⁷)

But most degrading of all was Trump's practice of filtering pageant contestants according to those he found attractive and those he did not. As one reported:

> *[Trump divided] the room between girls he personally found attractive and those he did not. Many of the girls found the exercise humiliating. Some of the girls were sobbing backstage after [he] left, devastated to have failed even before the competition really began ... it was as though we had been stripped bare.*²⁵⁸

◆   ◆   ◆   ◆

DONALD TRUMP ONCE MUSED: "PEOPLE WANT ME TO [RUN FOR PRESIDENT] all the time ... I don't like it. Can you imagine how controversial I'd be? You think about [Bill Clinton] and the women. How about me with the women? Can you imagine?"²⁵⁹ Given Trump's record, it was understandable for him to feel nervous about what might come out.

But as it turns out, Trump needn't have worried. Evidently people simply do not care very much what women have to say. Trump has spent his entire career demeaning, objectifying, and assaulting women. He has admitted to entering the dressing rooms of naked 15-year-olds to gawp at their bodies. He has admitted to grabbing women's genitals without their permission. He has traumatized women, over and over, through humiliating them verbally and assaulting them physically. Woman after woman reports that whenever Trump feels like it, he simply forces his tongue into strangers' throats.

Donald Trump has even made sexism part of his brand. He pitched FOX a television show called *Lady or a Tramp,* "in which girls in love with the party life will be sent to a charm school where they will receive a stern course on debutante manners."[260] (The show never advanced past the pilot stage, but no doubt it would have provided Trump with formidable new opportunities to enter changing rooms uninvited.) He calls women "dogs" and "pigs."[261] He exhibits an obsession with the anatomical, even to the point of sexualizing his own daughter, whose "body" he can't rave about enough. He is a man to whom women are "pieces of ass,"[262] no more than the sum of their physical parts.

Trump's treatment of women has proven no obstacle to his ascent. For a moment, it seemed as if the infamous "pussy" tape might unravel his campaign. Like everything else, it didn't.

In retrospect, it was foolish to have expected it to. Trump's relations with women show that we still inhabit a world in which men are free to abuse and harass at their leisure, and that the man who grabs and kisses whomever he pleases need expect no damaging repercussions. (Not only will you not go to jail, but they might even make you President of the United States.)

The odd thing about Trump's history of demeaning and abusing women is that everybody knows it. It's on tape. There are dozens of witnesses. It's in a sworn deposition. Trump has literally confessed to grabbing women "by the pussy" whenever he pleases. He went on the radio to talk about how he has burst in on teenage girls in their changing room so he can look at them naked. And yet while all of this drew national attention over the course of a single October news cycle, it has now receded into the background. Perhaps the truest thing Donald Trump has ever said was on the Billy Bush tape: "When you're a star... you can do anything."[263]

"If you don't win you can't get away with it. And I win, I win, I always win. In the end, I always win, whether it's in golf, whether it's in tennis, whether it's in life, I just always win. And I tell people I always win, because I do."
—DONALD J. TRUMP,
QUOTED IN TRUMPNATION: THE ART OF BEING THE DONALD (2005)

WHAT TRUMP STANDS FOR

THE PEOPLE OF SCOTLAND AND THE PEOPLE OF MEXICO ARE NOT necessarily known for sharing a unique cultural and spiritual bond. But the countries are united by their mutual antipathy for a certain common enemy: Donald J. Trump, a man loathed with equal fury from Aberdeen to Zacatecas.

When Trump came to Scotland in 2006, he came bearing ambitious plans. Trump wanted to build a new golf course on a stretch of sand dunes near the northeastern town of Balmedie. Trump promised Balmedie "the greatest golf course anywhere in the world," which would come with "a 450-room hotel with a conference center and spa, 950 time-share apartments, 36 golf villas, and 500 for-sale houses, and accommodations for hundreds of full-time employees."[264] The project, Trump told them, would "pump millions of dollars into the local economy and create 6,000 jobs — maybe even 7,000 jobs."[265]

Initially, the Scots were elated. The local press were dazzled by Trump's plans, concluding that Trump's arrival in Scotland "could turn out to be as economically historic as the discovery of oil under the North Sea."[266] Trump talked of investing billions in the country, and of turning a sleepy village in the sand dunes into an internationally-renowned destination.

Some were skeptical of Trump's intentions. "Mr. Trump's promises were extremely implausible," recalled the leader of the Balmedie planning council. "The number of jobs seemed ridiculously high, and the amount of money seemed also to be implausibly large."[267] But many were anxious for investment, and resolved to give Trump whatever he wanted. The allure of thousands of jobs was too strong for people to seriously question the feasibility of Trump's proposals. A nearby university gave Trump an honorary degree, and local bagpipers stood by him as he gave press conferences from the dunes.

The golf course plans were controversial, though. Trump had proposed to build on an environmentally protected site, an ancient and unspoiled coastal area home to various species of rare birds.[268] Many locals warned that flattening the dunes to build a golf course would be a criminal desecration of a beautiful piece of Scottish wilderness. As resident David Milne describes it:

> It's the serenity… You can hear the waves, the birds, the sea. It's pretty close to being an untouched landscape – or at least it was… The dunes were a very strange and beautiful place… It was an evocative site, and isolating – there were spots where you could see nothing else. We used to walk down through the dunes every weekend, then up the beach to Newburgh. It was a perfect place to live…[269]

Because of the damage Trump's course would do to a protected site, the local planning council refused Trump permission to build the course. But Scottish ministers, concerned about the potential loss of investment, intervened to overturn the council's decision. They concluded that "the economic benefits of the project outweighed the damaging environmental effects."[270] In return, Trump "promised to set up and fund an expert group to oversee compliance with a number of legal conditions designed to protect wildlife."[271] Trump's representatives failed to attend meetings of the oversight group, and it was eventually dissolved amid controversy.[272]

Birds were not the only residents of the dunes whose habitats were threatened by Trump's golf course. Residents of Balmedie who lived near the course soon found themselves at war with Trump, who resolved to make their living situations intolerable. Michael Forbes, a farmer and salmon fisherman who lived near the course, had spent forty years living by the dunes, wandering down to the water to fish. The arrival of Trump's course obliterated Forbes' water access, with Trump's private security forces dealing strictly with any attempt to pass through the Trump land. Worse, for Forbes, Trump felt that Forbes' nearby farm was an eyesore, and wished to force him out.

"I want to get rid of that house," Trump said. "We're trying to build the greatest course in the world; this house is ugly… Nobody has a problem with it… I guess maybe the people that live in the houses [do]."[273] In interviews, Trump called Forbes' home a "pigsty," "slumlike," and "disgusting."[274] Trump had his workers install high trees in order to conceal Michael Forbes' home from the view of the golfers, as well as building an enormous wall of earth around Forbes' home. (Forbes has noted that Trump seems to have a fondness for wall-building.) Forbes and other residents, "repeatedly lost power and water supplies during the development of Trump's golf course." Local residents Susan Munro and David Milne also reported being blocked in. As Anthony Baxter documents, "At the crack of dawn one morning in 2010, the billionaire's bulldozers sprang into action and began dumping thousands of tons of earth around the [Munro and Milne] homes… after the tycoon had branded their houses ugly."[275] The construction of the course ended up contaminating the Forbes family's water supply:

The faucets began pouring sludge, their only drinkable water poisoned. Despite their pleas and increasing scrutiny from local media and officials, Trump and his people refused to repair the contaminated water line, forcing the 92-year-old Molly Forbes to collect water from a stream she carted back to her home in a wheelbarrow. For four years.[276]

The Daily Beast, in an article entitled, "Meet a 92-Year-Old Woman Whose Life Was Ruined by Donald Trump," documents Trump's total disregard for the residents (whom he has personally dismissed as living like pigs), noting that Trump is "quite content to preside over a situation whereby he is in effect denying a neighboring landowner of their legitimate supply of fresh water."[277] This, despite the fact that Trump is "legally accountable for fixing his neighbors' access to water that lies on his land—and is violating Scottish law by refusing to do so."[278] Trump's strategy in Scotland has been to simply flout the law, and bully those who question him.

Trump's security forces were particularly brutal. A photographer who went to visit Susan Munro to document Trump's attempt to box her in said she was "threatened by Donald Trump's security" and that "it was quite frightening," and they threatened to smash her camera. Munro herself was "forced to spreadeagle over the bonnet of her car by Trump security guards, while attempting to reach her home."[279] Trump's spokespeople openly swore to deal with opponents of the project "very harshly—and we will continue to be strong to anybody that stands in our way."[280]

(Trump's tactics in Scotland were not out of character. In the 1990s, Trump attempted to seize an elderly widow's home using eminent domain, planning to bulldoze it to make room for a limousine parking lot at the Trump Plaza casino.[281] Trump pursued the widow, Vera Coking, in court for years, in an attempt to seize and flatten her house.

"He doesn't have no heart, that man," Coking said of Trump, calling him "a maggot, a cockroach, and a crumb."[282])

The Balmedie development itself produced few of the anticipated benefits. Years later, having bulldozed the dunes and intimidated the neighbors, Trump's resort "employs fewer than 100 people and has lost millions of pounds since it opened."[283] According to the *Washington Post*, the course is "lonely and desolate," having attracted "no major tournaments," and with a parking lot that is "rarely, if ever, full."[284] Officials had allowed Trump to flatten an environmentally protected area because the benefits Trump promised to the region outweighed the anticipated cost in damage to rare coastal habitats. But the benefits turned out to be illusory.

As a result of Trump's swindle, public opinion in Scotland turned strongly against him. Robert Gordon University revoked the honorary degree they had given him.[285] For taking on Trump, Michael Forbes beat out tennis star Sir Andy Murray in a vote for "Scot of the Year."[286] (Forbes now flies a Mexican flag from his farm next to the golf course, as a gesture of anti-Trump solidarity.[287]) Former Scottish National Party leader Alex Salmond, who had initially championed Trump's golf course project, accused Trump of "sociopathic behavior."[288] "We welcome all Americans - minus Trump," Salmond said.[289] Filmmaker Anthony Baxter, who has made a documentary about Trump's battle against the Scots, has suggested the project was a "disaster to the environment and a callous disruption of people's lives by a ruthless one-percenter run amok."[290] Over the course of the project's development, Trump "battled with homeowners, elbowed his way through the planning process, shattered relationships with elected leaders, and sued the Scottish government," but "has yet to fulfill the lofty promises he made."[291]

David Milne concludes that the golf course project ruined something irreplaceable: "It was a perfect place to live... It was a unique and valuable wilderness, valuable to Scotland, to the UK and to those of us who live here. This development is a tragedy."[292] 92-year-old Molly

Forbes, whose water was cut off and never restored, says: "He promises the world. It never happens. Never trust Trump… I pity America if he's president."[293]

◆   ◆   ◆   ◆

DONALD TRUMP'S ONGOING WAR WITH THE PEOPLE OF SCOTLAND IS a bizarre footnote in his long history of pissing people off around the world. But parts of the story are usefully illustrative of Trump's pattern of treatment toward ordinary people, and his indifference to trampling on the rights of those he sees as being of lesser social importance to himself. The Balmedie tale shows Trump at his Trumpiest: issuing grandiose false promises, calling people names, betraying trusts, preying on people's hope for his own self-enrichment. It demonstrates quite plainly how little Trump actually cares about fulfilling the promises he makes to people, or about the pain and inconvenience his schemes cause to others.

It also, incidentally, shows another common Trump trait: horrible business sense. When Trump announced the golf course's location, a puzzled local columnist called Trump's plan "fabulous news [for] knitwear manufacturers, who will make a killing when the world's top players step out on the first tee and feel as though their limbs are being sawn off by a north-east breeze that hasn't paused for breath since it left the Arctic."[294] The golf course was a failure, ruining protected land without actually producing anything of use. It is a classic Trump story: smashing everything to pieces, insulting anyone who gets in the way, and ultimately producing… nothing of worth, except massive inconvenience for anyone who isn't Trump and massive wealth for Trump himself.

Fundamentally, Trump sees other people as a means to his ends, rather than valuing them as ends in themselves. That means he doesn't mind telling them lies, and getting up their hopes, if doing so will get the result he seeks (e.g. securing planning permission, or convincing them to vote for him). But Trump has never been about the fol-low-through; every promise is just a device to secure a desired effect, rather than an actual bond of obligation. Every word Trump speaks is designed to use and manipulate people, yet they persist in being surprised when he betrays them.

◆   ◆   ◆   ◆

In one sense, "What does Donald Trump stand for?" is a question without an answer. If we are trying to figure out what Trump *believes*, we will have a difficult time. Trump's inner core is inscrutable, even to himself. Reading his books is not much of a help; Trump himself appears to have a very limited role in actually writing them (Tony Schwartz, who ghostwrote *The Art of the Deal*, says Trump had no hand whatsoever in the writing process, and limited himself to spending "a couple of hours" reading a draft of the book once Schwartz had completed it.[295]) And so much of Trump's public persona is cultivated. As he puts it:

> *I've read stories in which I'm described as a cartoon… A comic book version of the big-city business mogul with the gorgeous girlfriend and the private plane and the personal golf course…. My cartoon is real… I am the creator of my own comic book, and I love living in it.*[296]

By trying to understand what Trump "stands for," then, we are more interested in asking: "What does Donald Trump *represent*?" It's less fruitful to look at what he himself *thinks* he signifies than to look at what he does, in fact, signify. Trump, for example, would think he stands for the tasteful and elegant rather than the gilded and schlocky. He would think he stands for the humble and cautious rather than the egotistical and erratic. But his thinking it does not make it so. More productive than trying to figure out what makes Trump tick is understanding the philosophy that he has publicly espoused, the character that he has created and foisted upon us all. That character is "Donald Trump" the "comic book" super-mogul. Since the 1980's, his name has been synonymous with the ostentatious display of riches, the totally shameless embrace of an ideology of self-love and self-enrichment.

The Trump philosophy of life is simple: life is a competition. The one who gets rich wins. The ones who don't lose. It's a world of winners and losers, and Trump wants to be a winner. Wealth therefore measures worth. And to Trump, there's nothing wrong with bragging about those riches, if you've got them. Besides, perhaps, Ayn Rand (who wore a gold brooch in the shape of a dollar sign[297]), nobody has ever so openly promulgated a philosophy of wealth, selfishness, and competition.

Trump has attempted to pass this philosophy onto his own children. His son Donald Jr. recalls that before school in the morning, Trump used to tell him that only losers ever trust anyone:

> Seven o'clock in the morning, I'm going to school—hugs, kisses, and he used to say a couple things. 'No smoking, no drinking, no drugs.' I think a great lesson for any kid. But then he followed up with: 'Don't. Trust. Anyone. Ever.' And, you know, he'd follow it up two seconds later with, 'So, do you trust me?' I'd say, 'Of course, you're my dad.' He'd say, 'What did I just—' You know, he thought I was a total failure. He goes, 'My son's a loser, I guess.' Because I couldn't even understand what he meant at the time. I mean, it's not something you tell a four-year-old, right? But it really means something to him.[298]

One might be justified in believing this a perverse thing to tell a young child. But it is a logical outgrowth of Trump's core convictions, such as they are. Dylan Matthews of *Vox* suggests that Trump essentially sees the world as zero-sum and dog-eat-dog: there is a pie, and some people get more of the pie than others, and if you're getting more of it then you're a winner, and if you're getting less of it then you're a loser, and everyone is trying to stab you in the back to get a bigger piece.[299] It may be somewhat sick to tell your child they are a failure because they trust people and because they love their father. But such is Trump's view of humanity.

Perhaps, though, we can break down the Trump philosophy of life a little more, to understand where he is coming from and what it means to embrace Trump and Trumpiness. If we wish to produce an orderly classification, we can roughly divide the Trump outlook into four core qualities: ego, revenge, prejudice, and bullshit.

1. EGO

"Show me someone without an ego, and I'll show you a loser..."[300]
—DONALD J. TRUMP

IN OCTOBER OF 1989, SEVERAL OF DONALD TRUMP'S TOP CASINO executives died in a horrific helicopter accident on their way to Atlantic City, shortly after leaving Trump's office. When Trump received a phone call from a reporter informing him of the deaths, he was stunned. But in crisis, he also saw opportunity. Quickly recovering his composure, he pressed the mute button on the phone. Turning to the others in his office, Trump said: "You're going to hate me for this... But I just can't resist. I can get some publicity out of this."[301] Returning to the reporter on the phone, Trump said "You know, I was going to go with them on that helicopter..."[302]

According to "half a dozen" sources close to Trump, this is a "barefaced lie."[303] Trump had never had any plans at all to ride with the executives on the helicopter. He never flew chartered helicopters to Atlantic City, only his personal one. Nevertheless, biographer Wayne Barrett says that Trump "planted stories" in major newspapers about his supposed near-death experience, knowing that he would be sympathetically profiled. (Trump would also use the helicopter accident to justify leaving his wife a short time later.[304])

A similar instinct to see others' deaths through their implications for his own self-image was on display after 9/11. On the very day of the attacks, asked to comment on the disaster, Trump observed that with the World Trade Center gone, he himself now owned the tallest building in New York City, 40 Wall Street. Speaking to local news mere hours after the attacks, Trump said:

> *40 Wall Street actually was the second-tallest building in downtown Manhattan, and it was actually, before the World Trade Center, was the tallest, and then, when they built the World Trade Center, it became known as the second-tallest. And now it's the tallest.[305]*

(A few days later, Trump decided it was time to remind people who missed the Twin Towers that "to be blunt, they were not great buildings."[306]) The disturbing thing here is just how little Trump seems to understand or be affected by harm that comes to other people. It simply doesn't register with him that other people are people, that they suffer and die. Having three of his deputies die in a helicopter accident was an inconvenience, certainly. But as former Trump casino lieutenant John O'Donnell wrote, "It was clear to me…that Donald would not be reaching for a handkerchief at any point through this ordeal."[307] O'Donnell recalls that when Trump attended one of the executives' funerals, and saw the deceased's brother break down into uncontrollable tears while giving the eulogy, Trump observed "I could just never get up in front of people and look like such an asshole."

When O'Donnell responded: "Well, there was a lot of love in that eulogy," Trump replied "Yeah, I know. But I would never want to look like an asshole. I'd never let myself be put in that position."[308]

O'Donnell appears to have been shocked that Trump couldn't even understand *why* death would affect people, that the *only* prism through which he was capable of viewing tragedy was that of his own image. (Indeed, the eulogy Donald gave at his father's funeral only mentioned his father in passing, focusing largely on Donald's own career and upcoming real estate projects.[309])

This is the extraordinary thing about Donald Trump's ego: it is not just a devotion to self over others or a disregard of other people's lives and well-being. Fundamentally, it is a failure to comprehend that other people even truly exist other than insofar as they help or hinder the life goals of Donald Trump. Trump cannot conceive of the existence of selflessness. (He believes Mother Theresa and Jesus Christ must have had "far greater egos than you will ever understand."[310]) Hence *Trump* magazine had to have a picture of Donald Trump on the cover of every issue, since Trump would be unable to think of anything else to put on it. For Trump there is nothing, and nobody, outside of Trump.

We should note, however, that *ego* is only loosely related to *greed*. Donald Trump's obsession with himself does not necessarily entail a corresponding devotion to the pursuit of money, as is often assumed. Trump is a narcissist; that means if he had to choose between wealth and fame, he would likely choose fame. More than he likes money, he likes being in charge, and in our society the people with the most money are the people who are in charge.

The fact that Trump is ruled by ego and the desire for power has implications for how we understand him as a political operator. It means that one should not assume Trump is simply going to use the office to make a large amount of money. Trump is not necessarily *corrupt*, though one might almost wish he were. After all, corrupt leaders just want to enrich themselves. Megalomaniacs want to be worshiped. Trump is a megalomaniac. He believes he would have made "one of the greatest" Mafiosos,[311] and wants to be obsessed over.

2. REVENGE

"My motto is: Always get even.
When somebody screws you, screw them back in spades." [312]
—Donald J. Trump

Donald Trump is not a "forgive and forget" kind of guy. He has made that clear. In Trump's books and speeches, he elaborates a philosophy of merciless, unforgiving, gratuitous revenge. As he says: "Get even with people. If they screw you, screw them back 10 times as hard. I really believe it."[313] Trump realizes that this advice is unorthodox in the business world, where the usual principle is to prioritize pragmatic self-interest over petty feuding. But Trump's view is that the world is full of enemies who need to be showed what's what. As he explains:

> *There are a lot of bad people out there. And you really have to go…If you have a problem, if you have a problem with someone, you have to go after them. And it's not necessarily to teach that person a lesson. It's to teach all of the people that are watching a lesson. That you don't take crap. And if you take crap, you're just not going to do well…But you can't take a lot of nonsense from people, you have to go after them.* [314]

It may seem, from this, as if Trump has some kind of theory for why "not taking crap" is actually an effective way to serve one's self-interest;

that he screws people back ten times over *not* because he enjoys it, but because it helps build his reputation. Yet Trump will even pursue revenge at great personal and political cost to himself. When Khizr and Ghazala Khan, the parents of a deceased Muslim soldier, criticized Trump for his remarks about Islam and Muslims, Trump relentlessly attacked the family on social media and in interviews.[315] The move was deeply unwise from a public relations perspective; the gracious thing to do would be to have said "The Khans and I may disagree, but I respect their son's sacrifice" rather than Trump's strategy of insisting that he had made plenty of sacrifices of his own. But the "when they hit you, hit back harder" philosophy allows no exceptions, even for the grieving family of a dead Army captain. Trump was willing to sabotage his own reputation among military families, purely so he could continue to demonstrate that he *does not take crap.*

Trump's own descriptions of his vengeance-first philosophy make it clear that it is about little more than his own satisfaction at seeing other people get hurt. In one of his books, Trump describes how he asked a former employee to call someone she knew in order to secure a favor. When the woman refused, citing ethical concerns, Trump vowed to destroy her, seeing her unwillingness to help him as a traitorous act. As he writes: "She ended up losing her home. Her husband, who was only in it for the money, walked out on her and I was glad… I can't stomach disloyalty…and now I go out of my way to make her life miserable."[316]

When Virgin billionaire Richard Branson met with Trump, he was appalled by Trump's "vindictive streak," later writing that Trump's obsession with revenge had frightening implications for his use of political power. Branson said that over lunch, Trump "began telling me about how he had asked a number of people for help after his latest bankruptcy and how five of them were unwilling to help. He told me he was going to spend the rest of his life destroying these five people."[317] Branson was "baffled why he had invited me to lunch solely to tell me this" and left the meeting "disturbed."[318]

The actress Salma Hayek also reported encountering the Trump philosophy of "payback." At one point, Hayek told a Spanish-language radio program, Trump obtained her personal telephone number and began to call her to ask her on dates. When Hayek rebuffed Trump's advances, Trump allegedly called the *National Enquirer*, planting a story about Hayek.[319]

Trump's own family have also been on the receiving end of his vengeance. At the time Trump's father died, Trump's nephew's infant child was sick with a severe degenerative disorder, with medical bills in excess of $300,000. The nephew's family had always received health insurance through the Trump family's company. But when Trump's sister in law challenged the father's will, Donald Trump instantly canceled the health insurance as an act of retribution, leaving the sick child without coverage. "Why should we give him medical coverage?" Trump said at the time.[320] Trump's sister-in-law said that intentionally revoking the child's insurance, merely because of a property dispute, was "so shocking, so disappointing and so vindictive."[321]

Trump's "philosophy of getting even" is perhaps one of the most ominous aspects of his ascent to the presidency. When the most formidable weapon Trump had was an army of lawyers, he used them to relentlessly pursue and harass those that made critical claims about him. Now Trump has an *actual* army, the world's most powerful, and a network of tanks, missiles, prisons, prosecutors, and nuclear arms. Thanks to the precedents set by George W. Bush and Barack Obama, the American president can assassinate whomever he pleases, even American citizens, with little judicial oversight. It remains to be seen how the man who "doesn't take crap" from his critics will deploy this formidable and terrifying power. As one Trump aide put it: "Every critic, every detractor, will have to bow down to President Trump. It's everyone who's ever doubted Donald, who ever disagreed, who ever challenged him. It is the ultimate revenge to become the most powerful man in the universe."[322] For Trump, with his philosophy of "making his enemies miserable," to have become the most powerful man in the universe should probably scare the universe shitless.

3. PREJUDICE

"Laziness is a trait in blacks. It really is, I believe that." [323]
—DONALD J. TRUMP

IS DONALD TRUMP A RACIST? HE CERTAINLY WOULD VIGOROUSLY deny the charge. After all, Trump affirms racial equality in principle and (eventually) disavowed the Klan and the alt-right. And many conservatives have objected to the left's persistent attempts to apply the word to Trump. Blogger Scott Alexander has argued that calling Trump "openly racist" (as many on the left do) dilutes the meaning of the term; it "cries wolf" by failing to distinguish between Trump and, say, an actual white nationalist or neo-segregationist.[324] After all, if Trump is a racist despite professing to love people of all races, then what does it actually *mean* to be an "open racist"?

The question is complicated by Trump's seeming lack of any sincere convictions. Racists, after all, generally have a set of beliefs. Trump, caring only for himself, could be too unprincipled to qualify as racist. As biographer Wayne Barrett says: "It could be he's not an authentic racist—there's almost nothing authentic about him."[325] If we consider racism to be holding a strong sincere belief that some races are inferior to others, perhaps Trump is excused simply because he holds no sincere beliefs whatsoever other than the belief that he, Donald Trump, should be in charge.

At the same time, there is considerable evidence that Donald Trump holds a set of racial prejudices, or is at least deeply racially insensitive. He has been quoted in the press referring to "Japs" (as in "Who knows how much the Japs will pay for Manhattan prop-erty?"[326]) A former Trump casino worker recalled that "When Don-ald and Ivana came to the casino, the bosses would order all the black people off the floor. ... They put us all in the back."[327] Of accoun-tants, Trump said: "I have black guys counting my money ... I hate it. The only guys I want counting my money are short guys that wear yarmulkes all day."[328] John O'Donnell recalls that Trump "pressed him to fire [Trump's] black accountant, until the man resigned of his own accord."[329]

Of black people generally, Trump said: "Laziness is a trait in blacks. It really is, I believe that."[330] Indeed, the only black *Apprentice* win-ner, Randall Pinkett, recalls that "He described me as 'lazy'... He described my white female fellow finalist as 'beautiful.'"[331] *Celebrity Apprentice* participant Penn Jillette confirmed this, saying "the way [Trump] would address African American candidates and so on, was not the way I would."[332] Trump also continued to describe black contestant L'il Jon as an "Uncle Tom" even after the show's produc-ers begged him to stop.[333]

Black season 1 *Apprentice* contestant Kwame Jackson has publicly come out and denounced Trump:

> *I have had an over-a-decade relationship with Donald Trump... I think [he] is, at his core, racist... I was one of the first people to say 'racist.' Before, people were flirting with the idea, [saying] 'Oh he has racist tendencies' or 'Maybe he is echoing racism,' and I was like: No, actually he is a racist!*[334]

Jackson says he was appalled by Trump's infamous support for the "birther" movement, which, to many black people, was a nasty slap in the face, with its attempt to prove—after so much histor-ical struggle—that the country's first black president wasn't *really* the president at all. Trump's relations with black people had also been damaged by his 1980's campaign against the "Central Park Five," black teenagers who were falsely accused of raping a white female jogger. Trump had run a full-page newspaper at the time of the original case calling for the reinstitution of the death penalty, and reading "CIVIL LIBERTIES END WHEN AN ATTACK ON OUR SAFETY BEGINS!" "Muggers and murderers should be forced to suffer," he wrote.[335] (Usually even law-and-order types say that muggers should "face justice" rather than "be forced to suffer.") Trump contributed to a "show trial" public atmosphere that helped to convict the Five. Even after they were exonerated years later by DNA evidence, and a report from the Manhattan district attorney's office had confirmed that they almost certainly had no involvement whatsoever in the crime, Trump remained firmly convinced of their guilt, tweeting: "Tell me, what were they doing in the park, playing checkers?"[336] (As if there were zero innocuous explanations for a group of black friends to be hanging out in a park at 9pm.)

One largely forgotten Trump racial incident arose from a conflict with Native American casino owners. When Mohawk Indians announced their intention to open a casino in the Catskills, Trump went to war against them, funding a vicious ad campaign suggesting that the community should fear the arrival of Mohawks. The ad said that the casino would bring evils such as "increased crime, broken families, bankruptcies and, in the case of the Mohawks, violence,"[337] and "featured a picture of cocaine lines and drug needles and listed alleged abuses by the Mohawk Indian Nation, asking 'Are these the new neighbors we want?'"[338] A Mohawk lawyer called Trump's ads "about as racist as you can get."[339] The New York State Commission on Lobbying ultimately "fined Trump a record $250,000 and ordered him to pay for a new round of ads to apologize."[340]

◆   ◆   ◆   ◆

THEN THERE WAS ALL THE BUSINESS WITH MEXICANS AND MUSLIMS. Referring to Mexican immigrants in 2015, Trump said:

> *When Mexico sends its people, they're not sending their best. They're not sending you. They're not sending you. They're sending people that have lots of problems, and they're bringing those problems with us. They're bringing drugs. They're bringing crime. They're rapists. And some, I assume, are good people.*[341]

The statement landed Trump in serious trouble. He was widely tarred as a racist, and several companies associated with him canceled their business relationships.

Yet people on the right profess not to understand how this could be *racist* to begin with. It may not be "political correctness," they say, but it is not strictly *racism*. After all, Trump says Mexico is sending rapists, Trump isn't saying that *all Mexicans are bad*. Just the rapists. And he's not saying Obama doesn't deserve to be president because he's *black*. He's saying Obama might not have been born here.

But here's the point: Mexico *isn't* sending a bunch of rapists. There's nothing racist about saying that rapists are rapists. But Trump creates the impression that people who are *not* rapists are rapists. And he does this by singling out the country of Mexico rather than, say, Canada. Also, note Trump's use of "they're not sending you." Trump delineates a difference between the type of people "you" are and the type of people "they" are, as if Mexican immigrants are nothing like "you." His definition of "you," the American people, doesn't include the type of people who come here from Mexico. The language treats immigrants who cross the border from Mexico as uniquely crime-prone, even though their crime rates are lower than those of natural-born citizens.[342] Trump's statement about Mexicans is not *inherently* bigoted, in that it could hypothetically be factually and statistically true. But because it *isn't* factually true, it reflects an unfair and damaging set of prejudices, prejudices that view poor people from Latin American countries as being dangerous and immoral.

Trump's remarks about an Indiana-born judge of Mexican parentage, Gonzalo Curiel, were similarly prejudiced. Trump argued that Curiel could not be fair in judging the lawsuits against Trump University, because his heritage would make him take a natural dislike to Trump.[343] Here, once again, Trump shows an instinct to judge people by their demographic characteristics, and make assumptions about people based on their nationality, rather than finding out what they actually think.

Likewise, with the "birther" controversy. There's nothing racist about questioning whether *a* president is constitutionally qualified for office. But Trump singled out the first *black* president. Why should Barack Obama's heritage attract unique scrutiny? Is it simply because Obama had a parent born outside the country? Yet Trump's mother was born in Scotland, and nobody would suggest there was anything peculiar or suspicious about Trump's circumstances of birth. Obama is worthy of scrutiny because Obama is *strange*, because he seems somehow *more* foreign. And the only reason he seems *more* foreign then Trump is because Obama had a parent from Kenya rather than Scotland.

The same logic explains why Trump's attitude toward Muslims is so particularly unpleasant and unfair. Trump called for a ban on *all* Muslims entering the United States,[344] meaning that people would be *pre*-judged as suspicious solely on the basis of their demographic characteristics, the very definition of bigotry. Leaving aside the practical impossibility of Trump's suggestion (that something is impossible has never prevented Trump from advocating or attempting it), it involves reducing people to their religious faith and treating ordinary adherents of Islam as a unique threat to the world and the country.

◆   ◆   ◆   ◆

RACISM IS A SERIOUS CHARGE, AND THE WORD SHOULD BE DEPLOYED with great care. Some may be tempted to give Trump the benefit of the doubt, concluding that he is "guilty of insensitivity rather than outright bigotry."[345] But his actions and words bespeak some deep, and crude, ethnic prejudices. Not only has he said that blacks are "lazy," but he has unfairly suggested that populations of Mexican immigrants are disproportionately overflowing with rapists and drug criminals. He believes there is a difference between *those people* and *you*, even though in reality, people from all countries and of all immigration statuses are roughly similar.

Whether Donald Trump "is" a racist depends on our definition of the term: if we think a person has to believe they are a racist in order to be one, then as someone who does not think himself racist, Donald Trump cannot be racist. But if we believe that racism consists of a set of prejudiced beliefs, of a worldview defined by inaccurate and unfair stereotypes, then Donald Trump is deeply and disturbingly racist.

The issue is worth discussing in depth, because the consequences of Trump's racial attitudes are serious. Words like "delegitimize" and "dehumanize" may seem like abstract pieces of social theory. Indeed, they are, and abstractions should generally be used extremely cautiously. Ultimately, though, these words are attempts to describe real phenomena that wound people in real ways. People speak of the birther controversy "delegitimizing" Barack Obama because by eroding the soundness of his claim to the office, the birthers made him seem less like the actual president, and undermined his ability to govern. This was particularly insulting and aggravating to black Americans, who felt as if *even when* they had at last, after many years of struggle, finally managed to elect a black president, the victory was being hollowed out by a group of people who refused to accept that Obama legitimately held the office. Thus Trump, by spearheading the movement to demand Obama's birth certificate, attempted to spoil a moment of great and powerful historical significance to African Americans.

Trump's "dehumanization" of Mexican immigrants is similarly hurtful. By associating them in people's minds with rape and drugs, Trump builds a stereotype of such people as being a particularly low form of life. He doesn't treat them as the full and complex human beings they are, but as little more than a set of offenses against the laws of the nation. The truth is that Mexican immigrants are like everybody else: they run the entire spectrum of morality and character. Most are decent and kind, and work hard for their families and communities. Some are not. But when Trump looks at these people, he sees a swarm of crime and drugs. He does not see a set of mostly hopeful human beings who are trying their best to improve the lives of themselves and their loved ones. They certainly do not seem to make him think of his mother, Mary Trump, and her own journey from Scotland to Queens.

One can debate whether the term "racist" is *strategically* useful as a descriptor of Donald Trump, and whether the term has gradually lost value in conveying coherent meaning. But the debate over the *term* is secondary to the debate about the underlying facts. The fact is that Donald Trump frequently adopts cruel stereotypes about people different from himself. Whether it's that black people are lazy and make bad accountants, or that Muslims are inherently untrustworthy and belong on a registry, Trump judges people by their demographic characteristics first, rather than seeing them as individuals. By whatever word we call this tendency, it is simplistic, unfair, and dehumanizing.

4. BULLSHIT

"Give them the old Trump bullshit..." [346]
—Donald J. Trump

"Oh, he lies a great deal... But it's sheer exuberance, exaggeration. It's never about anything important." [347]
—Philip Johnson, architect

DONALD TRUMP HAS ALWAYS BEEN SET APART FROM OTHERS BY HIS willingness to engage in what has charitably been called "shameless—and totally unsubstantiated—hyperbole."[348] As he has said himself, he frequently departs from the literal truth of the matter, for the sake of successful promotion:

> *A little hyperbole never hurts... People want to believe that something is the biggest and the greatest and the most spectacular. I call it truthful hyperbole. It's an innocent form of exaggeration — and a very effective form of promotion.*[349]

Because of this proclivity for that oxymoronic guff he calls "truthful hyperbole," Trump is frequently accused of being a serial liar. But this is not quite right. For one thing, it misunderstands what lies and bullshit are, and who Trump is. In *On Bullshit*,[350] the philosopher Harry Frankfurt tells us that the difference between the liar and the bullshitter is that the liar is deliberately trying to tell us something he knows to be false. The bullshitter, on the other hand, simply does not *care* whether what he says is true or false. He will say whatever is necessary to persuade his audience. That means it will include a mixture of truth and falsehood. The bullshitter may even end up saying a lot of true things. But he doesn't say them because they're true, he says them because they work.

Donald Trump is a bullshitter. He is best classified as a bullshitter rather than a liar because *he himself* does not believe he is issuing falsehoods. He doesn't necessarily think that he's telling the truth either. What he does is find the words that will produce the effect required at any given time; he finds the most effective promotional tool. Sometimes these things are lies. Sometimes they are not. But Trump's intention is to produce consequences rather than either to deceive or enlighten. Trump will feed you whatever bullshit it takes to get your money or your vote.

Trump's usual tactic, captured in his notion of *truthful hyperbole*, is to take something with a kernel of truth, and exaggerate it *almost* to the point of being totally false, but still connected in some vague way to *something* resembling reality. As one random example among zillions, Trump claimed that Hillary Clinton "destroyed 13 iPhones with a hammer." *The Toronto Star*'s fact-checkers instantly swooped in to correct the record: in fact, it was two BlackBerries, and it was an aide, rather than Clinton herself, who did the hammering.[351] The "13 iPhones" statement is characteristic of Trump's exaggeration: every number doubles, then doubles again. If he received $400,000, he'll say he was paid $1,000,000. If 12,000 people show up to an event, he'll say it was 30,000. The architect Der Scutt, who designed Trump Tower, was once told by Trump exactly how the rhetorical tactic worked: "Give them the old Trump bullshit," Trump told Scutt. "Tell them it is going to be a million square feet, sixty-eight stories." ("I don't lie, Donald," replied the architect."[352]) Donald Trump exaggerates everything, including his net worth,[353] and always has. It has been part of his sales tactic: every building he builds is the biggest, the most beautiful, the most luxurious. Trump operates in extremes. He's going to make America the *greatest*, while Hillary Clinton is the *worst, most corrupt* politician on earth.

Technically, much of this could count in fact as lying. But the label doesn't quite fit, because it ignores the fact that many of Trump's ostensible "lies" are grounded in *something* true. Those who accuse Trump of lying often find themselves having to defend a truth that sounds *a little bit like* something Trump said, but not quite. For example, take the iPhone statement. It was treated as a "lie." But it sounds somewhat odd to say "Donald Trump is *lying* that Hillary Clinton destroyed 13 iPhones… in fact it was two BlackBerries." That's because the thing Trump has distorted is *not* the most important part of the claim. If the underlying point is that Hillary Clinton destroyed her phones, then the underlying point still stands, even if the details are off.

This is frequently the case with Trump's bullshit. *The Toronto Star* came up with a list of over 500 "lies" that Trump told on the campaign trail. But many of them are of this nature. Consider a few, with the *Star*'s responses:

> **Trump:** "Your premiums are going up 70, 80, 90 per cent and it's only going to get worse."
> **Star Fact-Check:** "ObamaCare prices are jumping, but Trump greatly overstates the hikes. Writes the *Washington Post*: "State-by-state weighted average increases range from just 1.3 percent in Rhode Island to as high as 71 percent in Oklahoma. But the most common plans in the marketplace will see an average increase of 9 percent."[354]

> **Trump:** "Worldwide, we have almost an 800 billon dollar trade deficit."
> **Star Fact-Check:** "The U.S. trade deficit was $746 billion only when services trade is excluded. Overall it was $532 billion."[355]

> **Trump:** "[Palm Beach is] probably the wealthiest community in the world."
>
> **Star Fact-Check:** "Palm Beach is nowhere near the wealthiest community in the world — it's not even the wealthiest in the United States (it's No. 3)."[356]

The *Toronto Star* made a big deal of its list of over 500 Trump "lies," and many other media outlets also latched on. It was used as evidence that Trump is a serial fabricator. But if we look at how these fact-checks operate, we can see that many of these "lies" are structured around underlying true statements. ObamaCare premiums *are* going up a lot, there *is* a very large trade deficit, and Palm Beach *is* a very wealthy place. Calling Trump a liar for these statements doesn't seem quite right. Certainly they're wrong, and untrue, and he seems not to have cared that they weren't true. But if your exchange goes like this…

> **Trump:** ObamaCare is horrible. Your premiums will go up 60, 70, 80 percent.
>
> **Democrat:** That's a *lie*! Your premiums will rise *up to* 70 percent, but a *mean* of 9 percent.

…then you are probably going to lose the audience. Trump has a gift for making exaggerations that force people to issue incredibly complicated and nitpicking defenses that do not register with people. (See, for example, Clinton's fumbling attempts to explain why she used a personal email server, or how the Clinton Foundation works.)

Of course, there *are* outright fabrications in the things Trump says. It's hard to think of *any* way in which, as Trump alleged, Barack Obama is the "founder of ISIS."[357] The rumors he spread about Obama's birth certificate were totally false and groundless. Contrary to Trump's claims, crime rates are *not* rising. And the idea that Mexico is sending America a horde of rapists is likewise false.

Trump *doesn't* actually care much about getting to the truth. As a lawyer who worked with him once observed: "Donald is a believer in the big-lie theory… If you say something again and again, people will believe you."[358] (The "big lie" theory in question—that it's better to tell a large lie than a small one—originates with Adolf Hitler. Indeed, Trump has notoriously kept a book of Hitler speeches by his bed.[359]) One can see this at work with the "Obama founded ISIS" remarks. Trump simply says it and says it, refusing to back down or qualify it, with the hopes that it catches on.

But Trump also knows how to take small truths and spin them into big bullshit.

◆   ◆   ◆   ◆

PERHAPS ABOVE ALL, THOUGH, TRUMP STANDS FOR IMPUNITY: THE notion that you can get away with absolutely anything. For his entire life, Trump has been testing to see just how many rules he can violate without facing consequences. He'll stiff his contractors, assault women, lie about his building projects, mistreat his tenants, misrepresent his past. And he knows that nothing will happen, because he's Trump. In fact, he knows that he will be rewarded. The more codes he violates, the more brazen he is in disregarding every norm of kindness, taste, and good manners, the more success he will find. It doesn't matter what people say, because ultimately, all that matters is that they're paying attention to him. Nobody can destroy him, nobody can hold him accountable. Trump stands for complete immunity from consequence.

Trump has spent his life proving definitively that if you're a white guy with a pile of money, and you throw away every ounce of your shame and decency, all of your wildest dreams can come true, and you can become as powerful as you've ever wanted to be. In the school-yard, you can throw rocks at the other kids. What are they going to do about it? When it comes to paying your workers, you can just refuse to pay. What will they do? Sue you? Good luck with that, you'll keep them tangled up in litigation for years. Do you want to find out what a woman's legs feel like? Just touch them and find out. What's she going to do, call the police? Who will believe her? Trump knows that the rules governing society are mostly matters of convention. Ultimately, they're not backed up by anything but approval and disapproval. If you don't care about experiencing disapproval, then the rules simply don't apply to you.

Trump tested this during the presidential debates. He would interrupt the other candidates over and over again. He would call them names. He would cut off the moderators. He would say things under his breath. He would lie. But Trump knew that there was nothing anybody could do about it. They weren't going to fling him off the debate stage. They weren't going to cut off his microphone. So why should he let anybody else talk? There was nothing to be gained from letting anybody else say anything. Certainly, after the fact, commentators could *criticize* him. They could give the candidates letter grades, and hand Donald Trump an "F." But why would he care about that? That F doesn't actually *mean* anything.

Donald Trump recognizes that ultimately, *you can do what you want* and generally, nobody will do anything to stop you. If you don't like the truth, why not just lie? Oh, sure, people will call you a liar. But you can just call them a liar as well, and claim they're out to get you. Then nobody will know what to believe. And you will have won. The message Donald Trump sends to every young man is as follows: if you want something, take it. If people complain, fuck 'em. Rules are for losers.

This is why the election of Trump is such an infuriating culmination to his career: it proves him right. Trump thought that he had no need to listen to experts, that there was no need to apologize for anything. And he was right. You can do whatever you want, attack whomever you want. And as long as you double down, and make sure never to show a hint of compassion or self-reflection, you'll probably win in the end. The Trump philosophy can be summarized in two words: Fuck You.

All of this reveals something just as poisonous about *society* as it does about Trump, though. Because the lesson of Trump is that assholes finish first, that the people who are the most shameless and the least empathetic rise to the top. But that can only happen in a system that *rewards* people for Trumpian behavior. If Trump *had* been held accountable for breaking the rules, then he *wouldn't* be correct in believing there are no consequences. If people had listened to the women who accused him of sexual assault, then he wouldn't have been right that his fame allowed him to get away with it. If the Scottish government had scrutinized Trump's grandiose promises more, instead of expediting his planning permission, then he wouldn't have been incentivized to lie. If we didn't live in a world that offered sociopathic, predatory, capitalistic monsters total impunity for their crimes, then sociopathic, predatory, capitalistic monsters like Donald Trump wouldn't attain positions of status and power.

WHO MADE TRUMP

"Goddamn it! We created him! We bought his bullshit!
He was always a phony, and we filled our papers with him!" [360]
—ANONYMOUS JOURNALIST, on Donald Trump

"It may not be good for America,
but it's damn good for CBS..." [361]
—LES MOONVES, CBS CHAIRMAN,
on Trump's presidential run

THE ART OF THE DEAL IS NOT A GOOD BOOK. IT IS A TEDIOUS SLOG through a series of 1970's New York real estate deals. Donald Trump describes his phone calls and meetings in excruciating detail. Yet when *Trump: The Art of the Deal* was released, *The New York Times* gave it a rave review. While noting that Trump came across as a thoroughly crass and egotistical human being, reviewer Christopher Lehmann-Haupt felt that this did not diminish the quality of the reading experience:

> *Oddly enough, Mr. Trump's display of ego is not offensive*
> *to the reader. As one reads along, one takes inventory of*
> *certain qualities one might dislike about him... Yet for*

none of these qualities can you really blame Mr. Trump. He is the first to call attention to them. He makes no pretense to the contrary…He arouses one's sense of wonder at the imagination and self-invention it must have taken to leap from his father's shoulders and reach for the deals that he did. Jay Gatsby lives, without romance and without the usual tragic flaws…Mr. Trump makes one believe for a moment in the American dream again.[362]

The *Times* was not alone in seeing Trump as an ambassador for the "American Dream." *Fortune* magazine gushed with similar enthusiasm:

There is undeniably a Trump mystique. Some people love him, others despise him, but everybody talks about him. He has become a cult hero for many people around the world who seem to regard this flamboyant billionaire as the most heartening example of the American Dream come true since Ross Perot.[363]

Looking back over the coverage of Donald Trump in the 1970's and 80's, much of it is similar: Trump as role model, Trump as empire builder, Trump as king. The fawning began early and never really seemed to stop. The tenor of the coverage was set in the first *Times* profile: "Donald Trump, Real Estate Promoter, Builds Image As He Buys Buildings."[364] The media then steadily built Trump into an icon.

At every stage, Trump was working behind the scenes to encourage the coverage. Trump would feed his own mythology to the press, who would dutifully treat Trump as precisely the character he fancied himself. As Trump explained his methods:

Here's how I work… I call the society editor [of one of the

*New York tabloids] and tell them Princess Di and Prince
Charles are going to purchase an apartment in Trump
Tower. And they, in turn, investigate the source, call
Buckingham Palace. And the comment is 'no comment.'
Which means it appears to the public that Princess Di
and Prince Charles are going to purchase an apartment
in Trump Tower.*[365]

The press has been willing to participate in Trump's self-making
because of its mutually beneficial symbiotic relationship with him.
After all, the media need people to cover. Trump wants to be covered.
Trump gives them their story, and they give him his publicity. Everybody wins.

This was especially evident in the tabloids during the late 80s and
early 90s. Newspapers like *The New York Post* and *The New York
Daily News* did incredibly good business out of their Trump coverage. Browsing through old headlines, it is remarkable just how much
Trump was covered. Every last rumbling of a deal, every hiccup in his
marriages, made the front pages of the papers. His assets (Mar-a-Lago,
the Trump Princess) and his romantic partners (Ivana, Marla) became
nationally-recognized names. Media interest in Trump was at a level
many times that afforded to any other rich person, even those whose
wealth far exceeded Donald Trump's. Much of this was also positive,
or at least neutral. It was the *New York Times* who described Trump
in the late 70's thusly: "He is tall, lean and blond, with dazzling white
teeth, and he looks ever so much like Robert Redford."[366]

The coverage level was extraordinary. After all, billionaires generally
are not terribly interesting people. Their lives aren't really new. They
sell some things, they buy some things, they get divorces, then they
have new weddings. There is a reason that tabloids generally obsess
over the lives of celebrities rather than businesspeople. But Donald
Trump, through the force of his personality, has managed to will him-

self into a different category than any ordinary businessperson. The papers covered him as a heroic and fascinating American story.

Party of this came from Trump's own limitless savvy about the media. Even when he was in real estate, he knew he was really in entertainment. As he said to *Playboy* in 1990, "the show is 'Trump' and it is sold-out performances everywhere."[367] According to Trump, the glitzy trappings of his buildings are "props for the show."[368] Parts of Trump's outsized personality and lavish spending are carefully crafted for entertainment purposes. As many have observed, Trump is playing the character of Donald Trump. And he "seems to have an uncanny sense of the elements of a good story — conflict, money, and sex — especially when he's the subject."[369]

◆　　◆　　◆　　◆

OF COURSE, SINCE THE EARLY DAYS, TRUMP HAS ATTRACTED PLENTY of negative coverage as well. But the stunning thing is that the press consistently believe they are successfully criticizing him even as they give him precisely what he wants. They believe that by "exposing" Trump, they undo him. In fact, they make him even larger.[370] When Tony Schwartz wrote a highly negative profile of Trump, he was stunned to receive a phone call from Trump *congratulating* him on the story. Schwartz couldn't understand why Trump seemed elated, since what Schwartz had written was so damning. But Trump was pleased, because Schwartz's story had gotten Trump's image on the front cover of *New York* magazine. To Trump, that was all that mattered. As Jane Mayer recounts, Schwartz's article was:

> …*what Schwartz described as "a fugue of failure, a farce of fumbling and bumbling." An accompanying cover portrait depicted Trump as unshaven, unpleasant-looking, and shiny with sweat. Yet, to Schwartz's amaze-*

ment, Trump loved the article. He hung the cover on a wall of his office, and sent a fan note to Schwartz, on his gold-embossed personal stationery. "Everybody seems to have read it," Trump enthused in the note, which Schwartz has kept. "I was shocked," Schwartz told me. "Trump didn't fit any model of human being I'd ever met. He was obsessed with publicity, and he didn't care what you wrote." [371]

It was deeply naïve of Schwartz to believe that Trump would hate the coverage. Trump's regular outbursts at negative stories are partly calculated for show, and it is difficult to know whether he has any real feelings about the "haters" at all. As Megyn Kelly put it, "The vast majority of the controversy *he* generated, and in many instances intentionally — with the goal of being covered."[372] The comedians who put together a roast of Trump for Comedy Central discovered the same thing, initially being surprised that Trump was so willing to go along with vicious jokes at his own expense. As one of them recalled, "The more that we learned about Donald Trump along the way, the more it became obvious that Donald Trump is up for anything, so long as you are talking about him." This suggests that Trump's legendary "thin skin" is largely put on for show, and that the "Donald Trump" of Twitter feuds maybe as real as a pro wrestling character (indeed, Trump has appeared on pro wrestling, and knows well how the show works[373]).

Donald Trump is one of the people who has most successfully understood and applied the old saw about there being no such thing as bad publicity. Trump realizes that the only important question is whether he is in the papers, or whether he isn't. The papers, for their part, think that if they are issuing lengthy condemnations of Trump, they are doing their bit to counter him. They couldn't be more wrong. He is calculating their reaction precisely, and enjoying every last bit of it.

This same dynamic affects satire about Donald Trump. Trump is an easy target, because of his many outlandish and offensive qualities. But those who mock Trump seldom realize that they are frequently helping him. Helping him because while satire doesn't actually undermine his *power*, it certainly contributes to the further inflation of his *image*. (Again, imagine Trump as a wrestling villain.)

During the late 80's and early 90's, *Spy* magazine, the now-defunct satirical monthly, loved tormenting Trump in their pages. They are the ones who called Trump a "short-fingered vulgarian" after noticing Trump was afflicted with stubbiness of the digits. Trump would then send them photographs of himself with the fingers circled in gold Sharpie, alongside the words "See? Not so short."[374] To the editors, this was hilarious. Trump's ludicrous vanity makes him a figure of fun. But *Spy* helped to build Trump up even as it tore him down. Trump has essentially posed for the caricature artists. He is happy to play the most larger-than-life version of himself, even as he is relentlessly mocked for it, because as Trump became a "character" (even a grotesque one) he simultaneously became a celebrity.

It's hard to know, then, how much Trump's anger at people's jokes about his tiny fingers is an act. He is a narcissist, certainly, and so could conceivably care deeply. But he also knows that every burst of petty Trump-rage means an accompanying round of press coverage. He therefore has every incentive to appear as childish and vain as possible, because he knows that, for whatever else it does, it keeps attention focused squarely on Donald Trump.

Thus, while they are slow to realize it, the joke is almost always on those making fun of Trump rather than on Trump himself. It's difficult to resist the temptation. After all, Trump is one of the most absurd people on earth. Steve Martin has noted that "ego with nothing to back it up" makes for the funniest comedic characters (Think Inspector Clouseau, *Anchorman*, etc.) Bombastic and egotistical characters make great comedy. This is why Alec Baldwin's Trump impersonation is hilarious. But the last laugh is always had by Donald Trump. People seem to believe that by making Trump look ridiculous, they can somehow hope to undo him. But the opposite is true: they only make him stronger, and they fail to make it clear that he is far more frightening than comical.

◆   ◆   ◆   ◆

THE PRESS HAVE THEREFORE CONSISTENTLY SERVED AS TRUMP'S reliable stenographers, helping him get what he wants. The *New York Times,* which was regularly profiling Trump by the time he was in his mid-30s, early on ran an article on Trump suggesting that he had already negotiated a deal that he had not; once it was in the paper, it was on its way to being true.[375] By reporting everything that comes out of Trump's mouth, the press helps Trump create the world as he wishes it to be. Trump says "I make people believe in the American dream again." Then the *New York Times* dutifully writes "he makes people believe in the American dream again."[376]

We know Trump knows how beneficial the press is to him, because he has said it. Deborah Friedell says that during the 1980s, Trump "was realizing that his life could be an advertisement for his work."[377] As Trump described it:

> *It's really quite simple. If I were to take a full-page ad in the New York Times to publicize a project, it might cost $40,000... but if the New York Times writes even a moderately positive one-column story about one of my deals, it doesn't cost me anything.*[378]

Thus Trump is perfectly happy to confess that he uses the press carefully and strategically to cultivate his image. As Trump says, "the point is that if you are a little different, or a little outrageous, or if you do things that are bold or controversial, the press is going to write about you." In his words, "notoriety has real monetary value"[379] and even the divorces were "good for business."[380] Yet even though Trump announces this intention frankly, it does not actually prevent him from getting precisely what he wants. Trump says "I am using the press, who will print anything I say" and the next day's headline is "Trump is using press, says Trump." Journalists never learn. They have consistently given Trump precisely the attention he craves.

This is not to say that the press *shouldn't* have written about Trump. But it is important to acknowledge that stories about Trump have consequences, and that they are frequently the product of Trump's own manipulation. It's a serious task to figure out how Trump *ought* to be covered, rather than simply covering Trump using the ordinary rules of coverage, which Trump is so adept at manipulating.

◆   ◆   ◆   ◆

THE MEDIA'S CREATION OF TRUMP IS NOT JUST ABOUT NEWSPAPERS and magazines obsessively covering him. It is also about reality television. The "Trump persona" was manufactured in reality TV on *The Apprentice*; this is where he became "America's boss." Trump was already synonymous with "rich guy," but *The Apprentice* solidified the image; Trump's catchphrase "You're Fired" showed him to be a man whose will was done, with the infinite power to dispatch those who displeased him. Trump, in Trump Tower, was a king in his castle, dispensing favor to sycophants and exiling losers and ingrates. As Gwenda Blair says, "10 years of America looking at him as the boss, that is so, now, imprinted on people's ideas—that they can't get around that notion that he is the boss. If you say the word "boss," you think Trump."[381] Former *Apprentice* producer Bill Pruitt gives voice to some anguish and misgivings over the role the show had in turning Trump into an American icon:

I've been struggling with the whole experience of watching Trump go from punch line to GOP nominee… because of how it reflects on reality TV, which is the work I've been dedicating my life to for the last 10 years. The associations are glaring. Those in our business who hadn't already taken stock of what we wrought, we're doing it now.…. Those of us involved in the show are proud of our work. But we might have given the guy a platform and created this candidate. It's guys like him, narcissists with dark Machiavellian traits, who dominate in our culture, on TV, and in the political realm. It can be dangerous when we confuse stories we're told with reality.[382]

It's refreshing to see a reality television producer conduct some self-reflection on his social role. But Pruitt ought to go further: it's not just because reality TV gave Donald Trump himself a platform. It is also because reality television has slowly turned all of us stupid. The Republican primary debates actually *resembled* a reality show, with quirky minor characters being ejected by voters after poor performances and disappearing from the stage. It's reality television as a form, and the way it has affected politics, that bears responsibility, not just *The Apprentice* (which wasn't that bad of a show).

◆   ◆   ◆   ◆

DONALD TRUMP IS ADDICTED TO PUBLICITY, AS WE ALL KNOW. He needs people to be looking at him and talking about him. If they aren't, he's unhappy. The obvious course of action for any third-party is to simply refuse to pay attention to Trump. If a child is making noises and faces so that you will look at them, just walk away. Nobody is *making* you think or talk about Trump. Of course, if you don't, he'll do a series of even more outrageous things, with the hopes that *these* will make you take notice. But you don't have to pay attention to these either. No matter how interesting or controversial he makes himself, one is permitted to set one's own terms for how to talk about Trump. There is no need to give him exactly what he wants.

And yet for forty years, the press has reliably let Trump dictate terms. Trump would call the papers personally using a fake name ("John Barron") in order to plant stories about himself.[383] And they would dutifully print the stories. He would make outlandish claims, and they would be on the front page of *The New York Times* the next day. And now, he sends tweets, which immediately become headlines on CNN.[384]

Donald Trump *is* a self-made man, in the sense that he is the one who has made himself the center of attention. But the press has gone right along with it, suckers for a story that will sell newspapers. It has been impossible for them to resist the financial incentives. After all, Trump brings the ratings. He may have singlehandedly revived the flagging fortunes of CNN—the next four years promise to be an extraordinary ratings bonanza for the troubled news channel. CNN head Jeff Zucker said as much in October, calling 2016, "This is the best year in the history of cable news … for everybody. We've all benefited."[385] According to *Politico*, Zucker and CNN recognized early on that "Trump would be a ratings machine," and deliberately gave him "quite a bit of coverage," including broadcasting many of Trump's rallies and speeches in full.[386] Nevertheless, Zucker has no regrets, and reportedly "sleeps great at night."[387]

CBS head Les Moonves was similarly pleased with Trump's consequences for his industry, saying of the 2016 election that:

> It may not be good for America, but it's damn good for CBS…
> For us, economically speaking, Donald's place in the election
> is a good thing… The money's rolling in, and this is fun. It's a
> terrible thing to say. But bring it on, Donald. Keep going.[388]

It's worth considering the fact that the networks are also poised to do extremely well on the highly-entertaining Trump presidency, and have had no incentive whatsoever to cover him wisely. And it's worth assessing the significant responsibility the press bears for presenting the character of Donald J. Trump to the world. Moonves and Zucker's personal financial interests directly conflict with the well-being of the world's people. (One should always remember the perverse fact that wars and calamities are great for ratings.)

Thus until the press finds ways to resist the *incentives* that Trump creates by bringing eyes to the screen and clicks to the page, it will be difficult to get attention focused on things that matter. A profit-driven media cannot turn away from Trump, because Trump knows how to create a deeply entertaining spectacle. Trump cannot be gotten rid of until the media cancels the Trump Show, which will be difficult so long as the Trump Show is #1 in every time slot.

PART TWO
How It Happened

"I know what sells and I know what people want."
— Donald Trump, Playboy Magazine (March 1990)

TRUMP THE CANDIDATE

DONALD TRUMP HAD BEEN THREATENING TO RUN FOR PRESIDENT since the 1980s, endlessly announcing potential candidacies only to abandon them. Thus when Trump began publicly toying with the idea of running in the 2016 election, few in the press took him especially seriously. The consensus, early on, was that Trump was pulling his usual routine: building up a fictional presidential campaign as a way to further inflate the Trump brand. *BuzzFeed News* captured the general feeling of skepticism in a profile from February of 2014, entitled "36 Hours on the Fake Campaign Trail With Donald Trump," concluding that:

> *Trump can no longer escape the fact that his political "career" — a long con that the blustery billionaire has perpetrated on the country for 25 years by repeatedly pretending to consider various runs for office, only to bail out after generating hundreds of headlines — finally appears to be on the brink of collapse. The reason: Nobody seems to believe him anymore.*[389]

The *BuzzFeed* reporter suggested that Trump had a series of "confidantes and yes-men" who were fabricating a silly myth: that Trump had a singular appeal to "working-class men in flyover country." *BuzzFeed* quoted a Trump ally pointing out Trump's potential appeal as a candidate: "If you have no education, and you work with your hands, you like him… It's like, 'Wow, if I was rich, that's how I would live!' The girls, the cars, the fancy suits. His ostentatiousness is appealing to them." To the *BuzzFeed* reporter, this perspective was delusional, a product of echo-chamber thinking:

> *The more time I spend with the yes-men, the clearer it becomes that Trump has surrounded himself with a similar type. They are the outer-borough kids who made good, and they are hypnotized by his grandiosity. Trump's lavish lifestyle and his brash proclamations that everything he touches is the best, the greatest, the most incredible — all of it contributes to an illusion of electability within his inner circle.*[390]

Thus from the very beginning, long before the various scandals and outrageous remarks, Trump's campaign was dismissed as being either fake or deluded. The idea that Trump had a message that would resonate with working-class white people was simply part of a fabricated "illusion of electability" that had taken hold among the more sycophantic denizens of TrumpWorld. Sensible political analysts knew better.

❖   ❖   ❖   ❖

When Trump formally announced his campaign over a year later, the level of skepticism remained similar. In the speech announcing his run, Trump did little to alter the media perception of him as far more obsessed with listing his own accomplishments than with presenting a serious political agenda: "Our country needs a truly great leader... We need a leader that wrote *The Art of the Deal*."[391] Trump bragged about his golf courses, about having "so many websites." He insisted that he "beat[s] China all the time."[392] He even held up a sheet of paper and read his net worth aloud. But Trump also laid out the core of the argument that he would use to appeal to working-class voters:

> *Sadly, the American dream is dead... But if I get elected president, I will bring it back, bigger, and better than ever... [I will] bring back our jobs, bring back our manufacturing, bring back our military and take care of our vets.*[393]

For the press, it was not the "restoring the American Dream" aspect of Trump's pitch that defined the tone of his campaign. Instead, it was the braggadocio and lack of polish. (*The Huffington Post* called it "a rambling speech that strongly resembled performance art."[394] *Politico* said that the "rambling, hour-long stream-of-consciousness speech" was "God's gift to the Internet."[395]) But beneath all the talk of golf courses and *The Art of the Deal* was a serious message: *I am successful. I get things done. America is hurting. You are hurting. You need me, the successful person who gets things done, in order to make things better.* From the very beginning of his campaign, Trump had a clear and coherent message: he was #1, and only he could fix the country. America was being run by losers. It needed a winner.

The press reaction to the speech, however, did not spend much time considering the potential appeal of this message. Instead, Trump's announcement became notable primarily for his comments about Mexicans. The remarks made Trump's campaign outrageous from the very beginning. NBC, Macy's, and even NASCAR soon cut ties with him.[396] A series of dynamics were set in place that would characterize Trump's campaign throughout 2015 and 2016: Trump would say something egregiously offensive or provocative. The press would furiously denounce him. Mainstream corporations and institutions would distance themselves from him. And the news cycle would become increasingly dominated by things Trump said and the various fallout and criticisms that occurred in response. Meanwhile, Trump's rallies would begin to swell in size, and his poll numbers would climb, as people tired of "political correctness" came to relish the spectacle of Trump ticking off the establishment.

Even as it helped build up Trump's significance, however, the press refused to treat Trump as a serious candidate, and consequently failed to take him as a serious threat. (A naïveté that would last up until approximately 11pm on Nov. 8, 2016.) Mark Leibovich of *The New York Times* magazine spent the summer refusing to cover Trump at all, dismissing him as a "nativist clown" whose "conspiracy-mongering, reality-show orientations and garish tabloid sensibilities would make him unacceptable to the polite company of American politics," before Trump's rising poll numbers forced Leibovich to produce a long profile of Trump for the *Times* in September.[397] Early on, *The Huffington Post* decided that Trump's campaign was so silly that it didn't even merit coverage in the "Politics" section. In a statement, the *Post* announced that it would be taking the high road:

> *We have decided we won't report on Trump's campaign as part of The Huffington Post's political coverage. Instead, we will cover his campaign as part of our Entertainment section. Our reason is simple: Trump's campaign is a side-show. We won't take the bait. If you are interested in what The Donald has to say, you'll find it next to our stories on the Kardashians and The Bachelorette.*[398]

Conservatives were infuriated by the sudden disruptive arrival of

Trump in the Republican primary. *The Weekly Standard*'s Michael Graham said he was "crying" to realize that an "energetic, spirited, and worthwhile GOP primary" was now going to be turned into a "TV show fiasco."[399] Former Bush press secretary Ari Fleischer summed up the feelings of many traditional Republicans, saying that "Donald Trump is like watching a roadside accident. Everyone pulls over to see the mess. And Trump thinks that's entertainment. But running for president is serious. And the risk for the party is that he tarnishes everybody."[400] By a few weeks after Trump's announcement, *Politico* was reporting that the Republican Party was "officially afraid of Donald Trump," who had gone from being a "minor comedic nuisance" to a "loose cannon whose rants about Mexicans and scorched-earth attacks on his rivals will damage the eventual nominee" even though Trump himself "has virtually zero chance of winning the presidential nomination."[401] According to NBC's Chuck Todd, the general view among Republican insiders was that Trump was "a skunk at the garden party."[402]

In the press generally, Trump's candidacy was commonly described as a "circus" and "sideshow," a distraction from serious politics. When Trump announced his run, the *New York Daily News* used "Clown Runs For Prez" as the front-page headline, with accompanying graphic of Trump in white facepaint and red nose.[403] Conservative commentator Michael Reagan (son of Ronald) said that while "Trump will create lots of late-night laughs," ultimately "everyone knows Trump can't win. He knows it, too."[404]

Professional political forecaster Nate Silver concurred in this judgment. "Trump's campaign will fail by one means or another,"[405] Silver predicted in August. In July, James Fallows of *The Atlantic* was unequivocal: "Donald Trump will not be the 45th president of the United States. Nor the 46th, nor any other number you might name. The chance of his winning nomination and election is exactly zero."[406]

But from the very beginning, there were signs that it was unwise to write Trump off. A CNN poll taken just a few days after his announcement showed Trump in second place for the GOP nomination behind Jeb Bush.[407] Despite Trump's high "unfavorable" rating among prospective Republican voters, he was also viewed as the least likely to "act like a typical politician" and was well ahead of candidates like Scott Walker, Rand Paul, and Marco Rubio, despite their far greater political experience and stronger backing among party elites.

Some people did notice this, and gave warnings about the folly of dismissing Trump. When Trump entered the race, *Salon*'s Heather Digby Parton cautioned against treating him as a "clown" too radical to have any serious political prospects. Parton suggested that journalists who treated Trump as being out of the mainstream may have a biased understanding of what the "mainstream" actually is:

> *Donald Trump may not make sense to the average journalist — but to the average Tea Partier, he's telling it like it is, with a sort of free-floating grievance about everyone who doesn't agree with them mixed with simplistic patriotic boosterism and faith in the fact that low taxes makes everybody rich... Sure, Trump is a clown. But he's a very rich and a very famous clown. And he's really not much more clownish than many of the current contenders or some serious contenders in the past... Donald Trump has the potential to be a serious 2016 player.*[408]

"Serious player" quickly turned out to be an understatement. From the moment of his entry into the race, Donald Trump dominated press coverage, and confirmed every establishment Republican's worst fears about turning the primary into a Trump-centric reality-show spectacle. As new wild comments poured forth from Trump's piscatorial lips, seemingly every television camera stayed fixed on Trump for the duration of the primary.

Trump certainly knew how to tick off large numbers of people with small numbers of words. In July, a month after joining the race, Trump set off a scandal with a remark about John McCain's time as a prisoner of war during the Vietnam War: "He's not a war hero," Trump said. "He was a war hero because he was captured. I like people who weren't captured."[409] Trump's attack on McCain was a cruel and ungenerous slight against a man who had spent five years in North Vietnamese captivity, during which time he was regularly tortured, being bayoneted in the abdomen and foot, having his arms and ribs broken, and being repeatedly knocked unconscious. (McCain spent much of his time on the "verge of death," nearly being driven to suicide, and was left with permanent debilitating injuries that affect him to the present day.[410]) For Trump to mock and trivialize this, especially considering Trump's own questionable medical exemption from service in Vietnam, was considered appalling.

But the striking feature of Trump's attack on McCain was not its sheer cruelty. After all, it was consistent with a lifelong record of vicious bullying. Rather, what was notable about the incident was that political pressure and backlash did *not* force Trump to apologize or walk back his remarks. Of course, it was no surprise that Trump, when asked if he regretted his words, replied: "I don't… I like to not regret anything… There are many people that like what I said. You know after I said that, my poll numbers went up seven points."[411] Trump, after all, is a man who does not apologize. But the extraordinary fact was that Trump got away with it. For any ordinary politician, taking a nasty public swipe at a decorated veteran would lead to a cycle of outrage, followed by publicly professed remorse. Trump does not do remorse, which by the ordinary rules of politics should have discredited and destroyed him. Political figures are expected to use their words carefully, and when they do *not* use their words carefully, they are expected to issue statements apologizing for their words and promising to use more careful ones in all future public statements.

But Trump did the opposite. He trivialized a war veteran's service, suggesting that John McCain being tortured made John McCain a loser, because winners don't get themselves caught and tortured. Yet by doubling down and refusing to budge, Trump somehow managed to escape consequence.

The McCain incident was an early indicator that politics worked differently for Donald Trump than for everyone else. He could get away with more, because upsetting people was *part of* his appeal. By pitching himself as the one willing to offend people's sensibilities, and say outrageous things, Trump simultaneously kept the attention on himself *and* caused certain sectors of the American electorate to think "Well, I may not agree with everything Trump says, but I love that he's his own man and doesn't get pushed around." Trump realized that in a certain sense, the more outrageous he was, the better.

Throughout the early months, pundits continued not to have any idea what to make of Donald Trump. But from the very beginning, there was good reason to believe that Trump would end up the nominee. Immediately after entering the race, Trump rose to the top of polls, and before the first Republican debate, he was already in the lead. By the end of the summer of 2015, the *New York Times* reported that Trump's support was not just a mirage or press hype, but that Trump actually had a serious base among Republican voters:

> *[Aides to other Republican candidates] have drawn comfort from the belief that Donald J. Trump's dominance in the polls is a political summer fling, like Herman Cain in 2011 — an unsustainable boomlet dependent on megawatt celebrity, narrow appeal and unreliable surveys of Americans with a spotty record of actually voting in primaries. A growing body of evidence suggests that may be wishful thinking. A review of public polling, extensive interviews with a host of his supporters in two*

states and a new private survey that tracks voting records all point to the conclusion that Mr. Trump has built a broad, demographically and ideologically diverse coalition, constructed around personality, not substance, that bridges demographic and political divides. In doing so, he has effectively insulated himself from the consequences of startling statements that might instantly doom rival candidates.[412]

Sure enough, as the Republican primary unfolded, Trump squashed his opponents one by one. Developing derisive nicknames for his opponents (like "Lyin' Ted" Cruz and "Little Marco" Rubio), Trump made himself the center of attention, compensating for his comparative lack of endorsements and campaign infrastructure by managing to monopolize airtime on cable news. According to *Politico*, Trump "received by far the most [press coverage] out of any of his Republican primary rivals, earning 34 percent to 18 percent for Jeb Bush."[413] As a report from the Harvard Kennedy School noted:

Trump exploited [the media's] lust for riveting stories... He didn't have any other option. He had no constituency base and no claim to presidential credentials... Trump couldn't compete with the likes of Ted Cruz, Marco Rubio, or Jeb Bush on the basis of his political standing or following. The politics of outrage was his edge, and the press became his dependable if unwitting ally.[414]

Trump was aided by the fact that, with 17 total Republican candidates for the nomination, there was no other clear frontrunner. As candidates took turns in the lead, Trump would unleash a savage volley of insults and smears, to which few knew how to respond. Ben Carson, Trump said, had a "pathological temper," with an incurable violent disposition similar to that of a "child molester."[415] Lindsey Graham was "one of the dumbest human beings I've ever seen" and a "disgrace."[416]

Trump's assault on Jeb Bush, once the establishment frontrunner, was particularly brutal. Trump delighted in turning Bush into a figure of fun, successfully painting Bush as an effeminate, quivering jelly. Bush was "a poor, pathetic, low-energy guy."[417] Trump also launched his typical below-the-belt attacks. "Bush has to like Mexican illegals because of his wife," in reference to Bush's wife Columba.[418] Bush's responses to Trump did little to save him. "That is not how you win elections," he insisted, alternating between trying to keep the moral high ground and trying to give as good as he got.[419] But as it turned out, Bush was wrong. This was indeed how you win elections, and Bush spent $130 million for the privilege of being humiliated before the entire country and relentlessly emasculated by Donald Trump.[420]

It's easy to be puzzled by how Donald Trump did so well in both the primaries and the general election. After all, he knows little about policy substance, and has a tendency to behave indistinguishably from a wailing newborn. But watching his rallies and speeches, Trump's power becomes infinitely more understandable. Sit down and watch Trump for 40 minutes straight, and one realizes just how *compelling* a speaker he is. Not a *good* speaker. But a mesmerizing one. Trump was *funny*. He was the funniest of any of the 2016 presidential candidates. A lot of that comes from his willingness to say things everyone knows, but that nobody will say. He would make fun of Marco Rubio's profuse sweating, or of Ben Carson's sleepiness.

Republicans in the 2016 primary had little idea how to deal with Trump. They alternated between attempting to rise above him and responding to his insults with insults of their own, thereby joining him on his level. Neither strategy worked. When they attempted to keep their cool, Trump would continue to mock and deride them. When they responded with their own schoolyard taunts, the result was rarely helpful, and only further dragged the campaign into the sewer.[421]

Trump has a gift for bullying, in that he can find precisely what a person is most sensitive about, and will hit them where it hurts the most. Trump went after Ted Cruz's wife, making what appeared to be a reference to her experiences with depression.[422] Trump pointed out what everyone was thinking (but did not say) after Rick Perry began to publicly sport a pair of spectacles, observing that "Rick Perry put on glasses so people think he's smart."[423] As with McCain, Trump took what would ordinarily constitute rudeness and multiplied it by ten. When asked to apologize, he would not only not back down, but would often say something far worse. Eventually, there were *so* many outrages that people seemed to become numb to them, and reports of new Trump insults became a regular aspect of the day-to-day news cycle.

Trump deployed every trick from the playbook that had served him so well for forty years. He exaggerated the hell out of everything, bragged shamelessly, and insisted his opponents were a bunch of losers who would soon be kneeling before him and begging for his favor.

◆   ◆   ◆   ◆

By the end of the 2016 primary, Trump had set the record for most GOP primary votes ever. He had won 44% of the votes, 20% more than the next highest contender, Ted Cruz.[424] He had done so despite spending far less money on advertising than any other candidate, and running what Bernie Sanders called "the most unconventional campaign in the modern history of America."[425] Conventional wisdom about primaries had always been that "the party decides,"[426] i.e. that it is the people at the top of the party's organization, rather than the voters, who matter the most in determining the nominee. Donald Trump had proved this totally false; the party had despised him, and he had steamrolled them. Efforts to form a "Never Trump" opposition movement had fizzled laughably.[427] Behind him, Trump left the carcasses of over a dozen Republican candidates, many of whom were better-funded and better-connected. He had defied every piece of traditional advice at every turn, and it had paid off.

One should be careful, however, about concluding from this that Trump was too significantly different from an ordinary Republican candidate. Certainly, Trump's *campaign* and *personality* were totally at odds with conservative orthodoxy. But much of his platform was familiar: lower taxes, get rid of the immigrants, "bomb the shit out of" the terrorists.[428] Republicans' insistence that they were appalled by Trump rang hollow; Republicans had been endorsing these sorts of *policies* for years. What they were scandalized by was Trump's *vulgarity*. It seemed, frequently, that conservatives were more upset by Trump's willingness to swear and insult people than by the actual serious harm that his policies would do to human lives, from deporting Central American children to face deadly gang violence to allowing millions of the earth's residents to be driven from their homes by flooding as a result of climate change. "Sucks to you, I've got mine" has always been the Republican Party's policy on providing social welfare to the poor, and the consensus philosophy among American conservatives is that if someone is suffering under grinding poverty, it is probably because they failed to work sufficiently hard. For conservatives, the problem with Trump is that he says what is implicitly believed by the movement in terms that make it seem grossly unappealing and callous.

Thus the Republicans had made room for Trump. The Tea Party normalized extreme positions like the ones Trump held. There is very little difference between the cabinet Ted Cruz would have appointed and the cabinet Donald Trump ultimately appointed. Trump was a more vulgar version of a perfectly mainstream form of Republican politics. Granted, he was a dash more populist, with his criticisms of free-trade agreements. But the truly outrageous aspects of Trump's proposals, like the crackdowns on Muslims and the promise to throw more people into Guantanamo, were hardly aberrations or departures from popular Republican positions.

In certain ways, Trump's brand of "honest Republicanism" (honest insofar as it doesn't hide its ugliness beneath gentility, not in that what it espouses is true) is far more refreshing than that offered by orthodox politicians on the right. And one of the reasons that Trump was so successful was that the criticisms he made of the other candidates were often deliciously accurate. Jeb Bush *is* a bore and a product of nepotism, whose brother *did* start a catastrophic war. Ted Cruz *is* a dishonest sleaze. Rick Perry *is* clearly wearing those glasses so that people would forget how stupid he seemed during the 2012 primary. The candidates Trump was running against lacked the credibility to confront him effectively, because many of the criticisms he made of them were perfectly accurate. Lindsey Graham called Trump "a race-baiting, xenophobic, religious bigot."[429] In response, Trump pointed out that Lindsey Graham was Lindsey Graham. And people nodded, realizing that Lindsey Graham has no moral authority to be calling anyone anything. Similarly, Rick Perry called Trump "without substance." But nobody is less well-positioned to make such a criticism than Rick Perry, who famously forgot the name of one of the three federal agencies he wanted to eliminate.[430]

◆   ◆   ◆   ◆

FROM THE VERY BEGINNING, TRUMP BUILT HIS CAMPAIGN THE WAY he built his business: he impersonated a winning presidential candidate, and in doing so gradually became one. The evidence said Trump wouldn't be the President. Trump insisted otherwise, and preferred "the power of positive thinking"[431] to poll-watching and number-crunching: if you will it, it is no dream. (Dara Lind of *Vox* calls Trump "a lifelong member of the Church of Fake It 'Til You Make it."[432]) Trump's skill was in realizing that the pursuit of the presidency had finally become a reality show, and thus it would be won like one.

Perhaps this explains why he waited until he was nearly 70 in order to run, despite having talked about the seeking the presidency since he was in his forties. Trump was waiting cannily for the moment that the campaign cycle had become just the right kind of contest at which he could excel.

It's fitting that "Make America Great Again" wasn't actually a slogan of Trump's devising, but was cribbed from Ronald Reagan.[433] His political campaign was like his business dealings: a phony imitation of something that was already phony to begin with. Ronald Reagan was an actor running for president. Trump was a reality television star, yet another level down.

But there's still a serious mystery to Trump's dominance of the Republican primary: how did a man, detested by the entirety of the party establishment, destroy all of its favored candidates and totally crush its various attempts to resist him? Few Republican elected officials had supported Trump, and many had actively opposed him. He hadn't spent much money, his debate performances had been roundly criticized, he had hardly any existing organized campaign infrastructure, he seemed to operate his campaign almost entirely from his office in Trump Tower, and his public messaging consisted mostly of Tweets. As an act of successful political maneuvering, Trump's trajectory from long-shot clown to Republican nominee has no obvious modern precedent.

Perhaps, however, the fact that this seems mysterious just speaks to faulty assumptions on our part. It has always been assumed that party elites matter a lot in choosing candidates. Perhaps this is only true if all of the candidates are of a certain kind. Perhaps what matters most is personality and charisma. Or perhaps what matters most is media; the ultimate lesson here is that party apparatus, campaign spending, and organizations matter very little if you are a skilled entertainer with a lifetime of expertise on how to hog media coverage.

Of course, it's also true that he couldn't have picked a better race into which to insert himself. The Republican candidates were even drearier and less distinguished than usual. (Furthermore, there were a *lot* of them.) Perhaps the other contenders were simply weak and vulnerable, and the Republican electorate was in the mood for a major change. But however he did it, Trump's victory will necessitate a new evaluation of how presidential nominating contests work. His victory was an extraordinary demonstration that you don't necessarily need to follow the existing rules in order to defeat the party establishment. Democrats wishing to upend their own party may wish to take heed…

CLINTON VERSUS TRUMP

THE DEMOCRATIC PRIMARY WAS SUPPOSED TO BE A CORONATION. "It's her turn. I think it's her time,"[434] said former Obama campaign manager Jim Messina. Hillary Clinton received endorsements from 41 out of 46 Democratic senators.[435] There was a sense among Democrats that Clinton would face no serious opposition in the primary. She was, in the words of the *Washington Post*, "the biggest frontrunner for the Democratic presidential nomination ever."[436] Because of this, many Democrats thought, she would be uniquely well-positioned in the general election once she had (inevitably) won the primary. As she breezed through state after state, easily securing the nomination, Republicans would be tearing each other to shreds. As Justin Beach wrote at *The Huffington Post*:

> *Hillary will be able to outspend and out-campaign the Republicans. She'll be relatively unbruised from what*

*should be a cake walk of a primary. She'll be able to run
for President while the Republicans run for, what is likely
to be, a bitterly contested nomination.*[437]

Needless to say, this was not quite how it worked out. The entrance of a certain elderly socialist Vermonter into the race had a disruptive effect…

Few expected Bernie Sanders to pose a serious threat to Hillary Clinton's quest for the Democratic presidential nomination. In the Spring of 2015, the *Washington Post*'s Dana Milbank wrote that the contest was between "Clinton and … nobody — unless you think Martin O'Malley or Jim Webb or Bernie Sanders can make a serious run for the Democratic nomination, in which case you probably also believe in the tooth fairy."[438]

Still, there were signs that Hillary Clinton wouldn't necessarily have an easy time seeing off a challenger. At the same time as he waved away Bernie Sanders' chances, Milbank reported from a firefighter's union conference, relaying that there was a widespread sense of "buyer's remorse among the union faithful" about Clinton's inevitability.[439] Clinton evidently lacked the kind of fiery anti-establishment bona fides that working-class Democrats were looking for.

Two months *after* Clinton announced her candidacy, she planned a speech to make the case to "lay out her motivation for running" a candidacy that Democrats were worrying "lacked in inspiration."[440] The case for Clinton rested far more on *who she was* than *what she would do*, and while Donald Trump was making pithy (if startling and brutal) promises like building a wall and banning all Muslims, Clinton was not running on a particularly obvious set of proposals, beyond preserving the Obama legacy. She was pitched as *experienced* and *capable*, rather than as someone who would accomplish some particular thing. There was a sense that she simply deserved to be president, by virtue of being better qualified for the position (and wanting it more) than anyone else. "It's my turn" was not something Clinton herself said, but one could pick up this sense from her campaign's focus on the qualities of Clinton herself rather than particular issues or the voters themselves (using "I'm With Her," rather than, for example, "She's With You.")

Still, in the early days, virtually nobody believed Bernie Sanders posed a credible threat to Clinton. While, in the days after his announcement, some noted that Sanders "appears to be attracting bigger crowds than any other candidate,"[441] he was seen largely as an eccentric whose function in the race would be to "raise issues."[442] He would not stand a chance of coming near the nomination. Many had long been certain of Hillary's inevitability. Matthew Yglesias of *Vox* said in 2014 that the party was completely unified around her. "It is impossible to mount a coherent anti-Clinton campaign," Yglesias wrote, "because there is no issue that divides the mass of Democrats."[443]

As everyone now knows, this turned out to be false. Bernie Sanders won 20 states, and received over 13 million votes (Clinton received 16 million). The primary contest was brutal, and while Clinton never lost her lead over Sanders, the Democratic Party became bitterly divided. The unexpected surge of anti-Establishment sentiment among primary voters foreshadowed the general election, where some of the main contentious issues that had divided Bernie Sanders from Hillary Clinton would recur in the fight between Clinton and Donald Trump.

◆   ◆   ◆   ◆

IN THE GENERAL ELECTION, DONALD TRUMP HARPED ON THE SAME themes as he had during the primary: unfair trade deals, job loss, immigration, and ISIS (themes also laid out in his campaign book, the unpleasantly-titled *Crippled America*[444]). But he also went after Hillary Clinton with an extraordinary ferocity. Not only did he use typical charges of corruption and duplicity against her, but Trump promised his audience that under a Trump presidency, Clinton would be on her way to prison. Ominous chants of "Lock Her Up" began to erupt at Republican events.[445] At Trump's rallies, Matt Taibbi reported that attendees would come "dressed in T-shirts reading things like DEPLORABLE LIVES MATTER and BOMB THE SHIT OUT OF ISIS, and even FUCK OFF, WE'RE FULL (a message for immigrants)."[446] It was not an uplifting candidacy on Trump's part. It mobilized voters based on anger and fear.

But there was also a lot of fairly standard rhetoric about sticking it to Washington, and ending business as usual. Trump ran both on a unique outpouring of rage *and* a fairly generic set of populist bromides, all of which was transparently phony. Trump began promising to "drain the swamp" of Washington, a slogan that caught on quickly with his base, only to be completely abandoned soon after Trump won the election.[447] (Newt Gingrich confessed in December that Trump "now just disclaims that. He now says it was cute, but he doesn't want to use it anymore,"[448] while Corey Lewandowski admitted that swamp-draining was "probably somewhere down at the bottom" of Trump's list of presidential priorities.) Trump made very little effort to follow through on any of his disdain for the powerful and established, immediately installing a cabinet comprised disproportionately of billionaires (and several billionaire *children* of billionaires, meaning people who had literally never experienced a second of life in which they were not billionaires). Instead of draining the swamp, he immediately began filling it with all manner of new mutant critters. Rich Lowry notes just how transparently fabricated the populist aspects of Trump's candidacy always were: "It was always a fantasy. The oldest story in Washington is a new president elected on a pledge to clean up Washington, who then turns to old Washington hands and well-connected financiers to help shepherd his administration."[449]

◆   ◆   ◆   ◆

Yet from the look of the newspaper reports during the campaign, it didn't seem as if the snake-oil pitch was working especially well. Trump was making gaffe after gaffe, his popularity tanking. From prolonging his battle with the Khan family to a series of widely-panned debate performances (in which Trump skulked around the stage and sniffed uncontrollably,[450] as well as calling Hillary Clinton "such a nasty woman"[451]), Trump did not appear "presidential," thus it was easy to believe he could never be president. In October came the infamous Billy Bush/Access Hollywood "pussy" tape, which many believed had finished Trump off once and for all.[452]

As for Clinton, over the course of the campaign, her supporters became more and more confident that she was destined to win. The aura of inevitability surrounded her. Not only were polls good, but there was *something in the air*. *Saturday Night Live* began calling her "President Clinton."[453] In August the debate began to center around whether Hillary Clinton would win comfortably or in a total wipeout, with *Business Insider* reporting that the country was "starting to hear the faint rumblings of a Hillary Clinton landslide as her 10-point lead is further proof that Donald Trump is in a downward spiral as the clock ticks."[454] Prognosticators were all but certain of her victory.[455]

There had always been signs, however, that Clinton might be weaker than her supporters believed. A number of Sanders-supporting progressive Democrats from the primary still detested Clinton, and resented "having" to vote for her.[456] Tim Kaine had been an uninspiring choice as a running mate; if it was true that populist anger would drive the election, Clinton would have been better off picking Bernie Sanders than the milquetoast Virginian, who seemed to have been selected by an algorithm designed to select the least controversial human being who would also give a one-or-two-point bump in a critical swing state.[457] Clinton's fortunes weren't helped by a comment she made early in September, labeling half of Trump's supporters "deplorables." As she said: "You know, just to be grossly generalistic, you could put half of Trump's supporters into what I call the basket of deplorables. They're racist, sexist, homophobic, xenophobic, Islama-phobic—you name it."[458] Mitt Romney had learned in 2012, when he criticized the "47%" of people who supposedly lived on government handouts,[459] that it is unwise to issue blanket dismissals of wide swaths of the electorate. Clinton evidently had not taken heed.

Then there was James Comey's letter. Having successfully avoided criminal indictment during the FBI's initial investigation into her private email server, Clinton was faced with a nasty October surprise when FBI director Comey decided to send a letter to Congress, explaining that new evidence (found on Anthony Weiner's computer, no less) warranted further examination.[460] The letter was explosive and damaging, feeding new material to Trump with which to paint Clinton as a criminal, and leaving the country hanging as to whether there might be some hidden Clinton scandal about to come to light. (There wasn't.) The campaign had been dominated by reports about Hillary Clinton's emails (a stupid issue, but a self-inflicted one), and many argued plausibly that Comey's letter gave Trump a last-minute advantage.

Still, Clinton went into Election Day with great confidence, hosting a would-be victory party beneath a symbolic giant glass ceiling in Manhattan's Javits Center (not noting, perhaps, the significance of standing beneath a ceiling you were not going to break).[461] The result was brutal. Trump won decisively, 304 electoral votes to Clinton's 227 (though as Clinton's supporters would repeatedly remind the country over the next months, she had comfortably won the popular vote). Trump had taken nearly every swing state, including Michigan, Ohio, Pennsylvania, North Carolina, and Florida. And he had successfully become the first president in United States history to assume the office without ever having previously served in government or the military. Donald J. Trump had gone from pussy-grabber to President.[462]

◆   ◆   ◆   ◆

TRUMP:
The Great Communicator?

ONE THING THAT IS RARELY RECOGNIZED BY DEMOCRATS AND progressives (because they hate him) is how effective Trump is at communicating. Trump's speaking style, derided for its self-aggrandizement,
circumlocution, and lack of polish, is in fact devastatingly effective.
He's funny, expressive, and direct. He's extraordinarily good at driving
home a point. And he knows *who* he is speaking to, meaning that he
is willing to do things that alienate the people in the room but please
the audience at home. As he said in 1990: "There are two publics as
far as I'm concerned. The real public and then there's the New York
society horseshit. The real public has always liked Donald Trump."[463]

Trump speaks to his "real public" even as he makes elites despise
him. See, for example, his much-panned performance at the white
tie Al Smith dinner, a charity banquet where politicians are supposed
to be impeccably civil and put aside their differences. Commentators suggested Trump ruined the evening, by telling poorly-received
"not-really-kidding" jokes about locking Hillary Clinton up (as well as
telling the Catholic audience that Clinton "hates Catholics"), in what
was intended to be a cordial and chummy atmosphere of mutually
good-natured ribbing.[464] But Trump knew that to his supporters at
home, rather than the stonily silent bigwigs at the dinner, he would be
seen blowing a big fat raspberry at the elites in their own nest. What
looked in person like a disaster was an effective piece of political messaging.

Trump is particularly good at countering attacks on him. He's
not exactly skilled at repartee and wit, but he certainly knows how
to throw an effective schoolyard comeback of the "I know you are,
but what am I" variety. Witness the following ways in which Donald
Trump defended himself and deflected criticism:

Marco Rubio (on the campaign trail): Have you seen his hands? You know what they say about men with small hands?... You can't trust them.[465]

Donald Trump (at later debate): He referred to my hands – "If they're small, something else must be small." I guarantee you there's no problem. I guarantee.[466] (Rubio ultimately apologized to Trump for the remark.[467])

Hillary Clinton: It's just awfully good that someone with the temperament of Donald Trump is not in charge of the law in this country.

Donald Trump: Because you'd be in jail.[468]

Megyn Kelly: You've called women you don't like 'fat pigs,' 'dogs,' 'slobs,' and 'disgusting animals'…Your Twitter account –

Donald Trump: Only Rosie O'Donnell.[469]

(Kelly was then forced to wait 15 seconds to resume her question, while the audience laughed at Trump's reply.)

No, Donald Trump's replies were not especially dignified. But they did successfully disarm the accuser. Megyn Kelly had wished to begin the presidential debate with a bombshell, but Trump instantly won the audience by turning what should have been a serious question into a joke. Of course, liberals found Trump's reply reprehensible and false, and Kelly responded by pointing out that it *wasn't* only Rosie O'Donnell, but that was beside the point. Trump's reply was effective for being memorable and pithy.

Trump was similarly effective at dealing with the fallout from the Billy Bush "pussy" tape. Trump called it "locker room talk" and indicated that "Bill Clinton has said far worse to me on the golf course — not even close."[470] The "locker room talk" line received a lot of criticism (since *if* what Trump said *was* locker room talk, this would just imply that a lot of sexual assault is confessed to in locker rooms). But Trump's invocation of Bill Clinton was skilled. Trump knew that Bill Clinton's record as a notorious womanizer would make it difficult for Hillary Clinton to go after him with the force and persistence that anyone else could. And truthfully, one can imagine that Bill Clinton probably *has* said far worse to Donald Trump on the golf course. Trump's instant invocation of Bill (and his subsequent press conference alongside multiple women who had accused Clinton of sexual assault and rape[471]) made it impossible for Hillary to assume the clear moral stance on behalf of women that she should have been able to take following her opponent's confession to sexual assault. What should have been a devastating attack on Trump was partially neutralized by Trump's instinct for the correct reply.

Trump is made fun of for his constant lobbing of insults. But one thing that is rarely noted is just how rhetorically effective it is. Law professor Eric Posner goes so far as to suggest that Trump has rightfully inherited Ronald Reagan's title as the "Great Communicator." Posner writes that "those of us who do not like Trump or his policies need to concede that he is a brilliant tactician," who "has used Twitter to take his case to the public far more effectively than any president since Reagan if not before."[472] (Trump-supporting blogger and *Dilbert* creator Scott Adams calls Trump a "master persuader"[473]—this seems excessively generous, but Adams is onto something by pointing out that Trump *is* actually good at talking to people. Not the people who hate him. But the undecided and the indifferent.)

Plenty of people will find this laughable, surely. Trump's public speaking skills are frequently seen as being at or near caveman-level, with grunts and snorts replacing human speech. But this ignores the impressive ways in which Trump has communicated with and mobilized his base. In fact, looking back on the general election between Clinton and Trump, and its coverage in the press, what is startling is the degree to which nobody noticed how powerful Trump's appeal was capable of being. To look at press clippings about Trump, one would think he was spending his time doing little but sending insults on Twitter and bragging about his penis. In fact, however, he was giving rallies all around the country, and at those rallies he was giving speeches, and in those speeches he was saying things that carried strong appeal with a number of voters.

There was rarely any analysis of Trump's speeches, however. The press was content to extract the jokes, exaggerations, and outrageous statements, acting as if Trump was saying nothing else at his rallies. In fact, he was also laying out a very clear right-wing populist message, focusing on trade, jobs, immigration, and national security. Trump's speeches were not incoherent or off-message, as the press frequently implied. Certainly, they had humorous digressions. But ultimately, they had some fairly careful and focused points. A representative paragraph:

> *There is nothing the political establishment will not do. No lie they won't tell, to hold their prestige and power at your expense, and that's what's been happening. The Washington establishment and the financial and media corporations that fund it, exist for only one reason, to protect and enrich itself. The establishment has trillions of dollars at stake in this election. As an example, just one single trade deal they'd like to pass involves trillions of dollars controlled by many countries, corporations, and lobbyists.*[474]

This is powerful stuff, and one struggles to recall how Clinton even attempted to counter it. In fact, the Clinton campaign mostly *didn't* attempt to argue the point. Instead, they focused on Donald Trump's fitness for office. Thus, people saw the following:

Donald Trump: A corrupt establishment is robbing you blind, telling you lies, and ruining your life.

Hillary Clinton: Donald Trump is an unstable narcissist who is totally unfit to be president. I am a stable and competent person with a lot of experience.[475]

The response, then, doesn't successfully address the point. It almost seems to concede it. In fact, we know that Clinton didn't even *try* to take on Trump's critiques of the establishment. The strategy from early on was to paint him as "dangerous Donald," a man who shouldn't be president. ("Dangerous Donald" was actually a nickname the Clinton campaign pushed in ads. It was colossally misguided, making him sound like a badass.[476])

Witness how Trump talked about Clinton in his speeches:

> *Honestly, she should be locked up. Should be locked up. And likewise the emails show that the Clinton machine is so closely and irrevocably tied to the media organization that she, listen to this, is given the questions and answers in advance of her debate performance with Bernie Sanders. Hillary Clinton is also given approval and veto power over quotes written about her in the New York Times. And the emails show the reporters conspire and collaborate with helping her win the election.*[477]

Again, we see the Trump bullshit machine at work. A lot of this is *close* to true. Hillary Clinton *did* have a warm relationship with certain reporters, and a list was drawn up of sympathetic journalists. It's not quite right that reporters "conspire." But Donna Brazile did leak the debate questions to the Clinton campaign.[478] Trump's statements are wild, but they're not so far from the truth that one can dismiss them outright. The Clinton campaign *did* enjoy a cozy relationship with the press. The mixture of truth, hyperbole, and emotion gives Trump's words a powerful appeal. Witness how a Trump speech ends:

> *We will vote for the country we want. We will vote for the future we want. We will vote for the politics we want. And we will vote to put this corrupt government cartel out of business, and out of business immediately. We will vote for the special interests and say "lots of luck, but you're being voted out of power." They've betrayed our workers, they've betrayed our borders, and most of all they've betrayed our freedoms. We will save our sovereign rights as a nation. We will end the politics of profit, we will end the rule of special interests, we will end the raiding of our jobs by other countries. We will end the total disenfranchisement of the American voter and the American worker. Our independence day is at hand, and it arrives finally on November 8th. Join me in taking back our country and creating a bright, glorious and prosperous new future for our people and we will make America great again and it will happen quickly. God bless you. Thank you.*[479]

You may hate Trump, but it's important to concede that it's an extremely effective piece of messaging. Who doesn't want their sovereign rights restored? Who wants cartels? Who wants workers betrayed, or voters disenfranchised? Anyone who thought Trump had no appeal was thinking about how they themselves perceived him, rather than how an undecided voter who went along to one of Trump's rallies would interpret what Trump was saying to them.

The Democratic responses to Trump's rhetoric were extremely ineffectual.[480] They mostly focused on pointing out Trump's lies and character flaws. But these aren't Trump's actual weak points. For one thing, if you call Trump a liar, he'll just call you one in return, and then people won't know what to think. For another thing, by focusing on whether Trump's statements are literally true or false in a technical sense, one can miss their deeper significance. During the election, there were constant attempts to "fact-check" Trump (*The Washington Post* and *PolitiFact* even instituted "real-time" fact-checks during the debates). But as Clay Shirky put it, you can't "bring fact-checkers to a culture war."[481] Fact-checking the statements Trump makes is a good way to counter them *logically*, but not a useful way to counter them politically. It brings satisfaction, but it doesn't neutralize Trump, and it allows Trump to portray the media and the left as little more than a bunch of pedantic nerds who obsess over trifles but don't have a plan to bring back jobs. Thus there was something to what Kellyanne Conway said, ridiculous as it sounds, when she said that the media tend "to go by what's come out of [Trump's] mouth rather than look at what's in his heart."[482] Trump's rhetorical appeal to his audience is frequently emotional rather than strictly logical or factual, and it's necessary to counter that emotional appeal.

Trump always wins at his own game. In order to beat him, you need to play a different game. If presidential elections have become media spectacles, Trump is the ultimate presidential candidate, because he is the ultimate manipulator of media spectacles. But if you can change the way media operates, then his strategies won't work anymore. The strategy is not necessarily to fight him directly—at least not on his terms—but to ignore him and do your own thing, develop your own agenda and stick to it. As one attorney who battled him suggests: "The key to Donald, like with any bully, is to tell him to go fuck himself."[483] Of course, plenty of people regularly tell Donald Trump to go fuck himself. But they also fall into his traps, because they think that "telling him to go fuck himself" means *actually* telling him this, rather than showing him you don't care about him. By getting into publicity wars with Trump, people reveal that they *do* care about him and *are* willing to pay plenty of attention to him.

WHAT CAUSED IT?

IN THE DAYS AFTER THE ELECTION, AS DEMOCRATS TRIED TO FIGURE out what the hell had just happened to them, weeks of vigorous finger-pointing ensued. Everybody had their own answer to the question of why Clinton lost. Had there been an anti-Establishment revolt in the white working class? Had a bunch of racist deplorables been energized by Trump's appeals to bigotry? Had Clinton simply been a bad candidate? Had she been the victim of sexism and unfair smears? Had the Russians meddled? Had the FBI? Had Trump been unstoppable? Would Bernie have won?

Part of the problem in analyzing the election after the fact was that everyone could easily tell their own preferred stories, carefully selecting the facts that served their own chosen narrative. You could make the case that Clinton had lost by alienating core Democratic constituencies, or that she had lost by being unfairly targeted by forces she could not control. Consider three possible reads of the election:

- *Donald Trump's victory was a resounding repudiation of the Democratic Party. He won over 300 electoral votes, and Republicans swept to power in the House and Senate, as well as continuing to dominate in the states. Scandal after scandal failed to destroy Trump, because no matter how much people disliked him, they preferred anything to Hillary Clinton and the Democrats. There was a working-class revolt in which the establishment liberal status quo was upended. People were tired of being ignored, belittled, and mocked by coastal elites, and Trump swept to office on a tide of politically correct backlash from the "deplorables." Hillary Clinton was a bad candidate, widely detested. The fact that she could not beat Donald Trump, who literally confessed to sexual assault on tape, suggests the weakness was in the Democrats' choice to run Clinton.*

- *Donald Trump's victory was not a product of the failure or repudiation of Democrats. Millions more people voted for Hillary Clinton than Donald Trump; how can it possibly be the case that Clinton was a bad candidate, when she resoundingly won the popular vote? Hillary Clinton survived a vicious attack from the left during the primary, a silly, overinflated email scandal, and the sexism of the American media, and still managed to get more votes. The only reason Hillary Clinton lost the election is that James Comey decided to interfere in the election at the last minute, painting a false picture of Clinton as corrupt and disreputable. Furthermore, Russia selectively leaked information designed to undermine Clinton.*

- *Clinton lost because of strategic mistakes. She was a good enough candidate. But she ran a bad campaign. She failed to focus resources in Rust Belt states. She spent too much time with rich donors and not enough time with ordinary people in crucial states. She did not deploy*

Obama or Bernie Sanders effectively as surrogates. This was not about her platform, or the candidate herself. It was about bad management on the part of her campaign. She paid too much attention to fancy algorithms and to her wealthy donors, and not enough to grassroots activists.

Each of these cases was made after the election. Some people believed that Clinton was a weak candidate who had been vulnerable and complacent. Others continued to see Clinton as a highly qualified and well-positioned candidate, who essentially triumphed (by winning the popular vote) but suffered a series of unjust setbacks that could not have been predicted.

How does one figure out how to think about the causes of Hillary Clinton's loss and Donald Trump's victory? Which of these stories is correct?

The first, and obvious, point, is that in many respects there is no actual contradiction between differing accounts of what happened. Did Clinton lose because of James Comey's letter or because she was incapable of delivering the kind of populist message necessary to win over Rust Belt voters? Well, it could very easily be the case that both of these factors together caused the loss. If *either* of them hadn't happened, she would have won, but *both* of them happened, so she didn't. Thus a person who says that Comey's letter cost Clinton the election is correct (because if he hadn't sent the letter, she wouldn't have lost) but a person who says Hillary Clinton was insufficiently populist is also correct (because if she had been a more convincing populist, she also wouldn't have lost).

Every event in human history is the product of a million causes, the absence of any one of which would be sufficient for it not to occur. These are the "but for" causes; Event B would not have occurred *but for* Preceding Event A. If I run a stop sign, and hit a pedestrian, one "but for" cause is my failure to stop. Another is the pedestrian's decision to cross the street; if he hadn't been in the street, I wouldn't have hit him. (What *caused* it and whose *fault* it is are separate inquiries.) Still another cause is the invention of the motorcar; *but for* the invention of cars, I wouldn't have run anybody over. There is, therefore, a limitless set of causes. And so if we ask the question "What caused outcome X?" we will necessarily end up going in circles. That's because we can come up with a million reasons why Donald Trump won. *If* Hillary had not set up a private email server. *If* people who had stayed home had come out and voted. *If* John Podesta had taken security precautions with his email. In determining *which* causes to focus on, it is best to think about *why* one is diagnosing causes in the first place. Presumably, one is mainly looking to determine responsibility rather than cause. After all, the pedestrian's decision to cross the street may be just as consequential as my decision to run the stop sign, but the *responsibility* is mine.

But when it comes to politics, there's something even more important than responsibility: usefulness. Unlike in a traffic accident, we can't sue to determine responsibility. We don't get to re-run the election if we can prove that the outcome wasn't our fault. Thus even if we prove that the election of Trump was *James Comey's fault* or *Jill Stein's fault* it doesn't make a difference. Finding the most appropriate party to blame might be satisfying, but it doesn't change the result.

When discussing causes, it may therefore be most productive to focus on those that one can *affect in the future,* the ones that give useful lessons. Instead of finding the most satisfying explanation of who caused the situation we now find ourselves in, we might look to discover what could have been done differently, in order to make sure that what happened in the Clinton/Trump race does not recur in future elections. It's better to conduct strategic examinations of responsibility rather than merely cathartic ones.

◆   ◆   ◆   ◆

LET US EXAMINE THE CASE OF THE COMEY LETTER. THERE IS evidence to suggest that James Comey's letter to Congress, informing them that there were further emails related to the FBI's investigation of Clinton, had an effect on the election outcome.[484] Hillary Clinton's poll numbers dropped in the last days of October. Comey's letter was sent on October 28th. Because Clinton lost by small margins in a few key states, the letter could have made the difference.

Now, it is not entirely certain that Comey's letter was the main source of Clinton's drop in polls. The drop began on October 24th, and the letter was not sent until the 28th. Another important piece of news came out around the same time, which could also have damaged Clinton. On the 24th, it was announced that Obamacare premiums for 2017 would be going up by 22%. So, in late October, just a few days before the election, many people received the news that a key Democratic policy, one Hillary Clinton was running in strong defense of, was going to cost them and their families a *lot* more money in the next year. It is reasonable to think that the Obamacare premium spike had an effect on some voters' decision-making. In fact, on October 25th (again, days before the Comey letter), Chris Cillizza of the *Washington Post* wrote that "in an alternate universe, [the] Obamacare news is devastating for Hillary Clinton." Cillizza wrote that:

> *For Clinton, who has latched herself to President Obama throughout both the primary and general election, this should be a very bad development. Very bad. If you wanted to make the case that Clinton represents an extension of the bad part of the Obama presidency, this is a gift of epic proportions. EPIC.*[485]

Cillizza nevertheless concluded that the Obamacare premium spike was *not* a particularly bad bit of news for Clinton, because the election had turned into a referendum on Donald Trump, who was mired in scandal. And yet: in the days following the Obamacare news, support *did* shift crucially away from Clinton and toward Trump. Is it bizarre to assume that at least some of this was due to people's shock at discovering that a Democratic policy was about to raise their health insurance costs by possibly thousands of dollars? Why is it necessary to believe, as Cillizza did, that this would only matter in an "alternate universe"? Perhaps the "alternate universe" in question is, in fact, the real world, where people care far more about their health insurance payments than about whatever Donald Trump mini-scandal is occupying the media's attention this week.[486]

One should therefore be cautious about accepting the claim that James Comey's letter was solely responsible for the late shift from Clinton to Trump. But let us assume that Comey's letter *did* make a decisive difference. By suddenly reopening the investigation into Clinton, and dragging the sordid spectacle of Anthony Weiner back into the press, Comey handed Donald Trump an extraordinary gift. It may well have been enough to make the difference, in a few crucial close states.

The important question, though, is what the *implications* of this are. We can conclude, from this, that James Comey is a fiend who should not have meddled. But there's another, more disquieting point for Democrats to come to terms with: if they had not run a candidate who was under active investigation by the FBI, Comey's whims may have been of less importance in determining the outcome of the race. Precisely because Comey was able to upend the race with a stroke of his pen, it may have been foolish to put forth a nominee whose prospects were entirely dependent on how James Comey handled the ongoing investigation against her. By choosing to nominate someone whose fate hung on which choices the FBI director would make, an incredible level of risk was introduced into the campaign. Democrats knew, when they nominated Hillary Clinton, that the FBI was investigating her. They were therefore taking a *gamble* on what the FBI director was going to do.

If one wants to control political outcomes, rather than contenting oneself with assigning responsibility after the outcomes occur, it is therefore more helpful to focus on those things one can *affect*. Frequently, however, diagnoses of the causes of electoral losses end up trying to assign blame rather than trying to figure out how our own strategy could be changed in the future to achieve different results.

This is why it makes more sense, in looking back at the election, to examine and critique Democratic strategy rather than Republican strategy. We can criticize Trump as much as we please, and point out all of his low, underhanded tactics, along with his various lies. But criticizing Trump does not eliminate Trump. On the other hand, figuring out where Democratic choices went wrong, and how the election could have been won, will offer a set of lessons that can be implemented as Democrats attempt to rebuild their political fortunes. A useful framing question, in looking back at the election, is "Could it have been otherwise?" Clearly, certain factors were beyond the control of Democrats. Yet were there decisions that *were* in their control that could have been made differently? Are there lessons about what *we* should do in order to avoid similar outcomes in the future?

These are uncomfortable questions for Democrats. It is always easier to write something off as inevitable, or the product of external malicious forces, than to accept that one's own choices played a substantial role in bringing it about. It is far more comforting, if one is a Democrat, to blame the Russians than to blame failures of Democratic strategy. If the Russians are responsible, there was nothing we could have done. If *we're* responsible, then we must constantly live with the thought that we could have stopped Trump, but failed to do so. Democrats will understandably wish to move on, to avoid "re-litigating" old battles out of a need for party unity.[487] But without first looking backward, there is no way to figure out how to move forward.

1. STRATEGIC MISTAKES

FOR THE QUICKEST ENCAPSULATION OF WHY HILLARY CLINTON LOST to Donald Trump, one only needs to read this extract from a September *New York Times* article on the Clinton campaign, entitled "Where Has Hillary Clinton Been? Ask The Ultrarich":

> *At a private fund-raiser Tuesday night at a waterfront Hamptons estate, Hillary Clinton danced alongside Jimmy Buffett, Jon Bon Jovi and Paul McCartney, and joined in a singalong finale to "Hey Jude." "I stand between you and the apocalypse," a confident Mrs. Clinton declared to laughs, exhibiting a flash of self-awareness and humor to a crowd that included Calvin Klein and Harvey Weinstein and for whom the prospect of a Donald J. Trump presidency is dire. Mr. Trump has pointed to Mrs. Clinton's noticeably scant schedule of campaign events this summer to suggest she has been hiding from the public. But Mrs. Clinton has been more than accessible to those who reside in some of the country's most moneyed enclaves and are willing to spend hundreds of thousands of dollars to see her. In the last two weeks of August, Mrs. Clinton raked in roughly $50 million at 22 fund-raising events, averaging around $150,000 an hour, according to a New York Times tally. And while Mrs. Clinton has faced criticism for her failure to hold a news conference for months, she has fielded hundreds of questions from the ultrarich in places like the Hamptons, Martha's Vineyard, Beverly Hills and Silicon Valley. "It's the old adage, you go to where the money is," said Jay S. Jacobs, a prominent New York Democrat. Mrs. Clinton raised about $143*

million in August, the campaign's best month yet. At a
single event on Tuesday in Sagaponack, N.Y., 10 people
paid at least $250,000 to meet her, raising $2.5 mil-
lion. If Mr. Trump appears to be waging his campaign
in rallies and network interviews, Mrs. Clinton's second
presidential bid seems to amount to a series of high-dollar
fund-raisers with public appearances added to the sched-
ule when they can be fit in. Last week, for example, she
diverged just once from her packed fund-raising schedule
to deliver a speech.[488]

Here, we see all of the most disastrous ingredients of the Clinton approach. Clinton jokes about things that matter seriously to working people. She is "more accessible to those who reside in…moneyed enclaves" than to the public at large. Instead of holding news conferences and town halls, she is hanging out with Paul McCartney. All of the most poisonous aspects of the Clinton approach to politics are visible: the money-for-access, the contempt for ordinary voters, the focus on safely blue states rather than swing states, the partying while people's lives fall apart, the belief that all you need is cash in order to win people's votes.

In many respects, Clinton's campaign style was downright bizarre. She did not seem aware of the "optics" of hobnobbing with rich Martha's Vineyard types, nor did she seem to spend a moment thinking about how to win over blue collar workers in Rust Belt states. And not only did she pointlessly spend time in solidly blue states, but she also went to solidly *red* states that she could never hope to win. Clinton herself was in Tempe, Arizona on November 2nd,[489] and Tim Kaine was in Phoenix on Nov. 3rd.[490] This means that Hillary Clinton spent more time in Arizona than Wisconsin, a state that she did not even visit once in the entire period from the Democratic primary to Election Day in November.[491]

Clinton's campaign staff also seemed to believe that they did not need to maximize the assistance they received from Bernie Sanders, Barack Obama, or Joe Biden. According to a particularly telling report from *Politico*'s Edward-Isaac Dovere:

> *Familiar sources say the campaign never asked the Vermont senator's campaign aides for help thinking through Michigan, Wisconsin or anywhere else where he had run strong. It was already November when the campaign finally reached out to the White House to get President Barack Obama into Michigan, a state that he'd worked hard and won by large margins in 2008 and 2012. On the Monday before Election Day, Obama added a stop in Ann Arbor, but that final weekend, the president had played golf on Saturday and made one stop in Orlando on Sunday, not having been asked to do anything else. Michigan senior adviser Steve Neuman had been asking for months to get Obama and the First Lady on the ground there. People who asked for Vice President Joe Biden to come in were told that top Clinton aides weren't clearing those trips.*[492]

Some decisions were totally inexplicable. Due to a "fear that Trump would win the popular vote while losing the electoral vote" millions of dollars raised by Donna Brazile "got dumped into Chicago and New Orleans," places where that money was guaranteed to be totally useless.[493] The campaign's advertising resources were similarly ill-deployed; the *Washington Post* reported that odd misallocations of the advertising budget "doomed" Clinton's campaign, which:

> *…aired more television advertisements in Omaha than in the states of Michigan and Wisconsin combined. The*

Omaha ads were in pursuit of a single electoral vote in a Nebraska congressional district, which Clinton did not ultimately win, and also bled into households in Iowa, which also she did not win. Michigan and Wisconsin add up to 26 electoral votes; she appears not to have won them, either.[494]

Edward-Isaac Dovere recounts the conflicts between union volunteers from the Service Employees International Union (SEIU) and the official Clinton campaign. Dovere says that, a week and a half before the election, when it became obvious that Hillary Clinton was going to lose Iowa, the SEIU decided to reroute its volunteers to Michigan. The SEIU had wanted to send organizers to Michigan since the beginning of the race, but had been ordered not to by the Clinton campaign, whose models told them the state was a sure thing. But when the SEIU told the Brooklyn headquarters of its plan to go to Michigan (where Hillary's victory was at risk) rather than Iowa (where Trump was sure to win), Clinton's "top campaign aides" were "furious":

Turn that bus around, the Clinton team ordered SEIU. Those volunteers needed to stay in Iowa to fool Donald Trump into competing there, not drive to Michigan, where the Democrat's models projected a 5-point win through the morning of Election Day. Michigan organizers were shocked. It was the latest case of Brooklyn ignoring on-the-ground intel and pleas for help in a race that they felt slipping away at the end...[495]

Other pro-Clinton activists on the ground in Michigan had the same experience. Dovere's report paints a picture of a totally out-of-touch campaign headquarters, driven by consultants and fancy analytics, with absolutely no concern for the needs or requests of activists on the ground:

> *Clinton never even stopped by a United Auto Workers union hall in Michigan.… The anecdotes are different but the narrative is the same across battlegrounds, where Democratic operatives lament a one-size-fits-all approach drawn entirely from pre-selected data… guiding [Clinton campaign head Robby] Mook's decisions on field, television, everything else… "I've never seen a campaign like this," said Virgie Rollins, a Democratic National Committee member and longtime political hand in Michigan who described months of failed attempts to get attention to the collapse she was watching unfold in slow-motion among women and African-American millennials… "It was very surgical and corporate. They had their model, this is how they're going to do it. Their thing was, 'We don't have to leave [literature] at the doors, everyone knows who Hillary Clinton is,'" said one person involved in the Michigan campaign.*[496]

Dovere uncovered stories from Michigan operatives indicating that the Clinton campaign was actively contemptuous of traditional methods of political organizing, and even spurned voters and volunteers who wanted to show their support. An elderly woman in Flint went to a Clinton campaign office to ask for a lawn sign and offer to canvas, but was "told these were not 'scientifically' significant ways of increasing the vote."[497] She left and never returned. The same thing happened to a "crew of building trade workers," who showed up to volunteer, but "confused after being told there was no literature to hand out like in most campaigns, also left and never looked back."[498] The Clinton campaign's "scientific" approach to politics made them hyper-confident and left them totally blindsided:

> *Most voters in Michigan didn't see a television ad until*

the final week. Most importantly, multiple operatives said, the Clinton campaign dismissed what's known as in-person "persuasion" — no one was knocking on doors trying to drum up support for the Democratic nominee, which also meant no one was hearing directly from voters aside from voters they'd already assumed were likely Clinton voters, no one tracking how feelings about the race and the candidates were evolving. This left no information to check the polling models against — which might have, for example, showed the campaign that some of the white male union members they had expected to be likely Clinton voters actually veering toward Trump...People involved in the Michigan campaign still can't understand why Brooklyn stayed so sure of the numbers in a state that it also had projected Clinton would win in the primary.[499]

◆   ◆   ◆   ◆

ALL OF THIS COULD BE WRITTEN OFF AS "MONDAY MORNING quarterbacking." Everyone has an after-the-fact diagnosis of what Clinton should have done differently, but it's far easier to say this after the fact than during the election. But these criticisms *didn't* just suddenly spring up after the election; they were being made at the time. Local Wisconsin news was puzzling over why Clinton hadn't set foot in the state during the primary.[500] And Michigan field offices were begging Hillary Clinton's Brooklyn headquarters for reinforcements.[501]

Sanders activists in Rust Belt states were also rebuffed by the Clinton campaign, when they attempted to warn Clinton's staff of the potential cost of ignoring states like Michigan and Wisconsin. *The Daily Beast* reported that Sanders' people were "offering Clinton's team their plans—strategy memos, lists of hardened state organizers, timelines, data, the works—to win over certain voters in areas she ultimately lost but where Sanders had won during the primary."[502] However, in the words of one former Sanders organizer:

> *They fucking ignored us on all these [three] battleground states [while] we were sounding the alarm for months… We kept saying to each other like, 'What the fuck, why are they just blowing us off? They need these voters more than anybody… We were saying we are offering our help— nobody wanted Donald Trump… We were painting them a dire picture, and I couldn't help but think they literally looked like they had no idea what was going on here.*[503]

Michael Moore was raising similar concerns. In July, Moore wrote the most prescient and perceptive analysis of the entire election cycle, entitled "5 Reasons Why Trump Will Win." Moore first cautioned people against complacency:

> *This wretched, ignorant, dangerous part-time clown and full time sociopath is going to be our next president…I can see what you're doing right now. You're shaking your head wildly – "No, Mike, this won't happen!" Unfortunately, you are living in a bubble that comes with an adjoining echo chamber…You need to exit that bubble right now. You need to stop living in denial.*[504]

Moore then explained precisely how Trump would win. Reason #1? "Midwest Math":

> *I believe Trump is going to focus much of his attention on the four blue states in the rustbelt of the upper Great Lakes – Michigan, Ohio, Pennsylvania and Wisconsin… In 2012, Mitt Romney lost by 64 electoral votes. Add up*

*the electoral votes cast by Michigan, Ohio, Pennsylvania
and Wisconsin. It's 64. All Trump needs to do to win is to
carry, as he's expected to do, the swath of traditional red
states from Idaho to Georgia (states that'll never vote for
Hillary Clinton), and then he just needs these four rust
belt states. He doesn't need Florida. He doesn't need Colo-
rado or Virginia. Just Michigan, Ohio, Pennsylvania and
Wisconsin. And that will put him over the top. This is
how it will happen in November.*[505]

Indeed, that was exactly how it did happen (although Trump got
Florida, too). And even as Moore had given the Clinton campaign the
clearest possible warning, it *still* spent the next months ignoring the
crucial states, and spurning the pleading of progressives in Michigan
to at least send some more canvassers or yard signs.

To call this "Monday morning quarterbacking," then, allows the
Clinton campaign to get off the hook for something that it bore full
responsibility for. This was not something that people noticed after
the fact. It was something people noticed at the time, and tried desperately to tell the campaign. But the Clinton camp was so pighead-
edly committed to its existing strategy that it refused to consider any
suggestion that it was making mistakes.

One of the reasons the campaign was so adamant in refusing to
conduct critical self-examination was that it had an extremely high
level of confidence in the ability of math to produce better strategy
than any humans were capable of. *Politico* reported in September on
the "computer algorithms that underlie nearly all of the Clinton campaign's most important strategic decisions," saying that Clinton's data
expert, Elan Kriegel, was the "invisible guiding hand" upon whom the
campaign consistently relied to tell them what to do.[506] Kriegel used "a
proprietary computer algorithm called Ada," which determined "the
cities Clinton campaigns in and what states she competes in, when

she emails supporters and how those emails are crafted, what doors volunteers knock on and what phone numbers they dial, who gets Facebook ads and who gets printed mailers."[507] Strategists said they had "never seen a campaign that's more driven by the analytics," with data deferred to absolutely, even when it flatly contradicted common sense.[508]

This explains why both why Hillary Clinton's messaging seemed robotic and inhuman, *and* why her campaign made totally bizarre and irrational decisions. Clinton sounded robotic because every step she took was being dictated by a robot, and she spent the leadup to the election in Tempe rather than Milwaukee because the robot said this was the prudent course of action. Ada ran "400,000 simulations a day" of potential races against Trump,[509] and Clinton's people were convinced that the computer knew best. *The Washington Post* reported that "The campaign's deployment of other resources — including county-level campaign offices and the staging of high-profile concerts with stars like Jay Z and Beyoncé — was largely dependent on Ada's work, as well."[510]

Ada's apparent fondness for celebrities suggests that the algorithm, in many ways, simply reflected the biases and preconceptions that Clinton's team already held. Algorithms are the products of their creators, and Ada's role may simply have been to affirm the Clinton team's own wrongheaded beliefs, and make it harder for them to hear criticism even as facts in the world appeared to contradict the conventional wisdom.

Some of this strategy was a logical outgrowth of Clinton's own personal philosophy. The *reason* Hillary Clinton spent more time with rich donors than on the ground in Wisconsin is because, in a crucial sense, this is who Hillary Clinton is. It was no accident that Hillary Clinton believed that Silicon Valley data nerds and rich Manhattanites were the key to electoral success. Clinton believes that these people make the world go round. The campaign's flaws reflected Hillary Clinton's personal traits: it was aloof, furtive, self-contradictory, and lacking in clear principle. To some extent, then, these weren't simply strategic *mistakes*: they were the product of a type of Democratic Party *mindset*, one that has made inroads among the wealthy (Obama and Clinton have both received impressive amounts of support from Wall Street donors[511]) but has lost support outside traditional liberal strongholds. Democrats therefore need to do more than just apportioning ad-buys more strategically. They need to excise the specter of Clintonism *itself*. Many people dislike Hillary Clinton for good reason: they have the sense that she does not actually care very much about them, and does not have any serious plans for how to improve their lives. And frankly, this is accurate. Clinton didn't really pretend to care much about the lives of voters. She spent her time with rich donors, she didn't have any particular promises for her presidency, and she called a bunch of them "deplorable." (She also made some catastrophically stupid gaffes, like telling West Virginians she planned to put "a lot of miners and coal companies out of business."[512]) People are right to be suspicious of this kind of Democratic politics, which sees itself as responsible for telling the people what their interests are rather than listening to them to find out what *they* think their interests are.

We shouldn't focus too much, then, on the role of "strategy," even though strategy is essential to rebuilding progressive political fortunes. Strategy is one thing. But making sure that we *don't* produce self-enriching,[513] dishonest[514] politicians like the Clintons is also important.

2. THIRD PARTIES?

Was the election of Trump also partially the fault of Jill Stein and the Green Party? Probably not, though it depends how we determine what constitutes fault. Even if *every single person* who voted for Jill Stein had voted for Hillary Clinton instead, Clinton still would have lost the election. While the amount of votes received by the Green Party was less than Trump's margin of victory in several swing states (Michigan, Wisconsin), in other states the Stein votes simply weren't enough to make up the difference.[515]

The fact is that Jill Stein did *not actually get many votes*. In most of the states that mattered, her total was around 1%.[516] That means that there was not a particularly high mass defection to the Green Party among former Bernie voters. Perhaps these people stayed home, but polls suggested that people who were assumed to be "Bernie or Bust" did largely fall in line and end up supporting Clinton in the general election.

Furthermore, if we want to consider the role of third parties, we cannot limit ourselves to thinking about third parties on the left. Gary Johnson, the Libertarian candidate, frequently earned about three times as many votes as Jill Stein. If third-parties are treated as "siphoning" votes from the major parties, then Johnson siphoned many more votes on the right than Stein did on the left.

It's nevertheless true that third-party votes did have a "spoiler" effect in *certain* states, and that if enough people choose to vote for third parties rather than major parties, elections can be swung. We know that if 500 Nader voters in Florida had held their nose and voted for Al Gore in the 2000 election, the entire outcome would have changed and the Iraq War might never have happened.[517] It is therefore important to think very carefully before voting third-party, *if* (and really, only if) one lives in a swing state where third-party votes could have serious consequences.

Furthermore, if we believe that more Johnson votes would have gone to Clinton than Stein votes that would have gone to Trump, there *may* be an argument that third-party voting kept Clinton from victory. But recognize what this presumes: that the Democrats are *entitled* to people's votes, rather than having to win those votes by actually appealing to the voters. The "spoiler" theory has a certain arrogance to it, as Nader voters frequently point out.

Still, many third-party voters who hold progressive values can be reluctant to even admit the possibility that they could actually end up under-mining those values by refusing to vote for a "lesser evil" candidate. Those who defend Florida Nader voters often argued that they shouldn't be sin-gled out for blame among the various causes of the outcome. After all, if 500 *Bush* voters had changed their minds, this would likewise have altered the election result. Why blame Nader rather than Bush?

But it's the most progressive voters who are supposed to care the most about ensuring progressive policy outcomes. Nader voters, because they are further to the left than Bush voters, should probably care a lot about the possibility of war or the elimination of social programs, both of which are risks that come with Republican presidents.

There's a simple solution to the third-party spoiler question: *only vote third party if you live in a safe state.* Otherwise, vote for the "lesser-evil" candidate. That way, one avoids the possibility of repeating a situation like the 2000 election.

Fortunately, in the 2016 election, third parties played only a minor role. Still, because margins of victory or loss can be razor-thin, in cer-tain states progressives who vote for third parties may be playing with human lives.

3. RACISM/SEXISM, ETC.

At least in the very immediate aftermath, the conventional wisdom among liberals about their loss seems to be as follows: they underestimated the racism and sexism of the American people, and the degree to which this country was full of a dark and rotten hatred. As Paul Krugman summed up his own take-away:

> *People like me, and probably like most readers of The New York Times, truly didn't understand the country we live in. We thought that our fellow citizens would not, in*

the end, vote for a candidate so manifestly unqualified for high office, so temperamentally unsound, so scary yet ludicrous. We thought that the nation, while far from having transcended racial prejudice and misogyny, had become vastly more open and tolerant over time. There turn out to be a huge number of people — white people, living mainly in rural areas — who don't share at all our idea of what America is about.[518]

Krugman's perspective is that Trump's victory was a victory for his remarks about Mexicans and Muslims, and for Trump's many nasty remarks and attacks on Hillary Clinton. He won because a large percentage of the country is hateful and does not share progressive values.

First, we should note that this is always going to be a tempting story for people on the left to tell themselves. That's because it validates their preconceptions, it says that while they *thought* America was very racist and sexist, in fact America is *even more* racist and sexist than they believed. While ostensibly an admission of error, the actual gist is: "I underestimated the correctness of my own worldview."

This view also exonerates people on the left of any responsibility for the outcome. It suggests that their flaw was that they believed in people too much, *not* that they failed to actually run a decent candidate or offer a compelling and worthwhile political message. One should automatically be wary of stories like this, which do a lot to assuage us that the Paul Krugmans of the world are noble and fine and decent, and to the extent they have acted wrongly, it is solely in having had excessive confidence in their fellow human beings.[519]

Many progressives have adopted this view. They have suggested that Trump's support is about bigotry, and that *economic* explanations, which focus on diminishing financial prospects in the American heartland, miss the much darker reality: that Trump's election is the product of white backlash to a black president. David Masciotra of

Salon fully embraced this perspective. After Trump's victory, he totally dismissed the role of economics. If you wanted to understand Trump, Masciotra said, you needed to understand race above all:

> *It has little or nothing to do with economics. Studies demonstrated, in the Republican primary, that Trump supporters were actually wealthier than the constituencies for the Democratic candidates… Many leftists won't acknowledge the totality of what Trump has exposed about America, because it is too ugly and painful… The narrative that Trump deserved to win it because he responded to the legitimate economic anxieties of the working class is wrong.*[520]

Another frequently-made claim is that racism "predicts" support for Trump. For example, Sean McElwee produces data showing that racists are more likely to support Trump than Clinton.[521] If we know that you have certain racial prejudices, we can comfortably predict you are also probably a Trump voter.[522]

The first point to note is that each of these writers is making a blanket statement on an issue where some nuance might be useful. By offering mono-causal explanations and either/or dichotomies (is it race *or* economics?) they exclude the possibility that race and economics could both be important factors.

Indeed, there's good reason to doubt the "angry white racists" explanation for Trump's victory. First, as *FiveThirtyEight* has pointed out, economic anxiety *was* a factor in people's support for Trump. Trump performed best "in places where the economy is in worse shape, and especially in places where jobs are most at risk in the future."[523] Ben Casselman writes that:

> *The slower a county's job growth has been since 2007, the more it shifted toward Trump… Trump significantly*

outperformed Romney in counties where residents had lower credit scores and in counties where more men have stopped working The list goes on: More subprime loans? More Trump support. More residents receiving disability payments? More Trump support. Lower earnings among full-time workers? More Trump support. [Trump country] isn't the part of America where people are in the worst financial shape; it's the part of America where their economic prospects are on the steepest decline.[524]

Second, a few of the arguments that are advanced are misleading. For example, the use of averages: Trump's supporters may be *on average* wealthier than Clinton's supporters. We would expect that, because Democrats have a greater percentage of minority voters, and members of racial minority groups tend to have less wealth, on average, than white people. But if we want to determine the role of economics in causing the outcome of the election, we also want to know whether there is a *subgroup* of Trump voters that are economically suffering. It may well be that while many Republicans are well-off businesspeople with rosy economic prospects (distorting the average), there is another group consisting of poor or economically anxious people with limited prospects.

What about the claim that racism *predicts* Trump support? McElwee convincingly shows that if you can show that someone is a white racist, you can fairly comfortably predict that they will also be a Trump supporter. But the problem with data like this is that it doesn't tell us what we're looking to find out: it tells us that racists tend to be Trump supporters, *not* that Trump supporters tend to be racists. Distinguishing between these two claims is important. After all, if all racists are Trump voters, but racists still constitute only a small fraction of Trump's overall support, then there is a large group of non-racist Trump voters that Democrats can focus on winning over. Yet if the vast majority of Trump voters are racist, there are fewer opportunities for Democrats to make inroads without sacrificing their opposition to racism.

The truth is rather simple and mundane: there were people who voted for Trump because of racism, and there were people who did not. There were people who voted for Trump because they felt let down by Obama. There were people who voted for Trump because they recently lost their jobs. People voted for Trump for all kinds of reasons.

For example, listen to this explanation that a white female Trump voter gave for her decision. She said she supported Clinton in 2008 against Obama, and was skeptical of Trump because she had heard he was racist, but then went to one of his rallies with her son:

> *I expected him to be like what I'd seen on the news, saying hateful things. But his presence was very calming and I liked his talking points. We really are the middle class, and we kind of get swept aside.... In the past, [Clinton's] stance on abortion was more the way I feel, just for the first trimester, then she did a 360. She was here in the primary, having a debate with Bernie Sanders. He answered the question honestly. When they asked her the same question, she kind of danced around it. Then she went on "The View" and said she was for late-term abortions. Just take a stance, be honest. Same thing as with gay marriage, she wasn't for it, then she was. I'm 100 percent for it. It's ridiculous the way we tell people who they can and cannot marry. Don't go back and forth. Don't pander.*[525]

Thus the voter's choice was made because of (1) Trump's rhetoric about helping the middle class and (2) Clinton's evasiveness and pandering.[526] This is not a particularly unreasonable way of thinking. It certainly doesn't sound very deplorable.

Yet some progressives have actually argued that it doesn't even matter whether Trump voters had good intentions or good reasons. Because Trump himself adopted cruel and bigoted stances toward Mexicans and Muslims, his voters nevertheless bear full responsibility for the results, and should all be treated as bigots. Jamelle Bouie, *Slate*'s chief political correspondent, argued in a column that "There's No Such Thing as a Good Trump Voter." Bouie's argument is that Trump will hurt many non-white people, and that instead of empathizing with those who put Trump in office, we should empathize with the non-white people whom Trump will hurt. As he says:

> *To face [the consequences of Trump's presidency] and then demand empathy for the people who made them a reality—who backed racist demagoguery, whatever their reasons—is to declare Trump's victims less worthy of attention than his enablers. To insist Trump's backers are good people is to treat their inner lives with more weight than the actual lives on the line under a Trump administration. At best, it's myopic and solipsistic. At worst, it's morally grotesque.*[527]

But why not have empathy with both? A true progressive politics is capable of caring about *everyone*. Yes, it *would* be grotesque to care about Trump voters in West Virginia, but not about the Mexican immigrant families whom those West Virginians wanted Trump to deport. But nobody faces such a choice. There's no need to decide whether to empathize with black lung-afflicted miners or refugee families. A successful, principled, humanistic political agenda cares about *all* disadvantaged people everywhere. As Fredrik deBoer writes, liberalism stands for "the idea that everyone should be treated with human dignity, enjoy equal opportunity and equal rights, and live free of poverty and injustice," thus "chopping up the country into places that you think matter and don't – acting as though some places deserve hopelessness and economic malaise and some don't – is contrary to the basic moral architecture of the American progressive tradition."[528]

Another key point is this: even if we acknowledge that a person is racist, we should understand what the economic roots of racism can be. Often, prejudices bloom into bigotry because racism offers convenient explanations for people's life-conditions. It can be tempting to blame immigrants for the loss of one's job rather than blaming the structural economic forces that are actually, but less obviously, at play. One job of progressives is to help people understand that *people of different racial backgrounds* are not the source of social ills, and to point people toward true explanations and true solutions. Thus economic deprivation can *lead* to an exacerbation of people's racism, meaning that it makes far more sense to see "race" and "economics" as two parts of a complex picture rather than as competing, mutually exclusive explanations.

In fact, it's very easy to understand this if you spend time talking to the voters about whom pundits make countless speculations based on polling data. Real people are flawed and complicated, and frequently they will be both racially prejudiced *and* have difficult life circumstances. When we understand people in their fullness, we see that the job of progressives is not to *deny* the importance of either prejudice or personal financial situation, but to figure out how to get people to be less prejudiced *as well as* ensuring a universal guarantee of a decent standard of living.

Of course, it's easy enough to figure out that many Trump voters aren't monsters. But many Democrats in coastal cities know very few Trump voters.[529] Thus many in the press and the Democratic Party apparatus have a hard time making sense of these voters' motivations. In order to understand Trump's base of support, instead of trying to speak to and empathize with these voters, they look at statistical data. From the statistical data, they see that these people express anxiety about race and immigration, and that they are not disproportionately poor. They thus conclude that Trump voters are motivated primarily by prejudice, and mock the idea that it is economic concerns that matter most to them.

If you adopt this theory, then you reach a somewhat fatalistic conclusion about Trump supporters. You can't *persuade* them, because they're racists, and racism is an irrational feeling. Instead, you *fight* them, by mocking them, and trying to turn out your own base. By treating Trump's support as largely the product of racism, one gives up on any attempt to actually appeal to Trump voters' concerns and interests, since racism is not an interest worth appealing to. And this was what Democrats did. There was a campaign of mockery: Trump voters were treated with disdain. Hillary Clinton dismissed huge swaths of them as a "basket of deplorables." To be a Trump supporter was to be dumb, a redneck, a misogynist.

But the real dynamic of Trump voters is often different: many had a kind of undirected dissatisfaction and anger at the Establishment. They didn't really know the source of this dissatisfaction. For some, it was likely economics. For some, immigration. For others, it was probably simply an existential despair at the hopelessness of modern life, such as we can all feel. Trump came along and gave them a convenient narrative: the source of this anguish was ISIS, Mexicans, bad trade deals, and Hillary Clinton. It was a powerful narrative. Democrats didn't have a good counter-narrative. They lost.

It's important to recognize the extent to which support for Trump was this kind of blind anger *at* something rather than an affirmative vote *for* anything. Liberals didn't understand why none of Trump's scandals (the fraud, the tax evasion, the sexual assaults) seemed to dim his support. They didn't realize that Trump was, in Michael Moore's memorable phrase, a "human Molotov cocktail" to be thrown in the direction of D.C. with the hope of blowing it up.[530]

This meant that (in some sense) the worse he was, the more people liked him. A vote for Trump was not nuanced. It was designed to do as much damage as possible. Pointing out that the Molotov cocktail does not share the thrower's values, or cheats on its taxes, is not an effective rhetorical strategy. Because a vote for Trump is an attempt to blow up the government, it doesn't matter at all whether Trump is a sleaze, sex predator, or vulgarian. He pisses off the right people, and that is what matters.

◆   ◆   ◆   ◆

WHAT ABOUT SEXISM? TO WHAT DEGREE DID HILLARY CLINTON'S gender factor into her loss? It's difficult to know with precision. People's feelings about gender often operate in unpredictable ways. For example, one might expect that while Hillary Clinton's gender would make some sexist men hate her, it would also cause some women to be keener on having her as president than they would otherwise be. However, certain women seem to have been *put off* by appeals to the historic status of Hillary Clinton's presidential campaign, seeing it as patronizing to think that women should be excited about a female candidate merely because she is female.[531]

We know that gender *does* matter, that it factors in to people's perception of Hillary Clinton. There is clearly something gender-based in the "Trump that Bitch" shirts that could be seen being sported at Trump's rallies.[532] (Men don't tend to get called bitches, even though plenty of male politicians are far more conniving and soulless than Hillary Clinton!) But because sexism can be buried or subconscious, it's hard to measure its impact, even though we know that it certainly *does* matter.

The voting itself fell, to a significant extent, along gender lines. *Newsweek* reported after the election that the gender gap among the electorate was the largest since modern polling began in 1972, with less than a quarter of white men without college degrees voting for Clinton.[533] But gender doesn't explain everything: the majority of white women voted for Donald Trump, meaning that Hillary Clinton did not capture most of the voters who shared her own demographic characteristic. If the story of the election is about gender, it is a complex story, in which large numbers of female voters decided to vote for a man who has confessed to sexual assault against the first female major-party presidential contender...

4. COULD BERNIE HAVE DONE IT?

BERNIE SANDERS DID NOT NECESSARILY LOOK LIKE THE "PRAGMATIC" choice as the Democratic nominee. He calls himself a socialist. He is Jewish. He is old. These traits do not scream "electability." But after Clinton's loss to Trump, some began to think that there were good reasons why Bernie Sanders would have made for a more effective Democratic candidate. He had a populist appeal that was targeted toward voters in Rust Belt states, focusing heavily on the negative consequences of globalization for U.S. manufacturing, and the bread-and-butter issues affecting the American middle class. Since Hillary Clinton was seen by many as elitist, corrupt, and in the pocket of the wealthy, Bernie Sanders' anti-big business, anti-Establishment campaign might have been able to make the crucial difference in tipping the election from Trump.

Certainly, against Sanders, Trump would not have been able to run quite the same campaign. He would not have been able to direct quite so much fire at trade deals and the disappearance of American jobs, because these are precisely the same issues that Sanders himself has been concerned with over the course of his many decades in government. Furthermore, Sanders would not have had some of Hillary Clinton's particular personal vulnerabilities, such as the pending FBI investigation and the long history of (frequently exaggerated, but nevertheless persistent) political scandals. Finally, certain polls indicated that Sanders had a far better chance against Donald Trump than Hillary Clinton.

But there are also arguments for why Bernie Sanders would *not* have managed to do any better. Clinton-supporting Democrats said from the beginning that Sanders' strong poll numbers against Trump were artificially inflated, because he hadn't yet had to undergo a brutal opposition smear campaign. Theda Skocpol of Harvard's Kennedy School wrote a letter to the *New York Times* with the theme that she would very much like Sanders to consider shutting up and going away forever:

> *Mr. Sanders did not attract broad working-class support in the primaries: His base was overwhelmingly restricted to white liberals, especially in the cities and college towns. Mr. Sanders' refusal to concede in a timely way as Hillary Clinton won many millions more votes and his constant harping that she was "corrupt" furthered Mr. Trump's message and contributed to the con man's catastrophic victory. Mr. Sanders has much to apologize for...* [534]

But Skocpol is being disingenuous when she suggests that white liberals in college towns were Bernie Sanders' base of support. For example, in Wisconsin (where Clinton would ultimately lose to Trump in the general election), Bernie Sanders won all but one county. The only county Sanders lost was Milwaukee County, which, ironically enough, is Wisconsin's largest "college town." [535]

The idea that Sanders only had support among white leftist college students is a myth. In fact, Clinton/Sanders divide was more *regional* than anything else. But it's plain that Sanders support was not concentrated in "cities." In fact, in many states, the more rural areas went for Sanders, while urban areas went for Clinton. One can see this, for example, in New York and in Theda Skocpol's own state of Massachusetts:

NY/MA/WI Democratic Primaries, 2016

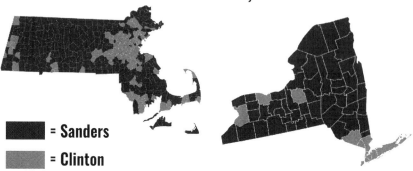

= Sanders

= Clinton

In many states it was, in fact, the wealthy Democrats in the cities who supported Clinton, while poorer rural Democrats supported Sanders. That is to say: the type of voter *more likely* to vote for Trump in the general election voted for Sanders in the primary. Thus there is good reason to believe that Sanders would have campaigned well in the sorts of areas that ultimately handed the election to Trump.[536]

We know that Clinton-supporting leaders of the Democratic Party were not especially concerned with courting these votes. Senator Chuck Schumer infamously declared that the party's strategy was: "For every blue-collar Democrat we lose in western Pennsylvania, we will pick up two moderate Republicans in the suburbs in Philadelphia, and you can repeat that in Ohio and Illinois and Wisconsin."[537] This turned out to be foolish. (Never rely on the "moderate" Republicans!) Schumer suggested that Democrats were not making any attempt to reach out to, or repair their reputation among, "blue collar" Democrats. Instead, they were simply attempting to convince wealthy Republicans that the Democrats were the real party of sensible, moderate businesspeople. (Ex-Pennsylvania governor Ed Rendell confirmed that the Clinton campaign intentionally rebuffed suggestions that it should campaign outside of Philadelphia and Pittsburgh, telling *The New York Times* that "We had the resources to do both… The campaign — and this was coming from Brooklyn — didn't want to do it."[538])

Sanders followed no such philosophy. For him, the "blue collar" Democrats are the very heart of his constituency. One can bet that he would  never write off entire swaths of Pennsylvania; the issues affecting those parts of the country are the core issues of his politics. In fact, Schumer's language is interesting: it suggests that he, and other key Democrats, are actually perfectly comfortable with the failure of the Democratic Party to continue to represent the working class. They don't necessarily see the party as being *for* working people; if you can pick up wealthy Republicans instead, that's just as good. This implies a lack of any serious core convictions other than a desire to get elected.

This is the key persuasive reason to believe that Sanders would have pulled off a victory where Clinton was defeated: the very parts of the country that Clinton neglected, the rural working-class in Rust Belt states, were the parts that Sanders concentrated on the most, and where he appeared to resonate most strongly. The election was close, and Michigan, Pennsylvania, and Wisconsin made the entire difference. Two of those (Michigan and Wisconsin) were strong Sanders states during the primary. In the other, Sanders won the very rural counties that Clinton would ultimately struggle in. It is far from unreasonable to think that this could have turned the general election for the Democrats, if Sanders had been the nominee instead of Clinton.[539] As Michigan congresswoman Debbie Dingell wrote after the election, Clinton ignored Dingell's district during the primary, and replicated the same mistakes during the general election:

Much of the district is Democratic and those voters strongly supported Bernie Sanders in the primary. That result didn't surprise me, but it did infuriate me that Clinton and her team didn't show up until the weekend before the primary, when it suddenly became clear they had a problem…was in my district 10 times during the primary. How would any sane person not predict how this one would go? [540]

Ultimately, it is impossible to know what would have happened if Bernie Sanders had run in Hillary Clinton's stead. Fictional alternate histories are enjoyable to indulge in, but it is ultimately fruitless to argue about them because we have no way of testing their accuracy. We *should*, however, carefully consider the possibility that Sanders would have done better, because it will affect what we do in the future. Democrats who want to move on and avoid reflection on the past are mistaken; it's only through examining *what happened and how* that we can learn vital lessons about political strategy that will return the party to a position of power.

At the very least, one should conclude that it would have been helpful to have a Democratic candidate who would have done better in particular parts of the Rust Belt. Certain compelling evidence points to the fact that Sanders *was* a candidate who would have done better in these parts. But no matter what conclusion one comes to on the question of whether Bernie would have won, the failure of the "Schumer strategy" is clear. If one gives up on "blue collar" Democrats, one does not have a sufficient coalition to guarantee victory.

◆   ◆   ◆   ◆

WHAT CONCLUSIONS CAN WE ULTIMATELY DRAW ABOUT THE CAUSES OF Clinton's loss to Trump, that might be productive for future attempts to rebuild progressive politics?

First, running Hillary Clinton against Donald Trump was probably a poor strategic choice on behalf of American Democrats. She had very high unfavorable numbers. She was under investigation by the FBI. (Probably a pretty bad sign.) She was a notoriously poor campaigner, who had previously made serious strategic blunders and lost the 2008 primary to a one-term senator with hardly any name recognition. She had plenty of material to feed Donald Trump's attack machine, and was the ideal foil for his bombastic approach. Yet many in the party were committed to the idea of her inevitability, with a sense that she *deserved* the nomination. (As Rachel Larimore writes, "Deferring to a person's 'turn' is a terrible strategy for picking a nominee and running a general election campaign."[541])

But even once Hillary Clinton became the nominee, she could have won the election. (The most disturbing thing to realize is that Trump's election *didn't have to happen.*) Yet she focused resources badly. She spent a lot of time raising money from big donors, but did not spend it particularly well. She never crafted a clear message for why she was running for president and what she wanted to accomplish. And she never managed to seem honest, authentic, and sincere.[542]

Doing things slightly differently might have saved Hillary Clinton's candidacy. Some better organization here, some more targeted ads there. But this ignores the crucial question: with Donald Trump having disparaged military families, conned his contractors, and sexually assaulted a dozen or more women, why was the race even close? Why wasn't Hillary Clinton 50 points ahead of Trump? Why did it come down to James Comey, or Michigan and Pennsylvania? Why did she lose in Florida and North Carolina and Ohio as well?

In answering this question, Democrats will have to face up to something disquieting: if you're in a close race with Donald Trump, you're doing something fundamentally wrong. Trump should be easy to beat; the fact that he wasn't suggests that Democrats are not selling something worth buying. It doesn't matter that Clinton won the popular vote; of *course* somewhat more people are willing to vote for the person who isn't a serial sex criminal who might blow up the earth. But the fact that so many people voted for Clinton grudgingly, or stayed home, considering who her opponent was, should cause the Democratic Party to thoroughly rethink its approach. If over sixty million people so disliked Hillary Clinton that they were willing to put Trump in the White House, Democrats have to change the way they court voters.

PART THREE
What It Means

DESPAIR LINGERS

AMERICA IN 2016 WAS IN MANY WAYS A CONTRADICTORY PLACE. The country had mostly recovered from the 2008 recession (albeit slowly),[543] the stock market was doing well,[544] crime was near an all-time low,[545] and millions of people had health insurance who had never had it before.[546] Judged by the aggregate numbers, the United States was performing solidly, as Democrats never tired of pointing out. Yet not everyone was feeling quite so optimistic and prosperous. Beneath the data on America's continued economic growth and overall lower levels of violence, for many people life did not appear to be going very well at all.

Job growth had rebounded under Obama. But most of the new jobs were not permanent; they were part time, insecure positions.[547] It was an Uber-ized economy, with work arriving inconsistently and the traditional benefit structure (health care, pensions) having all but disappeared for many workers.

Black families had nearly half their wealth wiped out during the 2008 recession,[548] and it hadn't come back.[549] The black-white income gap was at its highest point in 25 years.[550] What's more, while Obama had taken certain steps to slightly soften the impact of the criminal justice system, which ensnares so many young black men, prisons nevertheless continued to eat communities alive.[551]

For many millennials, with crippling debt burdens, the possibility of ever having a stable middle-class lifestyle seemed nonexistent. Two-thirds of millennials had at least one source of outstanding long-term debt (car loans, student loans, mortgages), and 30% of them had more than one.[552] They worry about debt, and struggle to pay it.

Overall, financial worries plagued the country. Credit card debt had reached its highest point since the recession, total average household debt had risen, and medical expenses had jumped significantly.[553] For many, income growth hadn't matched growth in the cost of living, leading to the taking on of even more debt.[554] And as people took on debt, they took on the corresponding issues of anxiety and a sense of personal failure.

Then there was the particular fate of the "white working class." Not only had jobs disappeared (due to a mixture of globalization and technological change, but mostly technological change[555]), and entire communities become ghost towns,[556] but poor white Americans were suffering from severe health issues.[557] Life expectancy for certain categories of white women was actually going *down*.[558] As doctor and health care commentator Adam Gaffney points out, there had been, for many whites:

> *...a general deterioration of health status: more middle-aged whites reported "fair or poor health," various chronic pains, and "serious psychological distress." Rates of heavy drinking and abnormally high liver enzymes — a marker of liver injury — also rose. Much of the uptick in mortality was due to various "external causes," such as poisoning (by alcohol or drugs), liver disease, and suicide. In sum: a demographic and social disaster has been quietly — almost invisibly — unfolding in America.*[559]

Furthermore, a "50-state epidemic" of opiate use was causing massive increases in drug overdoses,[560] with heroin addiction a persistent problem. And the suicide rate was at its highest point in 40 years,[561] with numerous populations of people in the throes of total hopelessness and despair. Dan O'Sullivan writes of an America characterized by the "evisceration of people by drug addiction, treatable health problems, overwork, malnutrition, foreclosure, infant mortality, slum housing, usurious loans — the sundry complications of poverty."[562]

Thus while aggregate statistics looked good, many people's actual lives were either getting worse or stagnating. Part of the paradox can be seen in the below chart. Incomes, on average, continued to grow. But the benefits of this growth were increasingly going only to people at the top 10% of the distribution. For people on the bottom, things

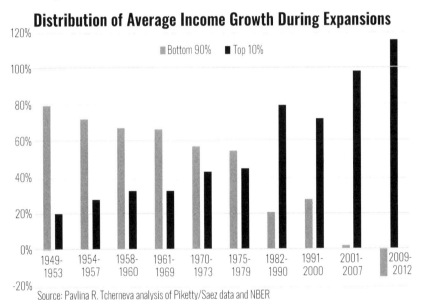

Distribution of Average Income Growth During Expansions

Source: Pavlina R. Tcherneva analysis of Piketty/Saez data and NBER

were getting better much more slowly.[563] As can be seen, this trend even continued to accelerate under Barack Obama, meaning that neither Democrats nor Republicans had successfully addressed rising inequality, and had in fact presided over its exacerbation.

Economic benefits were also unevenly distributed geographically. As Bourree Lam of *The Atlantic* writes, for the country's poorest communities "the recovery is a distant phenomenon, something taking place far away. Wealthy communities, by contrast, have been booming."[564] Many cities were prospering, even as many towns and rural areas remained in desolation. As Steve Glickman of the Economic Innovation Group confirms, "the data outlines two different Americas from an economic standpoint… The communities taking advantage of the knowledge economy are booming, but the areas where the industrial economy has traditionally held firmest have really suffered."[565] Large metropolitan areas recovered, but the manufacturing towns didn't.

The human reality was that people were watching the barriers between themselves and the height of prosperity grow and grow and grow. The more this happens, the more the American Dream becomes a lie, because one has no hope of ever making the leap between the bottom and the top. The country becomes more and more feudalistic; a small number of people have almost infinite wealth and complete power over the lives of others, while the mass of people toil and have little control over their conditions. Wealth is power, which means that inequalities in wealth necessarily erode any semblance of democracy.

It was amid these conditions, then, that the 2016 election took place. Whole swaths of the country were in despair and the grip of addiction. And while we may have been getting better off overall, nobody lives in the statistical aggregate. They live individual lives, and many of those lives felt more hopeless and futile than ever, the country's promises almost completely out of reach.

It was an ideal moment for populist candidates, then. Polls showed that people's top concern was the economy,[566] and that Americans largely had a bleak view of the economic recovery. Most people said that jobs were hard to find and that they were struggling to keep up with the cost of living.[567]

These facts undoubtedly explained at least a portion of Donald Trump's political success. As Jeff Guo of the *Washington Post* reports, support for Donald Trump was highest in the areas where white people had the highest increase in death rates; those areas that were ravaged the most by drug addiction and economic decline were most susceptible to his message.[568] Eduardo Porter of the *New York Times* adds that Trump's voters were "where the jobs weren't."[569] It's not difficult to see how Trump managed to capitalize on people's misfortunes with a promise to fix their economic troubles, combined with an appeal to their baser instincts.

Nor is it surprising that the Democrats' counter-message ("America Is Already Great") didn't play very well in many areas. It smacked of obliviousness—America is already great... for *me.* But while life certainly *is* great in Seattle and Brooklyn and Los Angeles, elsewhere not much has changed since 2008, and the Obama economy hasn't worked nearly as well for some people as for others.

The election should tell us something important about 2016 America, then: all is not well. Despair lingers, and if it isn't addressed, it can be capitalized upon by self-serving bigots.

Change in Number of Elected Democrats Since 2008
Source: The Washington Post

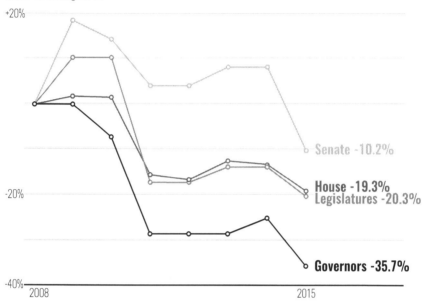

Senate -10.2%

House -19.3%
Legislatures -20.3%

Governors -35.7%

2008   2015

Republican-Controlled State Governments, 2016
Source: The New York Times

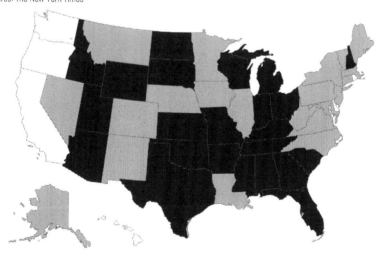

■ Complete Republican Control (Legislature, Governor)   ▨ Split   ☐ Complete Dem. Control

ORTHODOX LIBERALISM
HAS BEEN
REPUDIATED

SOMETHING HAS GONE TERRIBLY WRONG ON THE LEFT. LOSING THE Presidency, the House, and the Senate should be a sign that one's politics need a strategic rethink. Unless we think that everything, from the disappearance of the Congressional majority to the evaporation of Democratic power at the state level, is the fault of Vladimir Putin (and some do seem inclined to think this), the Democratic Party has a lot to answer for. Hillary Clinton's loss was not a mere regrettable blip. It was the culmination of an ongoing erosion in the Democratic Party's electoral fortunes, one that has occurred at the state and federal level alike. Since 2008, Democrats have been losing election after election.

The losses are stark. Witness, in the chart to the left, the change that has occurred over the last few years in the Senate and House, as well as state legislatures and governorships.

The numbers are dire. Only 16 of the country's governors are Democrats.[570] The party has lost over 800 seats in state legislatures since Obama took office.[571] The party now has less influence at the state level than at any point since 1920.[572] Matthew Yglesias of *Vox* noted solemnly in 2015 that "the Democratic Party is in much greater peril than its leaders or supporters recognize, and it has no plan to save itself."[573] And that was before Donald Trump became the president.

Oddly, the urgency of the situation has never really been appreciated by Democrats, likely because with Barack Obama leading the country, it seemed like Democrats were in the ascendance. But the presidency has been just about the only office Democrats have managed to hold onto, and the modest popularity of Obama has served to conceal a true political disaster occurring elsewhere. As Chris Cillizza of *The Washington Post* writes:

> *Barack Obama has been exceptionally good for the brand of 'Barack Obama' but far less good for the broader Democratic Party. His appeal was never transferable to down-ballot races, while some of his major accomplishments — especially the Affordable Care Act — turned out to be major negatives for the party's candidates for House and Senate.*[574]

Sam Stein of *The Huffington Post* concludes that Obama has essentially "destroyed" the Democratic Party; after all, "states are decimated, they lost control of the House and Senate, the governorships are decimated."[575]

This may seem deeply unfair to Obama. After all, the president is not singlehandedly responsible for the fortunes of his party, and a good portion of the rage and backlash against him was driven by racial resentment (including Trump's own attempt to paint Obama as an illegitimate president). But it's certainly true that Obama failed to use his considerable platform to try to mobilize the Democratic grassroots and encourage people to join the party. He dismantled the formidable organizing apparatus he had used to win the 2008 campaign, leaving ordinary Democrats with the impression that their role in the party was to show up and vote in presidential elections every four years. This failure to address and energize ordinary people was part of a philosophy shared by both Obama and the Democratic leadership alike. As party activist Lucy Flores (one of the first Hispanic women to be elected to the state legislature in Nevada) says, "There is no national strategy—we don't invest in sustained engagement with voters outside of the presidential election. I don't have a lot of faith in the current leadership."[576]

There were clear moments of policy failure here, too. Michael Grunwald of *Politico* documents the way that the Obama administration, concerned with marginally improving people's lives by technocratic policy adjustments, failed to actually convey to voters a sense of what they were getting and why it was valuable. Grunwald says that Obama's "guiding political assumption—that data-driven, evidence-based policy, at least in its center-left form, would inevitably turn out to be good politics—ended up being seriously flawed."[577] He gives as an example "Making Work Pay," an $800 tax cut provided to most workers. There was a debate over whether to give people lump sums of cash, or hide the benefit by dispersing it incrementally:

> *[Obama's] economists wanted to dribble out the cash to recipients a few dollars a week in their paychecks, because studies showed they would be less likely to spend the windfall if they realized they were getting it. His political advisers argued that it would be insanity to conceal middle-class tax cuts rather than send Americans fat envelopes with Obama's name on them. But Obama sided with his policy team, and later surveys showed that less than 10 percent of the public had any clue he had cut their taxes.*[578]

Thus hardly anyone in the country knew that Making Work Pay had even happened, because Obama's expert economists deliberately tried to prevent people from understanding what they were getting. This problem pervaded Obama policy-making, which was often complex and difficult to understand. As Sean McElwee of *Salon* characterizes it, "Democrats practice policy, not politics. Programs like Obamacare are wonk-approved, but pay insufficient attention to mobilizing beneficiaries as citizens and constituents."[579] But if you want to win elections, you have to—surprisingly enough—actually make people want to vote for you, rather than just nudging them gently toward progress without telling them and hoping they thank you for it later. McElwee suggests that Democrats should place much more emphasis on offering easy-to-use, non-bureaucratic, simple and effective government services:

> *Making post offices, DMVs and other government agencies function well is not sexy, but research shows that it can increase positive views of government, which increases support for services. Americans believe that government only works for elites and the wealthy, and the solution is to make government work better for average citizens. Policymaking should center on the direct provision of government services in a way that can help activists organize defined constituencies.*[580]

But some of this was not accident or incompetence on the Obama Administration's part. Instead, it emerged from a structural problem with the Democratic Party itself, which has increasingly come to be dominated by a "best and brightest" ethos. It believes in hiring the best experts rather then building mass participation. It has ditched the social democratic commitments that animated the party under Roosevelt and Johnson, to be dominated by a belief in governance by a meritocratic elite of Ivy League-educated wonks.

As Hal Walker describes this philosophy:

> *Within the party, the leaders and officials become enchanted by expertise. They throw aside easy to understand solutions for thousand page policies. Silicon Valley data wizardry is more trusted than shoe-leather campaigning and plain-voiced appeal to the masses of average people. To convince the public, they point to expert opinion rather than make emotional appeals to the lived experience of everyday life. The message behind the message is "listen up, we're smarter than you."... Rather than argue right vs. wrong, the battle is the smart vs. the stupid.*[581]

Other writers have documented this trend. Thomas Frank observes that what used to be "the party of the people" is now essentially a business party, progressive on social and cultural issues like LGBTQ rights, but fundamentally uninterested in changing the economic structure of an increasingly unequal country.[582] To the extent it runs on economic issues at all, it is purely based on improving the meritocracy, prioritizing things like giving people the ability to attend excellent colleges, rather than, say, raising the wages and living conditions of agricultural workers and kitchen staff. Because the top of the party has become dominated by wealthy people who care about advancing diversity (diversity on the board of Goldman Sachs, that is) but do not want to sacrifice any of their wealth, it is incapable of offering policies and messages with broad appeal to workers. The party has decided to compete with Republicans for the "middle class," even as increasing numbers of people find themselves well below middle class.[583] (Notice that Democrats constantly emphasize people in the middle rather than people at the bottom.)

As another consequence of this type of politics, the party has struggled to (some might say "given up on") actually organizing and engaging the public. In *Rolling Stone,* Tim Dickinson reports that Barack

Obama intentionally shied away from deploying the impressive activist infrastructure he had built in 2008 with "Obama for America." Instead of trying to maintain OFA after his election, Obama:

> ....began to pursue a more traditional, backroom approach to enacting his agenda. Rather than using OFA to engage millions of voters to turn up the heat on Congress, the president yoked his political fortunes to the unabashedly transactional style of politics advocated by his chief of staff, Rahm Emanuel. Health care reform — the centerpiece of his agenda — was no longer about mobilizing supporters to convince their friends, families and neighbors in all 50 states. It was about convincing 60 senators in Washington. It became about deals.[584]

Dickinson quotes disappointed OFA volunteers, who thought after the 2008 campaign that they would be called upon to "fight for something," but were instead told to go home, with the business of governing left to D.C. insiders like Emanuel. These volunteers were "demoralized"; they had felt like Obama wanted to give them an "ownership stake in the future of our country," but it turned out he just wanted to get elected.

Yet at the same time as Democrats have become more heavily dominated by moneyed interests, operating out of Martha's Vineyard and Silicon Valley rather than churches in Detroit and union halls in Indianapolis, they have tried to maintain their image as a people's party. One saw the effects of this in the candidacy of Hillary Clinton, who felt compelled by the Sanders insurgency to adopt a highly progressive policy platform despite spending her entire previous political career as a Wall Street-friendly, centrist war hawk. Every speech she gave tried simultaneously to appeal to young millennial progressives *and* Chuck Schumer's "moderate Republicans in the Philadelphia suburbs."

The resulting mish-mash was almost unintelligible, with voters having no idea what Hillary Clinton actually stood for beyond something about competence and experience and not being Donald Trump. She had opposed the Fight for 15's effort to get a $15 minimum wage (saying "Let's not just do it for the sake of having a higher number out there," and pushing for a $12 minimum wage instead[585]), before enthusiastically championing the Fight for 15 a few months later.[586] She had opposed Bernie Sanders' plan for free college tuition ("I am not going to give free college to wealthy kids…"[587]) before embracing an almost-identical plan in the general election.[588] The ultimate message that came out of this was totally incoherent, trying to appease left-wing democratic socialists while being careful not to threaten the party's supporters on Wall Street. As journalist Doug Henwood says, "The Democratic Party has a structural problem. It is a party of business that has to pretend otherwise sometimes. So that causes the confusion and weakness of message."[589] It needs to sound vaguely anti-Establishment without actually being so.

These efforts at "non-threatening" populism became downright ludicrous at times. Clinton released a famously mealy-mouthed statement about the Dakota Access Pipeline, which protesters had hoped she would condemn. It read:

> *From the beginning of this campaign, Secretary Clinton has been clear that she thinks all voices should be heard and all views considered in federal infrastructure projects… Now, all of the parties involved — including the federal government, the pipeline company and contractors, the state of North Dakota, and the tribes — need to find a path forward that serves the broadest public interest.*[590]

Far from making clear Hillary Clinton's position on whether or not the pipeline should be built, the statements simply said she hoped everyone would agree on something. *Jezebel* called the statement "meaningless" and environmental activist Bill McKibben pointed out that it "literally says nothing."[591]

Hillary Clinton's political messaging became even messier as it tried to incorporate language from "intersectional" feminist social theory,[592] which focuses on the manifold connections between various forms of human oppression. A campaign staffer evidently thought the following pair of tweets would usefully explain to voters how Clinton conceived of the causes of and solutions to social problems:

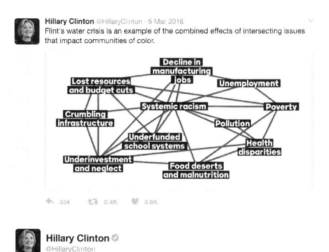

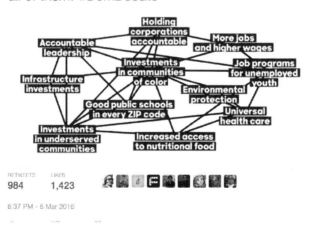

This cobweb of problems and policies showed just how unclear it was what Hillary Clinton was running on. She wanted to do everything and nothing, to be progressive but moderate. There wasn't some particular clear set of things that Hillary Clinton proposed to do, she just intended to address "complex, intersectional" problems using "solutions." (Joe Biden has explicitly suggested that Hillary Clinton didn't even know why she was running for president, other than feeling as if she would be quite good at it.[593])

◆   ◆   ◆   ◆

THE DEMOCRATIC PARTY'S INCREASING DOMINATION BY THE RICH and well-educated has led to a cultural problem too, captured in Hillary Clinton's "deplorables" remark. As unions play a decreasing role in Democratic politics, there has been a loss of understanding of how certain cultural attitudes play among working people. As Anthony Bourdain commented:

> *The utter contempt with which privileged Eastern liberals such as myself discuss red-state, gun-country, working-class America as ridiculous and morons and rubes is largely responsible for the upswell of rage and contempt and desire to pull down the temple that we're seeing now.[594]*

Hal Walker has a similar take:
> *[Democrats] simply will not hear criticism that does not come from the similarly credentialed. The loss is the fault of every stupid person. The voters were racist and sexist, those stupid hippy millennials didn't turn up, morons believed fake news. The front of the class don't need to change a thing, they've made good grades their whole*

*lives, they're never wrong, and they're going to just keep
on being right and losing fights.*[595]

And while the active *contempt* has been specifically targeted at the
white working class, the black and Hispanic working class are no less
excluded from the forefront of contemporary progressive politics.
Democrats have tended to embrace racial diversity while continuing
to place little emphasis on the needs, lives, or cultural tastes of *poor*
people of any race. After the election, the *New York Times* caught up
with black voters in struggling parts of Milwaukee.[596] What it found
were many people who didn't vote at all, and others who were disgusted by the Democratic Party despite its traditionally strong record
of black support. One voter blamed Bill Clinton's policies for sending
him to prison for 20 years, and another, speaking about why he preferred Trump's honest racism to Democrats' two-faced hypocrisy, said
of Trump: "He was real, unlike a lot of liberal Democrats who are just
as racist… You can reason with them all day long, but they think they
know it all. They want to have control. That they know what's best
for 'those people.'" The elitism of the Democratic Party has not just
involved talking down to rural whites, but totally ignoring African
Americans and taking their votes for granted.

◆   ◆   ◆   ◆

ONE COULD SEE THE PARTY'S ELITISM ON FULL DISPLAY IN THE
embrace of celebrity culture during the Clinton campaign. Donald
Trump's RNC was mocked for being unable to attract sufficiently
glamorous A-listers,[597] and the country was flooded with advertise-
ments in which movie stars sang Hillary Clinton's praises. The DNC
released a "Fight Song" in which dozens of celebrities all contributed
vocal parts to a pro-Hillary sing-a-long, and the cast of *The West Wing*
was dispatched to the campaign trail to stump for Clinton.[598]

The celebrity-first strategy was chosen over other approaches. Labor unions had recorded a series of anti-Trump ads featuring a multi-racial set of Trump hotel workers describing their mistreatment by his businesses.[599] Entitled "People who work for Trump are just like you," they recorded workers recalling that "he wrecked our livelihood" and "he left with all the money, left us high and dry. Jobs gone, health insurance gone, homes foreclosed."[600] These ads offered an effective anti-Trump narrative: it's not that Trump is a dangerous clown, it's that he's *every bad boss you've ever had* and will care about you and your family as much as he cares about the families of his casino workers, i.e. not at all.

Democrats did not push these ads. Instead, far more of them shared a different ad, in which Robert Downey, Jr. and "a shitload of famous people" (to use the ad's term) including Scarlett Johansson and Mark Ruffalo implored people to vote. (Joss Whedon gathered his famous friends for the campaign in order to "stop Orange Muppet Hitler."[601]) Robert DeNiro recorded an ad claiming that "I'd like to punch [Donald Trump] in the face."[602] In the last month before the election, the Clinton campaign itself decided to send Lena Dunham to North Carolina rather than sending Hillary Clinton to Wisconsin,[603] oblivious to whether a much-loathed HBO star who has spoken positively of "the extinction of men"[604] was the right messenger for the American heartland.

Thus the Democratic Party's drift toward valuing wealth and credentials over principle and authenticity has led to the embrace of celebrities as a vehicle for the part's message, even though many people simply don't like to be told what to do by famous people. It has resulted in the party having almost no presence in working-class communities of any race, and correspondingly causing mass disillusionment.

That needs to change. As Jon Hendren puts it, "we need to make it as embarrassing as possible to be a limousine liberal who is more excited about *Hamilton* than single payer healthcare."[605] (This characterization is not an exaggeration. The breathless quality of *Hamilton* coverage is difficult to overstate.[606]) The Democratic Party needs to realize that poor white voters notice when you trash them as morons. And black voters notice when you incorporate sophisticated analyses of diversity and intersectionality into your policy statements, but would pay tens of thousands of dollars a year to send your children to private school before you would allow them to attend a public school in a black neighborhood. And they don't necessarily buy it when you go from cheering the largest-ever expansion of the country's prison system[607] to embracing the Black Lives Matter movement.[608] Voters aren't actually stupid; they pick up on the messages that are sent, and the message the Democratic Party has consistently sent is: we talk like we care about you, but we don't actually.

There is a certain sense of *entitlement* that Democrats feel to working people's votes. Thomas Frank says that among those he knows in elite D.C. circles, there was a phenomenally arrogant sense that people *had* to vote for Hillary Clinton, that she *deserved* to be president: "They really think that they've got this thing in the bag. They think they're in charge."[609] After the election, Lena Dunham voiced her shock that something that was *meant* to happen had not happened, complaining "It wasn't supposed to go this way. It was supposed to be her job. She worked her whole life for the job. It's her job."[610] It's precisely because Democrats have felt that people are *supposed* to vote for them, rather than feeling like *they* are supposed to persuade people to vote for them, that people around the country, at all levels of government, have stopped voting for Democrats.

❖   ❖   ❖   ❖

UNFORTUNATELY, AFTER THE ELECTION, SIGNS WERE NOT PROMISING that Democrats had learned their lesson. Despite representing the worst tendencies of contemporary Democratic politics, Nancy Pelosi was swiftly reelected as the leader of the House Democrats, and declared that she didn't think there was any reason why the party needed a "new direction."[611] By January, people were encouraging Hillary Clinton to run for Mayor of New York, with Frank Bruni of the *New York Times* fantasizing about Clinton being able to slap Trump Tower with endless building code violations.[612] (Bruni did not seem to notice that he was dreaming of Clinton abusing municipal power for political ends, or realize that the fact Clinton could so easily be imagined doing this is probably precisely the reason why people view her so unfavorably.)

Some went even further than Bruni. Cultural critic Virginia Heffernan went so far as to insist that Hillary Clinton had done every single thing right and had no earthly faults:

> *When people told me they hated Hillary Clinton or (far worse) that they were "not fans," I wish I had said in no uncertain terms: "I love Hillary Clinton. I am in awe of her. I am set free by her. She will be the finest world leader our galaxy has ever seen."... More deeply still, I wish I had not reasoned with anyone... I wish I had said, flatly, "I love her."... Hillary Clinton's name belongs on ships, and airports, and tattoos. She deserves straight-up hagiographies and a sold-out Broadway show called RODHAM... Maybe she is more than a president. Maybe she is an idea, a world-historical heroine, light itself. The presidency is too small for her. She belongs to a much more elite class of Americans, the more-than-presidents. Neil Armstrong, Martin Luther King Jr., Alexander Fucking Hamilton. Hillary Clinton did everything right in this campaign, and she won more votes than her opponent did. She won. She cannot be faulted, criticized, or analyzed for even one more second.*[613]

Heffernan's reaction, while unusually extreme, showed the general direction of the reaction among Clinton supporters after the election: away from, rather than toward, self-examination. The election did not mean that one should figure out how Democrats could have acted differently, or whether it was a mistake to run the kind of candidate they had run. Instead, it was an excuse to double down: to insist that if the Democrats had lost, it had not been because of anything *they* did, but because they were the victims of external forces beyond their control. For Heffernan, Clinton supporters should not have "reasoned with anyone." Instead, they should write "hagiographies" about Clinton, i.e. refuse to acknowledge *any single fact* about Clinton that might undermine the conception of Clinton as "light itself." That means dismissing every single one of the reasons that progressives might have for not caring for Clinton (e.g. Haiti,[614] Libya,[615] Iraq,[616] Wall Street[617]), as well as every legitimate reason why voters more broadly might not have liked her (e.g. an FBI investigation, promising to shut down mines, pretending their problems didn't exist, calling them all deplorables).

◆   ◆   ◆   ◆

LIBERAL MESSAGING HADN'T GOTTEN ANY BETTER AFTER THE ELECTION, either. Confirming every possible stereotype Trump voters may have held about out-of-touch elites, Meryl Streep used the opportunity of the Golden Globes award ceremony to deliver a broadside against Trump. Streep insisted that her fellow Hollywood royalty were "most vilified segments in American society right now" (the scores of young black men in America's prisons might object to the idea that the stars of blockbuster films are the most disdained and despised of demographics). She dwelled on Trump's impersonation of a disabled *New York Times* reporter and declared that without Hollywood, "you'll have nothing to watch but football and mixed martial arts… which are *not* the arts."[618]

It was a moment perfectly encapsulating every misguided aspect of

American liberalism. A multi-millionaire Yale graduate, in a room full of famous people, was heaping scorn on the cultural tastes of Middle America *and* declaring herself part of a persecuted minority. What could better reinforce the worldview of Trump voters than to have the case for liberalism be delivered by an uber-wealthy Californian who can't keep herself from throwing in a slight at football?[619]

Trump, of course, immediately took to Twitter to throw some mud back at Streep, calling her an "over-rated actress" and "Hillary flunky."[620] But a few hours later, he followed this up with two tweets about car manufacturing:

> *It's finally happening - Fiat Chrysler just announced plans to invest $1BILLION in Michigan and Ohio plants, adding 2000 jobs. This after Ford said last week that it will expand in Michigan and U.S. instead of building a BILLION dollar plant in Mexico. Thank you Ford & Fiat C!* [621]

Thus, while the press covered the Trump/Streep Twitter fight, and progressives convinced themselves Trump had been "owned" and was embarrassing himself, Trump was telling his supporters that he had brought more of their jobs back. While Democrats dwelled on a two-second impersonation Trump had performed many months before, Trump was continuing his propaganda offensive on trade and jobs. The Streep episode is a classic example of the messaging failure of contemporary liberalism: it loses, even as it convinces itself that it is winning.

Instead, progressives should learn that it doesn't matter how *much* you criticize Trump, or how vigorously. What matters is that your criticisms *land,* that they are effective in speaking to people. The right message will not be delivered by Ivy League millionaires at awards banquets. It will be delivered by the working people whom Trump has spent his entire life screwing and robbing.

THE PRESS IS
DISCREDITED
FOREVER

REALISTICALLY ASSESSED, THERE WAS NO REASON WHY THE ELECTION of Donald Trump should have come as a particular surprise to anyone. After all, he was never *especially* far away from Hillary Clinton in the polls. And it was perfectly plausible that his protectionism and populism would play well in Rust Belt states.

And yet: on election night, Hillary Clinton's loss came as a total surprise to large numbers of people, who not only thought Donald Trump *wouldn't* win, but thought it was *impossible* for him to win. Clinton herself was preparing for a coronation, and had been so sure of victory that she hadn't even visited Wisconsin since the end of the Democratic primary. A glance at liberal Twitter and Facebook feeds from election night reveals confidence turning to panic turning steadily to denial and then despair. *It wasn't supposed to happen.*

How could anyone be so certain that Clinton would win, given that she did not? What made people think that the outcome was assured?

Part of this can be attributed to ordinary wishful thinking. Progressives didn't want to believe that it was *possible* for a man like Donald

Trump to be president. He was too horrible. There was simply *no way* that a person who had admitted to committing repeated acts of sexual assault could be elected President of the United States. This was not based on any particular *evidence*, but based on a firmly held desire for the world not to disappoint us.

But a large part of the responsibility for the complacency has to rest with the press. After all, a person who believed Trump stood no chance of winning was not merely projecting their own desires onto the news. They were, in fact, repeating exactly what they heard in the news. The messages coming from the press affirmed over and over and over that Clinton was a solid favorite to win, and that Trump would easily be vanquished.

Among some, the level of certitude was extraordinary. In October, *Slate*'s Isaac Chotiner wrote a column called "Donald Trump Could Have Been President" in which he told readers that, even though the danger had now safely passed, we should never forget how close Trump had come. Chotiner displayed no doubt that it was safe to speak in the past tense about Trump:

> *Donald Trump is never going to be the president of the United States. As we sit and digest each successive leak of damaging material, each un-endorsement, each Trump threat to attack Hillary Clinton in the most personal terms imaginable, the fact remains that Trump has almost surely destroyed his chance of ever becoming the most powerful man on Earth. The discussion will now slowly shift to Republican hopes of shoring up down-ballot races and (just wait) the creation of Trump TV...*[622]

Throughout 2015 and 2016, there was plenty of confidence among commentators that the election outcome was all but certain. A sample of the most catastrophically mistaken prophecies is worth reviewing.

The confidence began during the primaries.

- *"Any story based on the premise that Trump has **any** chance of becoming the nominee, let alone the president, is a disservice to the reader."*—James Fallows, "How the Press Should Handle a Candidate With No Chance of Winning," The Atlantic (July 13, 2015).
- *"Trump has a better chance of cameoing in another "Home Alone" movie with Macaulay Culkin—or playing in the NBA finals—than winning the Republican nomination."* –Harry Enten, "Why Donald Trump Isn't a Real Candidate, In One Chart," *FiveThirtyEight* (June 16, 2015).
- *"No, Donald Trump Won't Win"*—David Brooks, *The New York Times* (Dec. 4, 2015).
- "Trump Will Lose, or I Will Eat This Column"— Dana Milbank, *The Washington Post* (Oct. 2, 2015).

And on into the general election:

- *"There is no horse race here. Clinton is far enough ahead, at a late enough stage in the election, that what we have is a horse running by itself, unperturbed but for the faint possibility of a comet hitting the track. Place your bets accordingly."* — Jamelle Bouie, "There Is No Horse Race," Slate (Aug. 24, 2016).[623]
- *"The math is grim for Donald J. Trump: His rival, Hillary Clinton, has a 90 percent chance of winning the election, as of Monday afternoon. Wait, sorry — make that 91 percent, as of Monday night (and 92 percent as of Tuesday afternoon). It just keeps getting worse for him."* — Michael Barbaro, The New York Times, Oct. 18, 2016
- *"Donald Trump's chances of winning are approaching*

zero." — Chris Cillizza, The Washington Post (Oct. 24, 2016).

• *"With Trump facing a potential wipeout on November 8, there is a growing sense that he'll start a news network in 2017."* — Derek Thompson, The Atlantic (Oct. 18, 2016).

• *"Trump won't win Michigan, and I am frankly offended that people think this is even a possibility."* —Jonathan Chait, New York magazine (Nov. 7, 2016).

• *"It's time to admit Hillary Clinton is an extraordinarily talented politician."* —Ezra Klein, Vox (June 7, 2016).[624]

Truly, the number of extraordinarily wrong things said by well-educated and ostensibly sensible people is enough to leave one agog. Pundits speculated that Clinton might even win deep-red states like Texas and Georgia,[625] and spent countless column inches debating *just how much of a landslide* she would crush Trump in. Matthew Yglesias of *Vox* even went so far as to chastise people for making others nervous about Clinton's prospects, arguing that there was good reason to believe that polls showing Clinton ahead were actually *underestimating* her real lead:

> Some people seem to want to be nervous about it… The truth, however, is that by almost all accounts Hillary Clinton is leading in the polls and has been leading for essentially the entire campaign… So the search for doubt has settled on Nate Silver's forecast, an outlier among poll aggregators, that pegs Clinton as "only" a 65 percent favorite rather than the 85 percent or more she is favored by in other systems. But even if you buy Silver's main modeling assumptions (and I largely do), there's considerable evidence outside the realm of things captured by poll

aggregators that leads me to believe that if the polls are
wrong, they are more likely to be underestimating Clin-
ton's support than overstating it.[626]

Speaking of Nate Silver, the *FiveThirtyEight* statistics guru spent both the primaries and the general election issuing some particularly embarrassing declarations. Early on in the Republican primary, Silver had declared that Trump's odds of winning were minimal. And even as Trump continued to dominate the race and steadily pick off opponents, Silver produced lists of reasons why the public had no need to worry. In an article entitled "The Six Stages of Donald Trump's Doom,"[627] Silver explained the various ways in which Trump would inevitably be destroyed at some point during the primary process, with the only serious question being whether Trump would disappear somewhat sooner or somewhat later. Silver would even send tweets like "Dearest media, Please stop freaking out about Donald Trump's polls. With love, Nate."[628]

Some liberal commentators were so sure that Donald Trump was hopeless that during the primary, they even tried to *encourage* people to support him. Jonathan Chait of *New York* magazine wrote a headline entitled "Why Liberals Should Support A Trump Nomination."[629] Their certainty that Trump was an ignorant boob prevented them from entertaining the idea that Trump was a *serious threat* who shouldn't be joked about.

This pattern of error is worth reviewing not just for the sake of *schadenfreude*, delightful as it is to witness the humiliation of hyper-confident, self-important pundit-men (and they are, interestingly, all men). Collectively, these people bear a significant responsibility for what happened, because they told people not to worry, meaning that they discouraged their readership from taking political action. They essentially treated people who were worried about Trump like they were *crazy*, so assured were they of their own rightness. Nate

Silver used his authority as a skilled statistician to tell people concerned about Trump that they were "freaking out," and suggesting that they simply didn't understand math. And James Fallows of the *Atlantic* actually said that giving Trump any chance at all was a *disservice to readers*. This went beyond being wrong, then. It created an atmosphere in which all questioning was treated as madness, and in which Trump was repeatedly and dangerously underestimated.

One serious problem was that the press was uninterested in trying to seriously inquire into the political mood of the country. Just as with the unanticipated Brexit vote in the United Kingdom, political and media elites were oblivious to the level of hatred and resentment against them that was developing outside of the country's urban centers.[630] Trump voters were a curiosity, to be analyzed anthropologically as interesting specimens ("Who Are All These Trump Supporters?" a bemused and baffled *New Yorker* asked in July[631]). But at no point was the rising tide of Trump support seen as a threat that could actually engulf the country. It was a curiosity, certainly. But it was fundamentally fringe rather than mainstream.

This misleading approach arose, in part, from the way that political journalists, analysts, and commentators now operate. There is an obsession with poll data, and a lesser emphasis on actually going out into the world and discovering what the data may be concealing or failing to pick up. Many of the journalists who felt most assured of a Clinton victory seem to have never left Washington, D.C. during the whole election cycle. Here, one must recall the remark attributed—unfairly—to Pauline Kael, who is alleged to have said that she didn't know how Nixon could have won, because nobody she knew had voted for him.[632] Talk of bubbles and echo chambers may have become a cliché by now, but clichés are often clichés because they are true: people who work for major media outlets speak mostly to people who work for other major media outlets (or other people of the same general disposition and worldview). Yet since most people in the United

States do not work for major media outlets, the people who do are destined to have a warped impression of what the electorate looks like, and a series of biases in their perceptions that require considerable conscientious effort to account for.

As Michael Tracey, puts it, you've got to go out and talk to people if you're going to figure anything out: "Sitting around manically refreshing *FiveThirtyEight* all day doesn't give you any useful information. Talking to voters does. Because journalists ceased talking to voters, they could not discern the late shifts that were pivotal in tipping the race to Trump."[633] James Hohmann of the *Washington Post* admitted that during the last month of the campaign, national reporters had essentially stopped traveling, meaning they were unable to discern the critical shifts.[634]

There were cases of exceptional journalists who did go deep in trying to understand who supported Trump and why. Chris Arnade of *The Guardian*, a former Wall Street trader turned photographer, spent the year traveling Trump Country in a van, speaking to disaffected and hopeless people, who were turning to Trump in the hopes of waking up Washington. Arnade's portraits of the American small town are often heartbreaking, and he documented the lives of everyone from jobless white men who wanted "respect" to black families who insistently defied Trump's attempt to paint black communities as having "nothing to lose."[635] Arnade's reports from the American heartland documented a country filled with incredible pain, but also incredible determination, dignity, and resilience. Arnade pointed out that there was a revolt happening in the country against the "front-row" students, the kids who had gotten good grades and gone to the best schools, by the "back-row kids," who were often left behind in desolate towns to deal with the vicious consequences of globalization and technological change.[636]

Others attempted to sound the alarm about the seriousness of Trump. In December of 2015, Adam Wren of *Politico* went to an Indiana county that had been a "reliable bellwether" for presidential elections, and found significant Trump support. "If Trump can make it here," Wren said, "in this hollowed-out county of swing voters, union halls, three universities and a knot of CSX railroad lines, where voters seem to have a knack for predicting unpredictable elections—he can make it anywhere."[637] Paul Solotaroff, in *Rolling Stone*, profiled Trump and warned that Trump was smarter than he looked, and had potentially strong appeal to large numbers of voters:

> *You don't do a fraction of what he's done in life — dominate New York real estate for decades, build the next grand Xanadus for the super-rich on the far shores of Dubai and Istanbul, run the prime-time ratings table for more than 10 years and earn a third (or sixth) fortune at it – without being immensely cunning and deft, a top-of-the-food-chain killer.... What I saw was enough to make me take him dead serious. If you're waiting for Trump to blow himself up in a Hindenburg of gaffes or hate speech, you're in for a long, cold fall and winter. Donald Trump is here for the duration — and gaining strength and traction by the hour.*[638]

Yet at the same time as journalists on the ground, like Solotaroff and Arnade, were sending these warnings, the commentary factories in New York and D.C. continued to churn out articles like "Why Donald Trump Won't Be Elected President."[639]

The arrogance was damaging.[640] Liberal pundits bought into the myth of Clinton as an "inevitable" president. This idea should have been disposed of permanently in 2008, as well as by Clinton's weak primary performance against a socialist upstart. But there seemed to be a belief among the liberal press that if they just repeated it enough times, it would be destined to come true. By either explicitly or tacitly reassuring people that Clinton would definitely win, they diminished the sense of urgency among progressives. People could feel as if they didn't need to do anything, because nothing *inevitable* needs help coming to fruition.

The election of Trump bore some similarities with the surprise U.K. Brexit vote, in which pundits were likewise confident that the country *definitely wouldn't* vote to leave the European Union, only to have the country decisively vote to leave the European Union.[641] Elites in London simply *couldn't imagine* that there were enough people willing to make such a suicidal choice for the mere pleasure of delivering a middle finger to the Establishment. But they underestimated how much people hated the Establishment, having rarely traveled outside their insular cosmopolitan bubble.

Thus having failed to appreciate the degree of latent rage simmering in places distant from the country's urban centers, the U.S. press were likewise blindsided. America's liberal press *could not believe* that Donald Trump could ever be president. The outcome was so unthinkable that their inability to *imagine* it affected their assessment of its chances of occurrence. Progressives forgot that there is a distinction between media representations of reality and reality itself. If the press had done their job, rather than just bullshitting, perhaps we would have been as alarmed as we should have been. Liberal commentators made a crucial error: instead of trying to understand how the world actually was, they interpreted the world according to what they wished it to be.

❖   ❖   ❖   ❖

BEYOND ITS COMPLACENCY, THE PRESS WAS ALSO SIMPLY GARBAGE in a broader sense. Even more importantly than its failures of detection and prediction was its total stubborn failure to focus on things that truly mattered. As Bernie Sanders observed, "The less significant [an issue] is to ordinary people, the more attention the media pays."[642] The election cycle was not dominated by news about healthcare, jobs, and the environment, but about Trump's feuds with public figures, Hillary Clinton's emails, and the *horse race* between the candidates. *Slate*'s political coverage section, for example, actually explicitly devotes itself to focusing on the competitive aspects of politics, with the tagline "Who's Winning, Who's Losing, and Why."

There is empirical evidence to support the claim that media is dominated by stories about process and competition, "winners" and "losers," rather than matters of substance. As a report from the Harvard Kennedy School, which analyzed what the press focused on over the course of the race, concluded:

> *Election news during the primary period was dominated by the competitive game—the struggle of the candidates to come out on top. Overwhelmingly, election coverage was devoted to the question of winning and losing. Poll results, election returns, delegate counts, electoral projections, fundraising success, and the like, along with the candidates' tactical and strategic maneuvering, accounted for more than half of the reporting.*[643]

Let's be clear about why this is dangerous. Human civilization faces two possible existential catastrophes in the near future: climate change and nuclear war. If certain measures aren't taken immediately, with a coordinated effort among global governments requiring a tremendous amount of political will, either of these threats could present terrible consequences for billions of lives. Nuclear weapons, which can destroy entire cities instantaneously, and are possessed in the thousands by superpowers, probably ought to be taken somewhat more seriously as a risk. And climate change, which threatens the entire global ecosystem, is similarly consequential. (This is to say nothing of the increasing ease of developing biological superweapons…[644])

Yet from the degree of seriousness with which the press treats these issues, one would think it were safe to simply put them aside. *ThinkProgress* noted that "networks covered the New England Patriots' Deflategate scandal and the Superbowl about twice as much as they covered climate change."[645] *CNN* would broadcast Trump press conferences in their entirety, suspending all regular programming and filling the screen with Trump's jabbering head for hours at a time.[646]

Little has improved since the election, and liberal outlets have been especially disappointing. *Mother Jones*, a progressive watchdog magazine which should be at the forefront of the campaign to draw matters of civilizational self-destruction to public attention, ran a headline after the election on one of the issues it thought particularly significant: "Donald Trump Is Lying About His Weight."[647] Laurie Penny of *The New Statesman* wrote a column entitled "Yes, You Should Care That Donald Trump Is Attacking *Hamilton*," making the case for spending one's mental energy on Trump's feud with the cast of a hit Broadway musical.[648] And *Slate* ran a long explanation of why Donald Trump slipping away from the press to privately eat a steak with his family constituted a major national issue, under the headline "Why the Press Is Right to Freak Out Over Trump Sneaking to a Steakhouse."[649] Thus did the liberal press keep its reading public enlightened and informed of matters of global consequence…

If you care about issues like climate change, nuclear war, global poverty, and health, then you necessarily need to spend time talking about them. It should go without saying that if your post-election columns are on Trump's weight or his trip to a steakhouse, it is fair for the audience to conclude that you do not really care about the issues you say you care about.

◆   ◆   ◆   ◆

THIS DISASTER SHOULD CAUSE A MAJOR REEVALUATION OF THE POLITICAL media, who failed utterly to appreciate the seriousness of what was happening. There is a good argument to be made that the media is responsible for creating Trump in the first place. But the press also thoroughly failed the country, by distorting reality to make it appear as if Clinton was more likely to win than she was. In doing so, they allowed people to rest easy when they should have (and would have) been out trying to put the brakes on the Trump train. Trump's election should cause some serious self-reflection among members of the political press.[650]

The election of Trump is therefore a serious repudiation of media "experts." Websites like *Vox* position themselves as "explainers" of reality, disguising the fact that they are making an awful lot of things up in order to cover gaps in their knowledge. Trump's election has shown that believing these types of claims to expertise can be positively dangerous. And yet it is almost certain the experts will persist in claiming superior knowledge of the world, even as they refuse to leave their D.C. and New York enclaves. There are no consequences to false predictions, even if you end up getting Donald Trump elected president.

It is crucial, however, that the following lesson be learned well by progressives: *these people do not know anything.* Do not put too much stock in predictions, especially if the fate of the world may be on the line. No political commentator or forecaster can offer you any real certainty, because they don't have any special magic that the rest of us don't have access to. But more important than the silly pundits and their bullshit graphs were the matters the press *didn't* cover. The danger of the Trump era is that it will continue to fix all of the press's attention on Trump, and make it harder and harder to discuss things that matter.

CALAMITY LOOMS
(OR POSSIBLY DOESN'T)

"I genuinely believe that if Trump wins and gets the nuclear codes there is an excellent possibility it will lead to the end of civilization." [651]
—Tony Schwartz, ghostwriter, Trump: The Art of the Deal

WHAT WILL THE FOUR YEARS OF A TRUMP PRESIDENCY ACTUALLY LOOK like? If there's one thing that should have been (but won't be) learned from this election, it is that one should be very careful about making confident predictions about complex social phenomena. The best course of action is to consider various plausible futures, and try to account for their possibility.

We do know that for a leftist, liberal, or progressive, it is an extremely worrying political moment. There is complete Republican control of government. Soon the right may dominate the Supreme Court entirely. [652] The Republican Party almost has control of enough state governments to where it can pass amendments to the United States Constitution at will. Democrats have been almost completely shut out of power at the federal level, and their state power only remains especially strong in traditional blue states. Even there, they are frequently struggling. (Massachusetts has a Republican governor, after all.)

The dominance of Republicans means that the conservative agenda is poised to advance significantly. We may see the privatization of a number of traditional public functions, escalation of deportations, a more militaristic foreign policy, and a total abandonment of the social safety net. It is likely that inequality will worsen.

The worst case scenario for the Trump presidency is quite bad indeed. Trump is not a fascist, but he could well turn out to be an authoritarian strongman of the most sinister variety. Unfortunately, he has inherited an extraordinarily powerful office. Both Democratic and Republican presidents have, over the years, worked to expand the power of the executive branch, making the 21st-century Presidency an unusually powerful position with a lot of destructive potential.

The particular possibilities are unnerving to think about. *New York Times* journalist James Risen points out that the Obama administration has vigorously used the executive branch's capacities to prosecute whistle-blowers and monitor reporters' phone records. Risen argues that "If Donald J. Trump decides as president to throw a whistle-blower in jail for trying to talk to a reporter, or gets the FBI to spy on a journalist, he will have one man to thank for bequeathing him such expansive power: Barack Obama."[653] Given Trump's well-known distaste for the press corps, it doesn't seem implausible that press freedom could suffer in the Trump years.

More alarming still is the president's extraordinary ability to make unilateral foreign policy decisions. Both Bush and Obama expanded executive decision-making over war. During the election, the *New York Times* investigated the question of what would stop the president from dropping a nuclear bomb on whomever he pleased. The short answer, they said, was nothing.[654] Or rather, as writer Rachel Becker put it, the main barriers are "psychological, not legal."[655] (If one is relying on Donald Trump's "psychology" to rein him in and keep him rational, the world may be in for trouble…)

In *Foreign Policy*, James Bamford writes that the Trump presidency will have complete control over a formidable state apparatus, and wonders why nobody considered the possibility that an all-powerful state might be an unwise thing to construct:

> *Americans have been warned for decades about the potential consequences of the U.S. surveillance state — the largest, most powerful, and most intrusive in the world — falling into a would-be tyrant's hands. With Donald Trump's inauguration looming, I have to wonder: Was anyone paying attention?* [656]

Barack Obama maintained a so-called "disposition matrix"[657] (i.e. kill list) picking off various hostile targets for execution without trial (those killed included U.S. citizen Anwar al-Awlaki and, separately, his 16-year-old son[658]). Now Donald Trump has taken over the role, it is unclear what he will do with it. Bamford considers the possibility that Trump could institute "absolute power." Indeed, Trump's own words don't offer much confidence. Of hacking his political enemies, he said: "I wish I had that power. Man, that would be power."[659] And Trump has already suggested that he might support the surveillance of mosques[660] and the execution of Edward Snowden.[661]

But one should be careful about slipping into alarmism before anything has actually happened. Trump should only be treated as a dictator if he actually becomes one. And there is a tendency to blow Trump's statements beyond all proportion, and envision horrors that may not actually come to pass. Certainly, even if Trump simply doubles down on existing U.S. policies (such as mass deportations and surveillance), his government could be brutal and intrusive. But he is not necessarily Hitler (this is, of course, rather faint reassurance).

The truth is that Trump is highly unpredictable, and so the possibilities for what he will do range considerably, from "not that bad actually" to "the end of human civilization as we know it." And while many seem to believe the latter to be far more likely than the former, their evidence for their own doom is limited. They are frequently extrapolating from Trump's campaign rhetoric. Whether any of this rhetoric is transformed into reality depends on how serious Trump actually is. But since Trump is insincere and deceptive, most of his more extreme policy suggestions could have been little more than an electoral ploy. Almost as soon as Trump became president-elect, he abandoned his vow to "lock up" Hillary Clinton, for instance.

Regardless of whether Trump turns out to be ineffectual or barbaric, for people on the left, Republican control of government means that progressive policies face a grim few years. Even in the best-case scenario, in which Trump turns out to be mostly bluster, as incapable at organizing a dictatorship as he is at running a hotel, we may see every single progressive policy of the last eight years rolled back very swiftly. Goodbye, healthcare! Goodbye, moderate criminal justice reforms! Goodbye, mild attempts to rein in corporate malfeasance! Progressives are now going to be on the defensive. Instead of strengthening public schools and social welfare programs, we shall be trying to make sure that they continue to exist at all. Instead of expanding access to women's reproductive health care, we are going to be facing the possible elimination of *Roe v. Wade*, and subsequent outright criminalization of abortion in numerous states. It will not, in other words, be a happy few years.

And that might, of course, be an understatement. The rise of the white supremacist "alt-right" is certainly a terrifying development, though thankfully the movement seems largely confined to the internet, where its major weapons are meme-based.[662] But we have to be careful. They laughed at the Nazis in 1928, at the man with the funny moustache and his gang of silly brown-shirted thugs. They weren't laughing so much in 1933. Things could be the same when it comes to the man with the funny hair and the orange face. Hah... Hah...

Hah... Oh shit. Apocalypses are frequently closer than you think, and tend to take people by surprise.

For the sake of our sanity, it's necessary to assume that this isn't true. We must act as if we are not all about to die, as if the sky will not fall. (And who knows? It might not.) If we become *resigned*, if we start to feel doomed and hopeless, we are liable to produce a highly dangerous self-fulfilling prophecy. This has to be a moment of *action* rather than despair. Just how disastrous Trump turns out to be depends in large part on how progressives act in response. If they keep themselves focused on the issues where Trump is weakest, they can keep public opinion against him and sap his political capital. If they rebuild themselves into a persuasive and principled opposition, Trump may have to back down on some of his extreme policies. On the other hand, if the "resistance" is characterized by Meryl Streep telling Americans that football sucks, and Keith Olbermann draping himself in an American flag and ranting about Putin,[663] the left is unlikely to win many converts.

What, then, does the election of Donald Trump actually mean? Here is the important point: nobody knows. Anybody who says they know *doesn't know.* This election is, first and foremost, a repudiation of the establishment, which means that the wisdom of pundits, experts, and elites has been proven hollow. So in trying to interpret this event, *do not listen* to those who insist they know things, or who confidently offer a new round of predictions for what will happen. We've entered the Age of the Unpredictable.

"For Mr. Donald Trump we don't matter as workers or as human beings. For Mr. Donald Trump we're just a number…" [664]
—CELIA VARGAS, cleaner, Trump International Hotel Las Vegas

WHY TRUMP
MUST BE
DEFEATED

EDWARD FRIEL'S FATHER HAD BEEN A CABINET-MAKER BEFORE HIM, and the family had been in business together for over forty years by the time he landed a contract to make desks, bars, and slot machine cabinets for one of Donald Trump's Atlantic City casinos in the 1980s. But in the time since the company's founding, Friel had never experienced anything to match what happened with Trump. Customers may have complained, but nobody simply took the cabinets and refused to pay.

This is precisely what Donald Trump did, however. Having taken possession of all of the Friels' custom-made cabinets, Trump declined to hand over $80,000 of the sum he had agreed to pay. Instead, he called Friel in for a meeting, explaining that he was dissatisfied with the work and would not be paying the outstanding bill. He would also not be returning the cabinets. Trump did, however, offer to give the Friels more work in the future.

It was this promise of future work that most baffled Friel's son Paul.

"Why would the Trump family want a company who they say their work is inferior to work for them in the future?"[665] he recalled thinking to himself. It was difficult to avoid the conclusion that Trump was simply trying to get away with paying as little as possible. (In the event, the Friels did not end up continuing to work for Trump. Reeling from the significant loss of income, the company's fortunes declined and it went out of business.)

The Friels' experience was common among Trump's contractors. A *USA Today* investigation revealed that over the years, Trump had established a pattern of refusing to pay for work that had been completed, forcing those who performed services for him to undergo lengthy litigation in order to recover the sums they were owed.[666] According to *USA Today*, those that were stiffed included:

> *A dishwasher in Florida. A glass company in New Jersey. A carpet company. A plumber. Painters. Forty-eight waiters. Dozens of bartenders and other hourly workers at his resorts and clubs, coast to coast. Real estate brokers who sold his properties. And, ironically, several law firms that once represented him in these suits and others.*[667]

USA Today summarized the results of its investigation:

> *At least 60 lawsuits, along with hundreds of liens, judgments, and other government filings…document people who have accused Trump and his businesses of failing to pay them for their work… Trump's companies have also been cited for 24 violations of the Fair Labor Standards Act since 2005 for failing to pay overtime or minimum wage, according to U.S. Department of Labor data. In addition to the lawsuits, the review found more than 200 mechanic's liens — filed by contractors and employees against Trump, his companies or his properties claiming*

they were owed money for their work — since the 1980s. The liens range from a $75,000 claim by a Plainview, N.Y., air conditioning and heating company to a $1 million claim from the president of a New York City real estate banking firm.[668]

Those who did work for Trump tell common stories: they would land a lucrative contract, they would deliver the work. Trump would make the early payments. But when it came to paying the final bill, Trump would suddenly voice dissatisfaction, complaining that the work was substandard and should not be paid for. In 1990, according to the *Philly Voice*, casino commission records revealed "$69.5 million owed to 253 subcontractors on the Trump Taj Mahal." Of these companies, many "had already sued Trump, while others were attempting to recover what they could for work on everything from plumbing and lighting to ornaments including the casino's iconic minarets."[669] Many of the contracts were for large sums of money, and companies that did not get paid sometimes did not survive. When Trump was sued, he sometimes offered only "30 cents on the dollar."

Piano-maker J. Michael Diehl was one of those who, in his words, was "exploited and forced to suffer a loss because of [Trump's] corporation's shady practices." In an op-ed for the *Washington Post*, Diehl described his experience selling pianos to Trump:

> *I was thrilled to get a $100,000 contract from Trump. It was one of the biggest sales I'd ever made. I was supposed to deliver and tune the pianos; the Trump corporation would pay me within 90 days. I asked my lawyer if I should ask for payment upfront, and he laughed. "It's Donald Trump!" he told me. "He's got lots of money." [NOTE: This is bad lawyering.] But when I requested payment, the Trump corporation hemmed and hawed. Its*

executives avoided my calls and crafted excuses. After a couple of months, I got a letter telling me that the casino was short on funds. They would pay 70 percent of what they owed me. There was no negotiating. I didn't know what to do — I couldn't afford to sue the Trump corporation, and I needed money to pay my piano suppliers. So I took the $70,000. Losing $30,000 was a big hit to me and my family. The profit from Trump was meant to be a big part of my salary for the year. So I made much less. There was no money to help grow my business. I had fewer pianos in the showroom and a smaller advertising budget. Because of Trump, my store stagnated for a couple of years. It made me feel really bad, like I'd been taken advantage of. I was embarrassed.[670]

The habit did not die with Trump's casino bankruptcies in the early 1990's. Rana Williams, who sold hundreds of millions of dollars of property for Trump International Realty from 2009 to 2012, had to sue to recover over $700,000 in commissions that Trump's company was contractually required to pay but had failed to.[671] The experience of staffers at the short-lived *Trump* magazine was also a saga of bounced checks and suddenly canceled health coverage. (In the words of one staff member, who was left without insurance during her cancer treatment: "The people who actually put out the magazine—people like me—were left in the dust. The lack of accountability and responsibility was infuriating."[672])

Trump appears to see his refusal to pay his bills as a form of tough negotiating, rather than an act of theft. (And, to be clear, taking things without paying for them is theft.) This may be one of the reasons why he speaks glowingly of how shrewd his business bankruptcies were. He does not see what bankruptcy means for the small businesses or employees to whom one may owe money. As one online commenter put it, "Trump is the kind of guy that goes out to a nice restaurant, gets the steak and lobster, the finest wine, eats everything but the very last bite and then calls the manager over to say how awful everything was and he's not paying."[673] (Indeed, a woman who once went on a date with Trump confirmed that, after showing off his expensive new Cadillac, Trump suddenly found himself without any cash when it came time to pay for dinner. He promised he would pay her back. 40 years later, she was still waiting…[674])

Thus in Donald Trump's treatment of the small businesspeople he has hired, we see the same attitude as we saw with Trump University and the Scottish golf course: promises unfulfilled, ordinary people hurt and betrayed. Trump convinces people to trust him, and then leaves them with nothing. As Michael Diehl sums it up:

> *I delivered quality pianos, tuned and ready to go. I did every thing right. And then Trump cheated me. It's a callous way to do business.*

Beth Rosser, whose family company secured a $200,000 contract to install toilet partitions in the Trump Taj Mahal, remembers what happened when the payment never came after the work was complete. Her father, who had built the company from scratch, "nearly lost everything,"

> *We weren't this big company… we didn't have tons of money in [our] account to cover things… It's 27 years later. I grit my teeth every time I see him on television blustering about what a wonderful businessman he is… He stepped on a lot of people…[675] Trump crawled his way to the top on the back of little guys, one of them being my father. He had no regard for thousands of men and women who worked on those projects. He says he'll make*

America great again, but his past shows the complete opposite of that.[676]

◆   ◆   ◆   ◆

DONALD J. TRUMP IS AN EXTRAORDINARY MAN, INSOFAR AS HE MANAGES to embody everything bad about all of us. Trump is the person we would be if we all gave in to our worst instincts: if we used people instead of caring for them, if we mocked people instead of under-standing them, and if we dragged out the pettiest of feuds instead of putting aside our grievances.

The imperative to defeat Trump, then, is the imperative to defeat our worst selves and become our best selves. It is the imperative to be better people, who are actually nice to one another and don't rip each other off. So long as there is a Trump, there can be no justice. And so long as there is hate within our hearts, we are all our own Trumps to one degree or another.

There are plenty of ways one can convince oneself that this isn't true. Perhaps we don't need to defeat Trump. Perhaps, if you really think about it, Trump has already defeated *himself* by being such an awful person. *New York Times* columnist David Brooks says he feels little but "sadness and pity" for Trump:

> *Imagine if you had to go through a single day without sharing kind little moments with strangers and friends. Imagine if you had to endure a single week in a hate-filled world, crowded with enemies of your own making, the object of disgust and derision.*[677]

Of course, this does seem a bit sad. So we can tell ourselves that beneath it all, Trump isn't truly happy. How could anybody be happy without friends, love, and laughter? How could anyone be happy if they think only of themselves, if they cannot pause to appreciate the beauty of flowers or the laughter of children?

Actually, such people can be happy pretty easily. After all, Trump is the president. His life is probably great. He is universally feared. He can have anything he wants. He can grab whomever he likes by whatever parts of their anatomy, and one can be sure he is too busy enjoying being one of the wealthiest and most powerful people in the history of human civilization to lament the absence of "kind little moments with strangers" in his life.

It may be comforting to tell ourselves that Trump isn't *really* happy. He is unfulfilled, alone, bitter. And perhaps this is true. Love and warmth are very nourishing things. Having them is nice. But hatred can feel pretty great, too. And if we tell ourselves that Trump is crying on the inside, we may be (1) wrong and (2) making excuses for our own inaction. *If* justice works itself out no matter what, because people who are villainous end up unhappy, and people who are good end up happy, then there is nothing we need do; karma works everything out in the end. If, on the other hand, good people do suffer, and bad people have great lives and a good time, then it is incumbent on human beings to adjust the scale and make sure people receive the outcomes they deserve.

The truth is that nobody is out there making sure evildoers are punished. Evildoers make out quite well a lot of the time. The only way to make sure they don't is to actually stop them. Thus: if Trump's life doesn't end where it should (with Trump in prison, or fired into outer space), then there will be no justice. It is the responsibility of Earth's population to ensure that the story of Trump has a moral at the end. If they don't then the lesson of Donald Trump's life will be: act like an asshole and you can inherit the world.

Justice requires that Trump's career end in ruin. He can't be allowed to *get away with it*.[678]

PART FOUR

What To Do About It

DONALD TRUMP IS FREQUENTLY DISMISSED AS CLOWNISH AND A boor. He is belittled for his oblivious statements, or for not reading books. Trump has a brilliance, though. He is shrewd. One does not get elected President of the United States without having at least some understanding of what the people want and how to give it to them. Trump is a showman, and a good one. He knows just what he can get away with. Getting rid of him won't be easy. It requires figuring out how he works, and how to craft effective political messaging that can counter his all-consuming media show. Possibly the most difficult task is to take our eyes off him, to quit allowing the political universe to revolve around Trump to begin with.

The best thing progressives can do now is to ask themselves a series of questions: What do we stand for? Why do we stand for it? And how are we going to get it? Every political act should be framed in light of those questions. That means critical self-reflection. If some of the things we stand for don't seem to make sense, then we should refine our principles. If the actions we're taking don't seem likely to lead to achieving the things we stand for, then perhaps we should be taking different actions.

There are all kinds of examples of discussions on the left that seem disastrously self-destructive. One of them is the ongoing argument over "identity politics." Some people say that "identity politics" is destroying the left, by dividing people along racial and gender lines and causing counterproductive schisms and fractures. Other people say that "identity politics" is just a derogatory term for those who seek racial and gender equality, principles that are essential to any left agenda.

Both of those positions, in the abstract, seem perfectly reasonable. But both of them depend on tossing a term around without defining its meaning. Is "identity politics" useful? Well, it depends on what you mean. For example: *if* we mean that racism and gender discrimination, and other questions that affect people's personal identities, are extremely important issues, then obviously identity politics is an important part of any progressive agenda. But *if* we mean that people's political agendas should be entirely defined by their race and gender, with no sense of *common* human problems that cut across personal identities and affect us all, then identity politics seems like it will necessarily lead to the unhealthy splintering into factions and prevent us from offering broad appeals.

It should be perfectly possible to simultaneously fight against racism *and* appeal to working-class people of all races. There is no inconsistency between the principle that racial hierarchies are bad and that class hierarchies are bad. And yet sometimes, on the left, it can seem as if these two ideas are in tension: anyone who talks about reaching out to the white working class is excusing racism, and anyone who believes race matters is downplaying the importance of class. But these divisions can be avoided if we figure out what we actually believe, and why we believe it.

The new moment for progressive politics is going to require a serious attempt to figure out what we mean by things, what our principles are, whether we are applying them fairly and consistently, and how to apply them better. The problem with much of the reaction to Trump is that it doesn't appear to be in any way strategic. It's directed by our instinctual reactions to Trump rather than a pragmatic sense of whether it is actually useful in defeating him. For example, if Trump performs a bizarre caricature seemingly intended to mock a disabled reporter,[679] we will spend our time condemning his callousness in this particular instance rather than talking about the needs of disabled people more broadly. Instead of making the story about the lives of people who are not Trump, we allow the story to be about Trump and the bad things he does, and what a horrible human being he is.

In this final section of the book, I offer a few tentative observations and programmatic suggestions for dealing with Trump. I go through what I think are some weaknesses in the ways we think about him, and talk about effective strategies for opposing him. Finally, I very briefly delve into some of the present deficiencies of progressive politics, with suggestions for how to rebuild and retool it.

BAD WAYS TO CRITICIZE TRUMP

IT IS VERY EASY TO FIND WAYS TO CRITICIZE DONALD TRUMP. BECAUSE he has so many loathsome traits of character, Trump provides the prospective critic with ample possible lines of attack. It can be difficult to know where to start. Is it the bombast? The racism?[680] The massive serial sexual assault?[681] Is it the mob ties?[682] The fraudulent university?[683] The overstated wealth?[684] How about all of the lies?[685] Or the false promises?[686] What about the near-total lack of an attention span,[687] and the ignorance of global affairs?[688] Should we dwell on his childish personality?[689] On his bullying?[690] His vulgarity?[691] His sexism?[692] Trump presents a veritable buffet of appalling qualities, and it is nearly impossible to decide where to start.

But not all criticisms of Trump have equal effective force. After all, surely it matters more that he has actually committed serious sex crimes than that he has possibly made some bizarre reference to Megyn Kelly's menstrual cycle.[693] Likewise, his history of making it hard for his contractors to feed their families is far more reprehensible than his outlandish tweeting habits or his risible haircut. Trump's actions have hurt people in serious ways, and his behavior can be divided into that which is merely silly (such as his calling Rosie O'Donnell rude names) versus that which actively causes pain (such as his possibly having raped someone).

Unfortunately, media outrage about Trump frequently adopts a uniform level of outrage at his acts. Trump's history is treated as a *set* of bad things, meaning that few distinctions are made among which *kinds* of transgressions are worse. But there are lesser and greater crimes. Trump's constant theft of wages and payments from dishwashers, cabinet-makers, and servers is far more consequential than, say, his promotion of a failed mail-order steak franchise. Yet press coverage often treats such things as being of equal interest. For example, an *Atlantic* article compiling a definitive list of Trump's "scandals" lists both the sexual assault allegations *and* the fact that Trump may have once bought concrete from a Mafia affiliate.[694] Surely, though, grabbing dozens of women's genitals without their permission is worse than having purchased building supplies from someone vaguely shady. And *ThinkProgress* put as much effort into its comprehensive (half-joking, but carefully-reported) history of Trump Steaks as its coverage of the story of Trump's alleged brutal rape of his wife.[695]

Likewise, *Mother Jones* magazine ran a series on Trump called "The Trump Files." It included plenty of damning information about Trump's use of lawsuits and harassment to keep his critics quiet. And yet other entries in the series included: "Donald Thinks Exercising Might Kill You"[696] and "Donald Filmed a Music Video. It Didn't Go Well."[697] In the Trump files, one can find plenty of information about how Trump cheated the New York City government out of tax money,[698] or dumped his business debts on others.[699] Yet one can also find files on some of his more ludicrous reality TV show pilot ideas,[700] and "the time a sleazy hot tub salesman tried to take Trump's name."[701] There's a funny file about how Trump couldn't name a single one of his "hand-picked" professors for Trump University.[702] But the important point about Trump University is not that Trump lied about knowing who the instructors were, it's that it bilked people out of their savings.

Criticisms of Trump therefore need to be made carefully, because they can all end up bleeding together as noise. This is a good reason for, if not ignoring entirely, then at least giving very selective coverage to the rubbish Trump posts on Twitter. A Tweet is not, after all, the most consequential of communications. And while it may have been *interesting* for *The New York Times* to have two reporters compile a vast list of "the 289 People, Places, and Things Donald Trump Has Insulted on Twitter,"[703] a journalist's time may be better spent on more useful investigative work.

It's understandable why Trump's Twitter feed attracts so much attention. After all, it's outrageous, and frequently very entertaining. How can anyone resist finding out what he has to say about Glenn Beck ("mental basketcase"), Ruth Bader Ginsburg ("her mind is shot!"), or *Saturday Night Live* ("unwatchable!") The truth is, no matter how much we may deny it, on some level many of us *enjoy* watching Trump defy taboos and be nasty to people. After all, the entire reason for things like the *New York Times* Trump insult database is that it's amusing. People hate Trump, but they also love hating him.

There's also a convenient rationale for reading Trump's tweets, especially now: it provides closer access to the thoughts of the President of the United States than anybody has ever previously had. For journalists, there is good reason to cover Trump's social media outbursts: his words are now important. When the president speaks, it moves markets. It can create diplomatic incidents. Like it or not, Trump's tweets *do* matter.

The problem, however, is that Trump knows this. He knows that every noise he makes is amplified by the press. And he knows that, as journalist Michael Tracey writes, "his tweets will be instantly picked up by all the typical news outlets [and] everyone will frantically seize upon every crass Trump tweet, and use it to set the "tone" of their coverage for the day."[704] Thus Trump's rude and provocative tweets are calculated for maximum effect. And while members of the press may insist that they *understand* Trump is trying to get attention, they nevertheless end up granting him precisely the attention he seeks.

It's a difficult paradox to get out of. You can't ignore Trump's tweets entirely, because it's news if the President of the United States has publicly threatened or disparaged someone. But at the same time, by affording coverage to whatever Trump wants to say on Twitter, one allows him to set the agenda and make the news about himself.

Yet it's possible that a balance can be struck. Tracey offers a series of tips to journalists for how to deal with Trump's tweets, which balance the necessity of paying attention to the president with the reality that the current president is a manipulative attention-seeker. As he writes:

> *— You don't need to share, comment, react to, or write articles about every Trump tweet. Trump will do inflammatory tweets. Some might be in the middle of the night. Everyone knows that he does this. It's not surprising anymore. Therefore, it is not incumbent on the journalist to treat every instance of this as a major news item, just like you are not required to treat every politician's PR release as a major news item. Journalists should dictate the terms of their coverage, not Trump.*
> *— You don't need to treat every Trump tweet as 100% literal. Most of the time Trump is, pardon my French, just "bull-shitting." He muses, he riffs, he does these extemporaneous stream-of-consciousness rants…So if Trump muses about some nutty idea on Twitter, it doesn't mean that he plans to actually implement this idea in terms of*

government policy. He could just be trying to get a rise out of people. And it usually works.

– You are allowed to simply ignore Trump tweets. This may sound like a novel idea, but you are under no obligation to even pay attention to every Trump tweet. As a journalist, you are allowed to focus on other things… Hysterically over-reacting to every Trump tweet helps Trump. When you treat today's loony Trump tweet as the top news story… you are keeping him at the center of attention, which he obviously craves. But you are also… strengthening his grip over the media, and you are making the media appear helpless and servile.[705]

The core problem of Trump coverage, one that is rarely acknowledged or dealt with, is that because bad publicity helps Trump, there seems to be no way to criticize him without further inflating him. The moment you pay attention to him, he has won. And since it seems impossible not to pay attention to him, he will therefore always win.

That may make the situation seem impossible. It's only impossible, though, if the media continue to follow the same set of rules for coverage that they have always operated under. If it always merits attention when important people do outrageous things, then Trump will dominate the media forever, because Trump knows how to increase his importance and knows how to be outrageous. The rules of what's important must change if we are to successfully reduce Trump's dominance of the press. That means apportioning more coverage to, for example, Iraq, healthcare, and climate change, and less coverage to whatever 140-character idiocy Trump has most recently spewed. It should be recognized that Trump is *intentionally* trying to get people to pay as much attention to him as possible, and that one needs to find a way not to give him what he wants.

Finding effective ways to apportion critical attention to Trump means more than just ignoring some of his more rancid Tweets. It also requires ridding ourselves of certain *kinds* of criticism, which frequently *seem* damning in their content but aren't damning at all in their ultimate consequences.

Let's, then, go through a few insults and criticisms of Trump that don't seem to work very well. A few of the most obvious:

1. Trump is orange.[706]
2. Trump is vulgar.[707]
3. Trump is dumb.[708]
4. Trump has funny hair.[709]

These are all given frequent mention. They are also beside the point. One should care far more about what Trump thinks and does than what he looks like. Now, one could say that *what he looks like* is in some ways a reflection of who he is, since the ridiculous spray-tan with the little white eye-regions is the product and consequence of his vanity. But the broader principle of progressives should be: what someone looks like is of minimal relevance in evaluating them. That's what we believe. And we should be consistent in that belief. If someone made fun of our candidate's appearance, no matter what that appearance was, we would declare that as a matter of principle, image should matter less than substance. Such high-mindedness is both admirable and correct. But it has no force unless you maintain it consistently, even as applied to people whom you detest. (Furthermore, mockery of Trump's mannerisms and appearance has the perverse effect of building him up into more of an icon than he already is.)

This is why the "Naked Trump" sculptures,[710] which a group of anarchists erected during August in American city parks, were so politically useless. The sculptures depicted Trump as grotesquely flabby, his penis so minute as to be invisible to the naked eye. Entitled "The Emperor Has No Balls," the statue's artistic point was to humiliatingly "expose" Trump. But the message didn't really make sense. Some people critiqued it as "transphobic."[711] The real problem with it, though, was that it didn't actually make a serious point. Trump is fat. So what? Do we hate fat people? Do we want to reinforce the idea that being fat is gross? Trump has a small penis. So what? Do we want to maintain the cruel idea that penis size says something about one's dignity? And how would we feel about a similarly unflattering nude Hillary Clinton sculpture? Mocking his body is a *satisfying* form of lashing out at Trump, but it's not a particularly noble, persuasive, or progressive one.

In fact, one should also be wary of progressive attacks against Trump that are based on premises that progressives do not actually share. For example, there have been critical press articles (by liberals) about Melania Trump's skirting of immigration law,[712] Trump's lack of familiarity with the Bible,[713] and Trump's evasion of the Vietnam draft.[714] But progressives don't want immigration status to be an issue, and they don't care whether political candidates have read the Bible. And *we're* the ones who are supposed to be sympathetic to those who wanted to avoid being killed in Vietnam.

These attacks are therefore not honest reflections of our values. Of course, the progressive response is that these critiques of Trump are about *hypocrisy*, about *his own* standards. Because Trump is anti-immigrant, it makes sense to call out his wife's own violations of immigration law, or his own employment of unauthorized workers. Because Trump is pretending to be religious for the purposes of running for office, it makes sense to point out his pitiful knowledge of Biblical lore. Because he is warlike, we can point out that he's a chicken. (Likewise with the sculpture: because Trump is a narcissist, it makes sense to point out that he is unattractive. Not that *we* care. But *he* does.)

There's something a little bit uncomfortable about dwelling on these issues at all, though, because it's hard to simultaneously insist that something matters for the *limited* purpose of proving hypocrisy but ultimately doesn't matter in the least. If we call Trump a smallpenised, nonreligious, draft-dodging employer of illegal immigrants (and one who is *not even a billionaire* at that!), we are willingly adopting a set of values that we don't hold. And it may be difficult to turn around and insist that actually, those things are fine. Thus while it makes *logical* sense to make such critiques, it muddies progressive messaging. One's time is probably better spent pointing out how Trump doesn't live up to a set of *good* values that we *do* hold rather than a set of *bad* values that he himself pretends to hold.

A useful question to ask when criticizing Trump is as follows: would I care about Thing X if someone on my own side did it? For example, if someone on my side had bought concrete from a person with criminal ties, I would be taking pains to explain why buying concrete from someone unpleasant doesn't make you yourself unpleasant. Likewise, I do not care when Democrats have unfortunate haircuts. What matters to me is what someone believes, not whether their flesh is or is not the color of a ripe satsuma.

This is why John Oliver's mockery of Trump on *Last Week Tonight* was particularly toothless and pathetic. Having found out that Trump's German ancestors were called "Drumpf" rather than "Trump," Oliver led a campaign to "Make Donald Drumpf Again,"[715] wringing great amusement out of the apparent silliness of Trump's ancestral name. But what was the point of this joke? What did it say about Trump? Lots of people have foreign ancestors with unusual names. Do we care? Isn't progressivism supposed to have, as one of its principles, that *foreign names aren't funny just because they're foreign?* Isn't this the cheapest and most xenophobic of all possible jokes? Oliver's Drumpf campaign became extremely popular, but it was deeply childish. It fell into a common trap of Trump critiques: it descended to Trump's level, using name-calling and playground taunts rather than trying to actually critique the truly harmful and reprehensible things about Trump. (It is possible to do satirical comedy that is *actually* brutal. The best joke about George W. Bush was nothing to do with *My Pet*

Goat or his choking on a pretzel, but was the *Onion's* devastating headline: "George W. Bush Debuts New Paintings Of Dogs, Friends, Ghost Of Iraqi Child That Follows Him Everywhere.")

The critique of Trump as "vulgar" is another especially ineffective angle. Trump's vulgarity is actually one of his only positive qualities. Vulgarity can be refreshing. It can get to the point, and be emotionally honest. It's also nice to be told what politicians really think, it language that doesn't try to disguise cruelty beneath a thin cloak of civility. As Amber A'Lee Frost writes, vulgarity in itself can have a clarifying effect:

> *Trump's vulgarity is appealing precisely because it exposes political truths. As others have noted, Trump's policies (wildly inconsistent though they may be) are actually no more extreme than those of other Republicans; Trump is just willing to strip away the pretense. Other candidates may say "national security is a fundamental priority," whereas Trump will opt for "ban all the Muslims." The latter is far less diplomatic, but in practice the two candidates fundamentally mean the same thing. We should prefer the honest boor, as polite euphemism is constantly used to mask atrocities.*[716]

Frost also points out that "vulgarity is the language of the people" and can be "wield[ed] righteously against the corrupt and the powerful." Of course, much of Trump's vulgarity has no such redemptive quality, and is used in the service of power rather than to undermine it. But it's still more important to critique the underlying *sentiment* of Trump's views rather than the coarseness with which Trump expresses them.

The failure to distinguish between tone and substance afflicted coverage of the notorious Billy Bush tape. Multiple news outlets reported that Trump had been caught on tape making "lewd"[717] or "vulgar"[718] remarks about women. In fact, he had been caught on tape bragging about committing sexual assault. The problem wasn't the vulgarity. (After all, it would have been unobjectionable if he had been caught on tape saying "there's nothing I love more than when someone gives unambiguous and enthusiastic consent for me to grab her by the pussy.") It didn't matter that he had said the word "pussy," it mattered that he had admitted to a series of outrageous sex crimes. But the idea that "vulgarity" is what's unappealing about Trump suggests that if he did the same exact things, with a little better manners, his behavior would be beyond reproach.

Calling Trump dumb is a similarly futile line of attack. Nothing reinforces perceptions of liberals as snobs more easily than picking on stupid people. When Trump is mocked for his pronunciation of "China"[719] or compared with the president from *Idiocracy*,[720] critics miss something important: Trump may be an idiot, but he's no dummy. That is to say: treating Trump as if he is *slow* leads to underestimating the kind of genius he has for successful PR manipulation. People will analyze the reading-level of Trump's speeches,[721] and conclude that he has the mind of a fourth-grader. But if you treat Trump as a fourth-grader,[722] you may assume (quite wrongly) that he is easily outsmarted. Up until this point, underestimating Trump has produced nothing but misfortune for the under-estimators. Trump should be treated as what he is: non-literate, non-worldly, but media-savvy and ruthlessly cunning. "Trump is dumb" messages are likely to play about as well as "Bush is dumb" messages did during the Bush/Kerry fight. They make liberals seem haughty, and Trump can claim that the elites are sneering at him (and by, implication, the working class) for a lack of formal book-learning.

Some critics of Trump seem to almost want to goad him into being worse for progressives. For example, in the time following the election, Trump was attacked for refusing national security briefings[723] and retaining executive producer status on *The Apprentice*.[724] The premise here, apparently, is that we *want* Donald Trump to spend less time working on reality shows and more time exercising the power of the presidency. But that seems an insane thing to desire. For progressives, it would probably be better if Trump spent four years continuing his reality show act than if he started thinking about which countries he'd like to bomb. (Same logic applies to the wall. Here's a quick tip that all progressives should follow: if he doesn't make an effort to build the wall, *don't* tell him he's a hypocrite and a failure.)

Likewise with Trump's self-enrichment. A number of people have dwelled on his "conflicts of interest," suggesting that Trump will unconstitutionally use his new powers to seek new business opportunities abroad, exploiting the office for financial gain. But if we're being honest, this is probably the best outcome progressives could hope for. We should pray that Trump wants *money* rather than *power*, because building hotels in Singapore is one of the least destructive possible uses of his time. Corruption may be bad, but for progressives who care about human rights, Trump's corruption should be very low on our list of worries. As Noam Chomsky has pointed out before,[725] we should almost hope that strongman-leaders are corrupt. If they're corrupt, they might not do too much harm; you also can buy them off with money. But if they're sincere yet megalomaniacal, there's no end to the evil they will do. A corrupt con man will drain your treasury, but an honest ideologue could massacre six million people.

The question anyone writing about Trump should think about before making a criticism is as follows: does anybody *really* give a crap? For example, which do people care more about: Trump being friendly with Putin or about the potential disappearance of their Medicaid benefits? Do they care more about Trump tweeting some slur about a news anchor, or about the threat of nuclear war? Focus should be kept on those things that affect people's lives the most.

There are bad potential critiques of Trump at every turn. When

Trump negotiated with the Carrier air conditioner company in Indiana, arranging for them to keep 800 jobs in the United States in return for a tax break,[726] some pointed out that 800 was only a fraction of the jobs in Indiana's manufacturing sector.[727] But this was a foolish critique. After all, 800 may not be many jobs statistically, but it's a lot to the people working those jobs. Trivialize that number and you trivialize those people's experiences. And saving 800 jobs was pretty impressive for a guy who hadn't even been sworn in yet. Scoffing at the number seemed bitter and out-of-touch, and the grumbling appeared to implicitly concede that Trump had accomplished something.

There was a far better critique to be made: Trump had essentially arranged for the company to receive an enormous bribe as a reward for threatening to send jobs to Mexico.[728] It was a deal that looked good but set a terrible precedent, because it signaled to corporations that Trump would help to arrange for taxpayers to give them money to stay in the United States. The Trump Carrier deal was a PR masterstroke, but there was a serious and effective criticism to be made of it.

One person who understood how to criticize the deal effectively was Bernie Sanders. In the *Washington Post*, Sanders wrote:

> *Today, about 1,000 Carrier workers and their families should be rejoicing. But the rest of our nation's workers should be very nervous. In exchange for allowing United Technologies to continue to offshore more than 1,000 jobs, Trump will reportedly give the company tax and regulatory favors that the corporation has sought. Just a short few months ago, Trump was pledging to force United Technologies to "pay a damn tax." He was insisting on very steep tariffs for companies like Carrier that left the United States and wanted to sell their foreign-made products back in the United States. Instead of a damn tax, the company will be rewarded with a damn tax cut. Wow!*

How's that for standing up to corporate greed? How's that
for punishing corporations that shut down in the United
States and move abroad? [729]

Note what Sanders did *not* do. He did not criticize *every* aspect of the deal. He did not diminish what it meant to the workers whose jobs were saved. But he reversed the message: instead of a move to help workers, it was a handout to corporations. This is the correct approach. It doesn't treat *every aspect of everything Trump does* as necessary of the same criticism. Instead, it asks: how do Trump's actions affect people in the real world? And if Trump's actions affect people negatively, they should be criticized.

It's possible to conduct effective messaging against Donald Trump. Donald Trump has very low favorability ratings, and it should be relatively easy to expose him as a con man, one who offers working people promises that he has no intention of fulfilling, who says he will "drain the Washington swamp" and then stuffs his administration with parasitic billionaire elites.

But mounting effective attacks against Trump requires caring about being effective to begin with. The more Democrats spend time talking about things like, say, Trump angering China with a phone call to Taiwan[730] (isn't the left supposed to *favor* talking to Taiwan?), the less we'll zero in on Trump's true political weaknesses. Trump wants us to talk about his feud with the cast of *Hamilton*. He does not want us to force him to talk seriously about policy.

Criticisms should be of the things that matter: the serial sexual assaults, the deportation plans, the anti-Muslim sentiment, the handouts to the rich, the destruction of the earth. These are the things that matter, and if progressives actually do care about them, then these are the things we should spend our time discussing. Forget the gaffes. Forget the hypocrisy. Forget the hotels. Forget the hair. And don't bother calling him Drumpf.

A
NEW
APPROACH

WHEN WE THINK ABOUT THE TALKING POINTS HEARD FROM THE left during 2015 and 2016, and we think about how serious the threats of nuclear war and climate change are, and about the abuse, harassment, and violence people face daily, it's clear that something has gone terribly wrong. Instead of pushing a positive agenda, people on the left have largely spent their time talking about Russian hacking and Donald Trump's tweets.

In fact, during the entire 18 months leading up to the election, people on the left spent large portions of their time talking about things that didn't actually matter very much to humanity. Whether it was Melania Trump plagiarizing a speech by Michelle Obama, or Donald Trump making a remark about Megyn Kelly, progressives didn't necessarily stay focused on issues of the greatest significance.

In fact, large amounts of left-wing energy have been wasted on comparatively trivial matters. People erected a statue of a naked Donald

Trump with a small penis. This was a waste of time. Then other people criticized that statue as "transphobic." This was also a waste of time. We discussed whether serving bastardized Vietnamese food in the Oberlin dining hall is "cultural appropriation," and whether white authors should be able to write black characters.

Instead of these side-matters, the left should be focused on the issues that most affect people's lives. Our job is not to oppose the right. Our job is to create a better world for people to live in. Because, ostensibly, we like people. And so we want them to have nice lives rather than rotten, violence-ridden, impoverished ones. In this respect we are different from Donald Trump, who does not shed a tear if his colleagues die in a helicopter accident, and couldn't care less whether he knocks out an elderly lady's water supply and forces her to carry a bucket from a well.

In order to have a purposeful and politically successful agenda, first you need a set of underlying principles. Then, you need a set of political goals, designed to realize those principles in order to make a world consistent with them. Finally, you need a set of strategies for achieving those goals. But all too often, it seems as if the left (1) doesn't really know what it actually believes and (2) has absolutely no idea what it is trying to do or how to do it.

What, after all, is the fundamental principle of the political left? The most obvious candidate is a preference for equality over inequality.[731] But the left is about more than equality. After all, to ensure perfect equality, you could just make everyone equally miserable. If the left is about nothing more than "equality," the quickest way to achieve its goals is by taking everything everyone has away and leaving them destitute.[732]

What we're really about, then, is making life *better* for people, eliminating human suffering and creating better conditions for people to exist in. We're about taking the bad features of society, the pain and the torment and the exploitation, and replacing them with good things.

A small sample list of things we should probably dislike:

- **War –** War is a horror. It results in babies having their limbs torn off. It forces people to watch their children, siblings, and parents die in front of them. It exacts an incalculable cost in human suffering. If we are against anything, it is war. All wars. No more wars!

- **Climate Change –** As the planet heats, millions of people will be driven from their homes. They will suffer drought. They will be killed by natural disasters. Their cities will disappear beneath the ocean. This seems like it should be issue #1 or 2.

- **Murder –** All murder. Murder by police and the state, as well as murder by civilians. It's very easy for the left to combine its opposition to police brutality with an opposition to crime generally. There is a common principle: we detest victimization.

- **Prisons –** Since victimization includes throwing people in cages, we should also be skeptical of vengeful rather than useful rehabilitative punishments.

- **Rape and Sexual Assault –** Women across the world are routinely brutalized, attacked, and harassed. Every moment we are discussing something *other* than this is a moment we are wasting.

- **Racism –** Since all human beings are fundamentally the same, people shouldn't be subjected to different treatment or given different life chances on the basis of their race. The black/white wealth gap is inexcusable.

- **Ill Health –** When people die of preventable diseases because they have no money, this is an outrage. Health care should be a right.

- **Ignorance and Want** – Everyone should be prosperous (not rich) and have full access to the full range of knowledge and learning that humankind has amassed.

- **Discrimination, Cruelty, and Mistreatment** – Nobody should be subjected to cruelty. Thus, where there is cruelty, the left should oppose it.

- **The Meat Holocaust** – It is unfashionable to say it, but animal suffering is as real as human suffering. From a moral perspective, this is not an issue that can be put aside, no matter how difficult it is to get people to care about. Animals are beaten, starved, tortured, and inhumanely slaughtered by the hundreds of millions every day.

Notice what did not make the list. Donald Trump's various remarks about *Hamilton*, Megyn Kelly, and China are not on this list. White people wearing sombreros are not on this list.[733] The College Republicans inviting a *Breitbart* editor to campus is not on this list.[734] Instead, we prioritize those things with the greatest tangible consequences in terms of the suffering of conscious beings. This means making questions of language use and culture secondary, and making questions of material deprivation and harm primary.

By organizing our priorities around people's material wellbeing, we provide a unifying underlying set of principles to guide our political action. What is the left about? It is about making sure life has less suffering, cruelty, and exploitation in it. The world is a place where people must go through a lot of things they do not deserve. Parents are taken away from their children and deported. Mothers watch their children thrown into prison cells for decades for simple mistakes of youth. Girlfriends watch boyfriends bleed to death after being shot to death by the police. Factory workers in Bangladesh work long hours for miserable pay, and must live in constant fear of their safety. Miners die of black lung. Tomato-pickers live in overcrowded mobile homes, working dawn to dusk and never seeing their children. It is a world filled with heartbreaking occurrences, few of which are acknowledged or spoken of by people in power.

It is the job of the left to make life better, to care about improving people's conditions in tangible ways. This means helping people achieve decent wages. Making sure they have good schools. Making sure they're not tangled up in red tape as they try to get health care. Making sure that they're not lonely, or depressed, that they have a sense of community and purpose. Our job is to bring everybody *the good life*, to make sure they are able to eat good food, have great healthcare, have fulfilling and rewarding work, and maximize their potential. We don't want people stuck in dead-end tasks that they hate, we don't want them having to worry about whether they'll be able to pay for their children's medical needs, we don't want them blown to pieces in a needless war.

Yet consider how people on the left frequently talk: in abstractions, generalities, and theories, in ways that don't put our principles in intelligible terms. Partly because so much left-wing thinking originates in the academy, the language of the left frequently doesn't lend itself to mass appeal.

As an example, below is the abstract of an academic cultural theory paper by a leftist professor. It deals with a very serious issue, namely the death of Trayvon Martin, the unarmed black 17-year-old who was killed in 2012 by a neighborhood watchman. The author is trying to help us understand the nature of racism:

> In this paper, I read Trayvon Martin's murder at the hands of George Zimmerman and the ensuing debates surrounding Stand Your Ground law through Frantz Fanon's critical reformulation of Hegel's master-slave dialectic. For Fanon, the unacknowledged reciprocity of Hegel's dialectic obscures the sub-ontological realm—to

which Fanon and Martin alike were condemned—and Fanon's concept of comparaison [sic] sheds further light on Zimmerman's motivations as a liminally racialized subject. I argue that it is precisely by questioning the circularity of Hegel's formulation—in which to stand one's ground is to claim what one already has access to—and by diagnosing what lies beneath that ground that we can avoid mistaking the legal symptom for the underlying ailment and craft strategies for resisting white supremacy in the present.[735]

Could you make sense of it? I certainly couldn't, and I've spent over 20 years in school and specialize in social and political theory. And yet somehow numerous people on the left spend their time writing like this, even as they try to discuss serious issues that require urgent political attention. This kind of thinking doesn't clarify, it obscures. And yet moral clarity is the thing we need most of all in a world whose atrocities are constantly concealed beneath euphemism.

"Alright," you might well say, "but that's *academic* writing. They're trying to write for other academics, not a general audience." But should *anyone* be spending their time writing like this? Should even the tiniest fraction of the finite resource of human labor-hours be expended upon producing paragraphs like the one above? *If* one cares about the issue of young black men being killed, is there any sense in which writing like this advances us on the issue, or gets us an inch closer to having less of these killings happen? Do academics get an all-purpose exemption from having to be useful, relevant, and intelligible? Shouldn't it be *their job* to help us understand what's going on?

But it's also a problem that plagues left language more broadly. For example, instead of talking about suffering, cruelty, and deprivation, the left now frequently talks about "marginalization" and "exclusion." These terms don't really make the stakes clear; they *sound* like bad things because of their connotations, but aren't especially vivid. So instead of saying we need to bring prosperity, health, and happiness to poor people, we say we intend to "center the needs of the marginalized." But it's not obvious what you have to *do* in order to "center" something; we need terms that make clear to everybody what the problem is and what it would look like if the problem were solved. We should be careful about using language that is unclear or vague, because this makes our goals fuzzy.

It's important to believe in things that are real. Left-wing principles are often stated in abstractions. For example, "fighting oppression" or "creating equality." But the precise definitions of oppression and equality are difficult to specify. What would a world without "oppression" look like? What does true equality mean? These are difficult questions, ones whose answers are not obvious. But the words "oppression" and "inequality" are used so frequently on the left that they are assumed to be meaningful, without a careful inquiry into what the actual reality of these terms is.

This is *not* to say that our underlying concerns or values should shift. It's *not* to say we should be any less concerned with the *people* who are marginalized. It's to say that we should have clearer and less abstract ways of thinking. Sometimes, left-language gets so wrapped up in talk of "oppression," "domination," "symbolic violence," "privilege," etc., that it loses track of the underlying events that these terms have been created in order to describe. The more one uses *shorthand* terms (like "systemic injustice") rather than descriptors of the actual problems in people's lives that this shorthand term refers to (like "women being fired for becoming pregnant," or "factories closing and leaving hundreds of dads unable to pay for their children to visit the doctor," or "black men on the way home from their jobs being thrown against police cars and frisked," or "transgender people being bullied and beaten up and then crying all night believing they are totally hated and alone in the world"), the less we help people who are *not* leftists understand *what* we are actually concerned with. The majority of people are fairly apolitical; they do not even vote, let alone make politics part of their daily lives. This is perfectly understandable, because thinking politically often involves taking on profound feelings of hopelessness and despair, due to a recognition of the enormity of the world's problems and the difficulty there will be in solving them all. But in order to get people to feel a sense of urgency around matters like "systemic injustice" or "institutional racism" it is necessary to constantly be reducing these terms to the life-events that they are trying to capture.

Some forms of analysis are not especially helpful, or lead to dead ends when they are used to orient all political discussion. The concept of "privilege," for example, arose as a highly valuable way of describing the set of inherent advantages that some people have because of their demographic characteristics. For example, because I am a man, I might be described as "eccentric" or "brilliant" for exhibiting behaviors that would cause a woman to be labeled "crazy" or "unhinged" or "uncooperative." (And we know very well that women are frequently called "bitches" for acting tough in ways that men would be praised for.) It's helpful to think about this aspect of the world, because it makes you realize the various small ways in which social approval and economic benefits are being distributed unfairly to people based on characteristics over which they have no control.

But the "privilege" idea, if it becomes *too* dominant in one's political thinking, also doesn't lend itself to actually fixing very much of anything. The progressive activist website *EverydayFeminism.com* has an entire section devoted to documenting and discussing various kinds of privilege.[736] Mixed-race people can have "light-skinned privilege." Non-disabled people have "ability privilege," men have "male privilege." There is "thin privilege," "Western privilege," and "straight privilege." All of this just means that members of these groups have advantages over people who are not in these groups. That should certainly be remembered. Yet once rooting out privilege becomes an end in itself, one's political action frequently comes down to individuals "checking" privilege, without a particularly robust theory for how this will lead to real material improvements in human lives. People spend their (finite) political energy pointing out various instances of privilege and calling for it to be checked. Meanwhile the checking of privilege does not get society a single inch closer to the eradication of war, the elimination of poverty, or the provision of universal access to healthcare.[737]

At its worst, the politics of privilege-checking can actually *discourage* calls to real political action, as in the following explanation of why calls to protest are necessarily shot through with "class privilege":

> *Not everyone has the mobility – which is influenced by class – to spend their days in protest. So when activists call for people to go out and show up for prolonged protests or demonstrations, there is absolutely a classist (and ableist) element to it.*[738]

As a factual matter, this is of course true. The more well-off you are, the more free time you have for politics, and the less time you must spend trying to eke out a living. But what are we to conclude from this? If every call to arms is *ableist* (some people, after all, may not have arms), then are we trapped in permanent impotence? *Because* we exist in a world full of differential privileges and staggering inequities, anything one does will always have new "problematic" aspects to be uncovered and called out. But battles should tend to be picked in accordance with the consequences they have for human lives, after a careful evaluation of the stakes. If our organizing group becomes mired in divisive internal arguments over whether its call to "end the insanity and brutality of the Saudi bombing of Yemen" is problematic (because the word "insane" stigmatizes those with mental illness), then we are likely not going to win. If we're tearing ourselves apart over whether white people using Asian spices is "cultural appropriation" (an argument I have actually heard) or whether polyamorous people calling themselves "poly" is offensive to Polynesian people (an argument I have also heard), then we will lose badly.

Again, this is entirely separate from typical debates over whether progressives should focus on "race/gender/identity" issues or "economic" issues. It isn't to suggest that the white working class' concern over its retirement funds should come prior to transgender people's demand for acknowledgment and respect.[739] Rather, it's to suggest that as we integrate all of these concerns under a broad left-wing agenda, we should remain focused on our goal, which is to give as many people as possible decent and worthwhile lives. There's no need to jettison "identity politics," but there *is* a need to connect all political action toward the concrete rather than the abstract, academic, and theoretical. When people on the left focus on problems in conceptual terms (such as "delegitimization" or "erasure" or "appropriation") rather than material ones (such as death, impoverishment, imprisonment, terror, and abuse), they make it more difficult for people to understand the relevance of left ideas to the everyday, and to understand what we are actually talking about.

Thus there's no need to get lost in a debate over whether "class-based politics" or "identity-based politics" should define the left's agenda. Both can be accommodated, simply by prioritizing repairing the real harms and mistreatment people suffer in their daily lives. If we continue asking ourselves the questions "How much does this matter?" and "Given that every moment we spend on one thing is a moment we do not spend on another thing, do we have our priorities in order?", we will hopefully spend more time talking about the nuclear threat, climate change, our racially discriminatory immigration policies, the bullying and violence suffered by young transgender people, Native American poverty, domestic violence, healthcare access, the incarceration of millions of people, and violence in Chicago. And we'll spend less time talking about Trump's feud with Arnold Schwarzenegger over *Apprentice* ratings,[740] Mike Pence and the *Hamilton* musical,[741] whether transgender men *taking photos of themselves* in women's bathrooms "problematically erases nonbinary trans people,"[742] how eating certain foods from around the world may be a form of "cultural theft,"[743] or the difference between Karl Marx's early work and his mature thought.[744] This is not to say none of this can be interesting, or even relatively important, but that if one is spending more time writing about the symbolic politics of Beyoncé's music videos than about the threat of global nuclear destruction, a reassessment may be in order. When left politics devotes itself too much to high-level social theory, or the analysis of representation in pop culture products, it removes itself from the real world, and the serious issues affecting millions that urgently need dealing with.

This does not mean that there are no interesting debates to be had over cultural issues, or that films and television do not significantly affect the way we understand the world. If one goes too far in the direction of the material, to the neglect of the symbolic, we miss something important. It's not that people should never speak about the fact that, say, movies rarely have Asian lead actors (even when the film takes place in Ancient China![745]), or cultural depictions of Native Americans tend to reduce them to crass stereotypes. It's just that if we focus *largely* on the cultural, and don't care as much about, say, the steady self-immolation of the human species, we will be squandering important resources of time and political energy. Cultural appropriation debates may begin to seem somewhat beside the point if Donald Trump blows up the world.

◆   ◆   ◆   ◆

OUR FUNDAMENTAL PRINCIPLE, THEN, IS THAT WE WANT EVERYONE TO have the meaningful and fulfilling lives that they want, and to take away the various external obstacles that prevent people from having such lives. This principle can be consistently applied across scenarios. Why do we want nuclear arms control? Because if someone's city gets blown up and their children die, their life is less fulfilling. Why do we want to reform the criminal justice system? Because it destroys lives, too. Why do we want maternity leave and adequate child care? Because motherhood should be a rewarding and fulfilling and joyful experience, not a struggle for subsistence. Simple universal principles can therefore create a compelling moral framework for left-wing political positions. They do not involve fancy "dialectics" or social theory. All we need to do is reflect on what it means to have a good life, and those economic and social factors that stand in the way of people having good lives.[746]

Of course, there are plenty of disagreements over what constitutes the social good. It's worth having serious debates over the nature of our values, of interrogating them ruthlessly and seeing whether they are consistent and make sense. But the progressive left can nevertheless hopefully reach some consensus sets of goals, e.g. preventing the environment from falling apart, preventing nuclear war from obliterating humankind, trying to dismantle the prison system without causing new unintended harms, making it so that people don't have to toil and suffer, making people healthy, happy, sociable, and free, and keeping people from being discriminated against, mistreated, bullied, harassed, raped, and murdered.[747]

◆   ◆   ◆   ◆

THE LEFT HAS NOT DONE A VERY GOOD JOB OF COMMUNICATING ITS ideas to people. Perhaps that's because, at heart, we don't know our own ideas very well. In the 19th century, utopian socialists like William Morris and Edward Bellamy wrote elaborate fictional visions of what ideal future societies would look like.[748] Today, we know the future society we are fighting for largely in terms of what it is *not* (it is not sexist, it does not have white privilege in it) rather than what it *is*.

Perhaps it's a good idea, then, to think more about what our ideal world looks like. What is the best schooling like? What should jobs be like? (Should there be jobs at all?) What should cities look like? Should race and gender exist as meaningful categories? Should national boundaries exist? How should cultural divisions be dealt with? Should there be prisons? Tax collectors? Should we colonize space?

Utopian thinking is often seen as the height of uselessness, because it necessarily speculates on worlds that don't exist rather than dealing pragmatically with the world that *does* exist. But this misses a crucial purpose of these dreams: they help us understand what the end goal is, what the underlying vision is toward which we want to keep moving. By envisioning the promised land, you can chart a path toward it. You may not get there. But you will at least be heading in the right direction. (This is one reason why Martin Luther King's dream was such an effective image; it offered a vision of a seemingly impossible world and gave people something to look forward to and begin to build together.)

It's important, then, to have a clear idea of the world you wish to see. Otherwise, it will be difficult to explain clearly to people what you're fighting for. You might be able to tell them what you're fighting *against*. But proving that you're on the right side involves more than proving that the other side is bad: you have to prove that your own side is *better*. This is the fundamental problem Democrats have been making in their political pitches: they run on the grounds that they are *not Republicans*. Hillary Clinton tells you she is *not Donald Trump*. And this is an extremely compelling argument. For, as we have seen, Donald Trump is a monstrosity. But you still need an answer to the obvious follow-up question "Well, if you're not Donald Trump, then *what are you?*"

Progressives therefore need a meaningful vision. Why should people want a left-wing world? What does the left actually stand for? And what would it actually look like to have a world in which the things the left wants are implemented? If nobody gives people a clear answer to these questions, then we cannot expect people to sign on to our program. The first thing to figure out is what we are fighting for in the first place. Becoming successful requires becoming self-critical, understanding why people are not leftists rather than simply lambasting them for being so.

The good news for progressives is that Trump can be defeated. The bad news is that it requires them to do things they have never done before, like think about how to be politically successful. Fundamentally, it requires *having a clear set of objectives* and *deciding one's actions on the basis of whether they actually get us toward those objectives.* This means that progressives need a serious agenda, and need to have a strategy for actually getting it put in place.

DEVELOPING EFFECTIVE POLITICS

ONCE WE KNOW THE SORT OF THING WE STAND FOR, WE CAN START thinking about how to stand for it. We can go from believing that the world ought to be a more just and humane place to actually having a few ideas for how to make it so.

Fortunately, it is easy to find political ideas that flow from progressive principles. Compassion means making sure that people have adequate healthcare regardless of their means. Hence the need for a comprehensive national health insurance program. Having a decent life means not working long hours for crappy wages, hence the need for workplace democracy (i.e. having more of a say at your job). It means not having to work when you are elderly, hence the need for protecting and expanding Social Security and Medicare provisions. It means not having to be afraid that any time you meet a police officer, they might shoot you in the head, hence the need for serious reform of the way policing occurs, especially in black communities. It means not being harassed, mistreated, or discriminated against because of your race or gender identity. And it means being assured that the world won't be boiled to a crisp by the time your children reach adulthood, hence the need to coordinate serious global action to reduce emissions and stall the effects of climate change.

It's a relatively simple matter for the left to offer an appealing agenda. A good social-democratic program can win people over: single-payer healthcare, better labor protections, fixing criminal justice, and ensuring access to good schools when you're young, and a secure retirement when you're old. Such a program should emphasis the *universal*, "we're all in this together" aspect of left politics. Because these policies disproportionately benefit people who have the least, they are able to resolve the problem of balancing broad appeals with special attention to particular excluded groups.

In beginning to think about how to remake ourselves and become politically successful, people on the left should have a few broad goals on our mind:

- **Reformulate A Serious Progressive Platform** – No more Clintonism, no more technocratic politics. Politics should be based on a set of values that are clear and defensible. Those values should be articulable to everyone. We should not just focus on what policies we want, but explain why we care about them.

- **Offering Compelling Narratives** – Have clear goals, but don't get *too* wrapped up in policy details. It's important not to dwell in total fantasy, but it's also true that if you become too "wonkish," people aren't going to know what the hell you're talking about. To win political campaigns, you need to lay out broad principles and plans.

- **Moving Beyond Presidencies, Recapturing State And Local Power** – While the Democratic Party is relatively competitive at the presidential level, it has been roundly thrashed at every other level of government. It's important to remember that the U.S. presidency, while extremely important, is only a small part of the existing world. The president is often described as the most powerful person on Earth. This is true. But even the most powerful person on Earth isn't all-powerful, and you've got to be broadly competitive in order to get anything done. Your party can't consist of one person at the top, and a bunch of other people whose only job is to get that person elected. We have to have a serious presence at all levels of government.

- **Build Independent Media Outlets** – The existing large institutions are not enough. Fundamentally, they can't be fixed, because they have a direct financial incentive to continue promoting the spectacle that comes from Donald Trump. It's necessary to dismantle the dominance of corporate outlets obsessed with the horse race. While some media outlets still produce excellent work, we also need new voices. These should combine left-wing moral values with a commitment to empirical rigor, integrity, empathy, and joy. They should bring attention to serious issues that matter to people. We must figure out why previous efforts at producing left-wing media (Air America, Current TV) have been such failures. (I suspect it is less to do with the fact that there is no audience for those ideas than with the fact that they were boring.)

- **Trying New Things** – There needs to be a willingness for the left to do things it has never done before. For example, on the issue of climate change, it is very clear that the message of climate scientists is not being absorbed by the public with a sufficient sense of urgency. Thus climate scientists and experts should be going around to schools, churches, public libraries, inviting skepticism and taking *any and all* questions from the public. We shouldn't simply disdain those who refuse to accept the consensus; after all, it's perfectly rational to be a skeptic. Instead, we must think strategically about new ways to get people to understand the stakes, and try our best to understand why the message is failing.

- **Rebuilding The Labor Movement** – There is no future for progressivism without a functional labor movement, and the fact that Democrats have forgotten this is one of the reasons they are mystified at seeing their power erode. Unions are important, both in helping people negotiate better working conditions for themselves (in a world of unequal power between workers and bosses, it is impossible for workers to improve their fortunes unless they band together), and in getting people politically active.

- **Fixing Prejudice** – One question rarely asked by those who lament the racism they see in Trump voters is: "How do you actually make people less racist?" It's not enough to deplore racism. We actually have to end it. That means thinking about the processes in people's lives that cause them to develop bigotries, and intervening at those points.

- **Not Having Billionaires Be In Charge Of The World** – Upon being elected, Donald Trump immediately stuffed his cabinet with billionaires. As if to slap workers in the face as hard as possible, Trump chose as his Secretary of Labor the CEO of the Carl's Jr. hamburger chain, who has prominently opposed raises in the minimum wage for restaurant workers. But here's the irony: when Hillary Clinton's own cabinet choices leaked in January, it turned out that her own choice for Labor Secretary was…Howard Schultz, CEO of Starbucks.[749] One could not imagine a more perfect symbol of the current state of the Democratic Party. Republicans will give you the billionaire CEO of a hamburger chain, Democrats will give you the billionaire CEO of a coffee chain. Under Clintonism, the difference between left and right is the difference between Carls, Jr. and Starbucks. But a sincere left politics aims for a world in which billionaires *aren't* in charge of everything, rather than a world in which the "good" billionaires are in charge.[750]

- **Radical Democracy** – Democracy means that people should have a say in those things that affect their own lives. That means that they should have more control over their schools, workplaces, and legislatures. Instead of simply aiming for the policy that maximizes people's aggregate wellbeing according to the judgments of a set of experts, we should be aiming for inclusive institutions. The Democratic Party itself should be a membership organization where membership means something. It's bizarre that people don't know anything about how their state party officials are elected, or have any real say in this. Fundamentally, power within parties needs to come from the bottom (the members) rather than the top (the wealthiest donors).

- **Don't Move To The Right, Move To The Good** – When Democrats lose, they sometimes have a tendency to believe they should act more like Republicans in order to win. This is true in one sense, in that Republicans know how to accomplish their political agenda while Democrats do not. But it shouldn't be taken to mean that Democrats should adopt more right-wing political positions in order to attract a broader base of support. If you try to be both progressive and conservative, you'll end up being nothing at all. People are far more likely to respect sincere progressives who are truthful about their values than politicians who take the public's temperature via focus groups and adopt their political positions accordingly. Liberalism does not need to be more watery and compromising, it needs to be more principled and genuine. People dislike liberals not because their ideas are too radical, but because they are frequently hypocritical (say, by flying around in private jets while preaching about inequality) and because they are perceived to be elitist (say, by insisting that people who disagree with them are dumb and uneducated). We don't need to get rid of our commitments, we need to be persuasive in presenting them.

There is hope for progressive politics. One need only look to the activities of the Moral Mondays movement in North Carolina, which has built a diverse multi-racial coalition to fight against both racial and economic injustices, and has achieved impressive political successes in a state that did not seem naturally ripe for left-wing organizing. That movement "has brought tens of thousands of people into the streets and offered them a way to express their values so that elected officials are forced to take notice."[751] Or look at the Bernie Sanders campaign. Millennials, who were thought to be lazy, apolitical basement-dwellers, came out in droves to support a candidate who inspired them, offering a hopeful and constructive promise of major political change and an authentic (as opposed to merely rhetorical) rejection of "politics as usual." Sanders raised a fortune in small donations and managed to make a highly credible bid for the nomination, coming from total obscurity. When you're serious about fighting for your values, you can be very successful.

◆   ◆   ◆   ◆

BUT WHAT CAN PEOPLE DO PERSONALLY IN ORDER TO HELP REBUILD the fortunes of progressive politics? How do we act in our lives to bring about change? This kind of question requires a far more serious examination than is possible here. But below are a few suggestions for progressives, on how to think about being a politically active human being.

- **Care About Politics** – It is no longer acceptable not to think about politics, and not to act. Obviously different people have different capacities for political action. But what we must recognize is that, whether we participate or not, politics will go on around us. If we sit still, the country could elect Donald Trump. Both the Democratic primary and the general election had moments where small things made a big difference (a few more organizers in Iowa might have given Bernie Sanders a victory and a significant boost, and Hillary came extremely close to beating Trump). Everyone matters, and inaction is itself a form of action. If we care about issues, we have to ask ourselves what we are doing about them.

- **Talk To People Who Disagree With You** – It's a dead-end to talk only to people who already share your politics. People are lured to ideas because they hear those ideas coming from people they like and trust. Even if you think they're racist and sexist, try to figure out why they think that way.[752]

- **Take The Lead** – Don't wait for politics to come to you. It's not going to show up at your doorstep. Nobody is going to call. The "what can I do?" question often paralyzes people, who want to be shown where to sign up for a social movement. But things get started only through initiative. People have differing desires and abilities when it comes to taking charge, but we should consistently try to be more active and less passive in our politics.

- **Commitment To Truth And Integrity** – Integrity means freely acknowledging when someone on our own side does something wrong. If we have actual principles, we must apply them consistently. If we would condemn an act when Republicans did it, we cannot take great pains to defend it when our side does it. It's necessary not to be "partisan," not in the sense that we must be wishy-washy centrists, but in the sense that we must not allow our moral commitments to warp our factual assessments. Abuses of power by left-wing regimes are just as objectionable as abuses of power by right-wing regimes. And our own side is never going to be perfect.[753]

- **Be Clear, Meaningful, and Simple** – Communication must be effective if it is to be of any use at all. That means you need to always be clear and persuasive, and use messages that are understandable. Pithiness is valuable: Preserving the social safety net. Getting tough on the 1%. Saving the middle class.

- **Use Your Resources** – If you are wealthy, and a liberal, then you are probably not living up to your values as much as you could. After all, money is power, and the possession of money is the possession of the power to help people. Every dollar we keep is a dollar we don't spend, and every dollar we don't spend has costs in human wellbeing. So many people in this world struggle to simply feed themselves and find shelter. They struggle to pay for medical treatment. If we have money to spare, we are choosing not to help these people. Nor are resources limited to money: the time we *could* spend on helping make a better world is time we *should* be spending on it. None of us can be perfect, but all of us can be better.

- **Think Strategically** – What matters is what actually happens. Much political talk is cathartic without necessarily being strategic. If you join a group, make sure the group is actually accomplishing things, not just having a lot of meetings in which it talks about accomplishing things (this is most groups). Link political action to goals, not the mere expression of moral rightness. Certain things seem like resistance to Donald Trump, but aren't (for example, Keith Olbermann's online television show, *The Resistance*, which is, like most things Keith Olbermann does, more about letting Keith Olbermann make a lot of pompous noise than about actually moving a progressive agenda forward). "What will this actually accomplish? and

"Where is this leading?" are questions that should be asked at frequent intervals.

- **Try To Find Resolutions To Seeming Ideological Conflicts** – Many ideological differences are not mere "misunderstandings" and it will be impossible to find common ground.[754] Sometimes values are simply in conflict. But where resolutions are possible, we should try to find them before dismissing a clash as intractable. (For example, it is almost certainly possible for progressives to combine their opposition to race-based injustices with an opposition to economic injustices that go beyond race, and to address the concerns of *both* the black working class and the white working class.)

- **Don't Be Elitist** – This doesn't mean affirming the false idea that blue-collar white pickup-truck America is somehow the "real America." Nor does it mean a disdain for knowledge and learning. What it means is *not* assuming that you necessarily know what's good for everyone else. And it means that policy should be made accessible. A 900-page healthcare law is no good. (Even a comic book that tried to explain the Affordable Care Act to laymen ended up running well over 100 pages.[755]) People should be included in decision-making, which means abandoning the "trust us" model of governance.

- **Distinguish Between Empathy And Sympathy** – The question of whether progressives should "empathize with Trump voters" is easily resolved. Of *course* they should empathize with them. Empathy is just putting yourself in someone else's shoes in order to understand them better. We should be humanists who empathize with *all* people. That doesn't mean one needs to be *sympathetic* to someone's views. I can try to understand what made someone a racist without compromising my complete lack of sympathy for racism. Interestingly, progressives know how to do this. We are constantly insisting on this distinction when it comes to, say, terrorists and criminal defendants. You don't have to believe it's acceptable to join ISIS in order to try to understand why disaffected young Muslim men may do it. You don't have to think murder is justifiable to understand a murderer's background. It is absurd and hypocritical not to offer the same level of understanding to someone who voted for Donald Trump that we would extent to someone who committed a heinous crime. And it's perfectly possible to argue simultaneously that immigrants and people of color are the ones most in need of greater empathy in America, without suggesting that Trump voters are unique among all human beings in not deserving an ounce of human understanding or compassion. The key here is to be willing to listen to people and care about them, *without* ever sacrificing your fundamental values or condoning the indefensible.

- **Question Yourself Without Getting Wrapped Up In Guilt** – It's important to listen to other people's critiques and to stay humble. People who have different experiences from ourselves are likely to know things that we ourselves do not know, or have not noticed. At the same time, it's unhealthy to get totally consumed by worrying about what other people think. If you get too caught up in critical self-examination over your own role (am I contributing to X social problem by existing?) you'll end up paralyzed by inaction, which helps nobody.

- **Don't Spend Too Much Time Disparaging People Who Are On Our Side.** – We're all flawed. We need to be generous to one another. If you find yourself in a screaming match with someone who roughly shares your political orientation, something has gone terribly wrong. Vigorous criticism of our own side is important. But the more we fight within ourselves, the less we fight for the realization of values in the world.

- **Be Kind. Always Kind.** – Too many leftists are mean. We have to be a source of comfort, love, and compassion in these times. We are fighting for a nice world, one full of love. Be the change you wish to see in the world, and if the change you wish to see in the world is that the world is less mean, then we can start by being less mean ourselves. Hugs aren't, in and of themselves, a politics. But they are nice. So there's nothing wrong with giving more of them. The systemic injustices of the world make a lot of people lonely and afraid. And small acts of kindness will not eliminate the systemic injustices, but they may make living with them somewhat more bearable for a day.

- **Remember that the real world exists, and it's where politics happen** – So much political conversation occurs online nowadays that it's easy to forget that hardly anything that happens online actually affects the arrangements of political power in the external world. It's also easy to lapse into the delusion that by keeping up with the news and discussing politics a lot, you're an informed citizen doing politics. But of course, you're actually entirely passive, your effect no greater than those who *don't* read the news. Looking back on my own activity during the election cycle, I'm appalled by the amount of time I spent on social media. I'd like to think it wasn't much. But it was a lot. I, like many others, confused talking about politics with doing politics. Politics happens in the street, the voting booth, the town meeting, the legislature, and the workplace. We need to remember that when we're not in those places, we might be passionately expending energy thinking about and discussing an issue without affecting it in any serious way.

The key lesson from the election of Donald Trump for progressives is that we simply have to persuade people to join our cause and fight for it, or we will lose. It's not enough to know that you're right, or smarter than the other guy. It's not enough to know that you're very well-credentialed, or to be on the "right side of history," or to regularly check your privilege, or to read the newspaper and feel informed. One must translate these things into success.

This is, uncomfortable as it may be, going to involve speaking to and attempting to persuade some Trump voters. If one's politics are not winning elections, then one has a couple of choices: join the other side, or persuade some people on their side (or some indifferent, apolitical people) to join you. (Actually, there's a third choice, the one opted for by Bill Clinton in the early 1990's: adopt half of the other side's platform, but tell the people on your own side that you still care about them. This actually works reasonably well politically until people figure out what you're doing. It just happens to be immoral.) Thus, if progressives are committed to progressive values, they are going to have to bring new supporters to their cause. Persuasion is far more difficult than talking to people who already agree with you.

For Democrats, this means that instead of telling people that everything is alright, they need to acknowledge that for many, many people things aren't alright at all. Then, instead of offering terrifying doomsaying like Trump, they need to inspire people to believe things can get better. They need to run a campaign of hope rather than a campaign of complacency. If they want to successfully win Trump's voters over, they will need to stop treating such people as nothing more than delusional racists.

Many recoil at the idea of having to reach out and persuade Trump supporters. This is partially because they believe Trump supporters are incapable of being reasoned with, and partially because having productive political discussions is extremely difficult to begin with. There's also a popular line on the left, that the oppressed shouldn't have to be the ones to educate their oppressors. Unfortunately, in a world where political power has to be built rather than wished into existence, there is no alternative to having discussions designed to help people see your side.

Not all Trump supporters are the same, however, and progressives don't need to persuade *everyone* to agree with them, they just need to persuade *enough* people. Distinctions need to be made between those who should be part of a broad coalition and those who are totally hopeless. In fact, it was a failure to make these kinds of distinctions that caused Bill Clinton's 1992 and 1996 campaigns to be so poisonous to progressive politics. Clinton actively courted white racists, trying to forge a coalition between "Reagan Democrats" and the Democrats' traditional racially diverse base. In doing so, he ended up adopting a terribly regressive set of racial politics that ultimately harmed black lives.[756]

It's pretty easy, though, if you have a good sense of the values you care about and the values you won't compromise, to figure out who can be courted to the progressive cause. One online commentator offered the stories of two fictionalized Trump supporters, Michelle and Jon, to illustrate the difference:

Michelle and Jon both like Trump.

Michelle lives in a rural, working class, historically non-diverse town that has faced significant unemployment thanks to neoliberal financial policies and has been devastated by the opioid epidemic. She feels like politicians have forgotten about her.

Jon grew up with money and reads Breitbart. He thinks that first-trimester abortions are people, and that queer people are science experiments who should be electrocuted until they're straight and 'normal.'

Michelle, let's talk. Jon, go fuck yourself. [757]

This seems like the right approach. We empathize with people who are suffering or confused. We should be patient and listen, knowing that we ourselves likely have things to learn. Yet we are nevertheless willing to tell hatred and bigotry to go fuck themselves.

"Don't mourn, organize!" [758]
—Joe Hill

CONCLUSION

<small>OVER THE FOREGOING PAGES, I HAVE ATTEMPTED TO PROVE THAT</small> the following statements are true:

1. Donald Trump displays many of the worst tendencies that humankind possesses. We must not only rid ourselves of him, but of everything he represents.
2. Donald Trump is consistently underestimated. Much of what he does is calculated for effect, and we should be careful not to treat him as dumb.
3. If they are to defeat Donald Trump, progressives will need to reevaluate their approach to both Trump himself and politics generally.
4. Most importantly, we must focus on developing real solutions for people's problems, and communicating our ideas clearly.

Each of these is fairly easily demonstrated. First, Donald Trump's negative qualities are openly on display. He is greedy, vain, cruel, and vengeful. If there's a deadly sin, he probably regularly indulges in it. He has mistreated his contractors and workers, stealing their money and forcing them to suffer the consequences of his own bad business decisions. He has sexually assaulted scores of women, spied on naked underage girls, and may have committed outright rape. He lies, cheats, and steals, and uses his lawyers to threaten people who try to expose him. He is stingy, using his charity to buy portraits of himself instead of to help people. And he is prejudiced, making stereotyped and dehumanizing remarks about black people, Muslims, and Mexicans, and leading an effort to make the country's first black president seem like a foreign-born impostor put in place by affirmative action. But worst of all, Donald Trump is a ruthless predatory capitalist, using other people purely as means for his own self-enrichment and self-aggrandizing, selling them snake oil and preying on their desperation and aspirations. His very existence, and the example he provides, makes us all more stupid and selfish. He doesn't read, doesn't think, doesn't laugh, and doesn't display an ounce of charity, kindness, or humility. He has managed to acquire every single unpleasant human trait, and he displays them proudly and openly. Trump should probably be in prison: if not for the sexual assault and rape, then for the multiple instances of fraud and theft.

For everything Trump is, however, he isn't stupid. He's a vicious and ambitious predator. Lawyers who have had to negotiate with him have been impressed by his negotiation skills, including his ability to grasp and exploit his opponent's weaknesses. Nobody has had more success than Trump in crafting a personal brand, in turning modest financial success into an unprecedented amount of celebrity and power. He is both formidable and terrifying.

Thus *never underestimate Trump.* Do not treat him like he is stupid. He is not stupid. He may never have read a book, but he's no dummy. And if you are pleased with yourself for having "taken him down," think *very* carefully about whether you're the one being played. Donald Trump leaves behind a 40-year trail of the humiliated remains of those who have thought they could best him. He has just destroyed the entire establishments of the United States' two major political parties. One would be very, very unwise to assume that this was the act of a mere clown.

But one should also resist attempts to define Donald Trump himself as a uniquely monstrous human problem. Trump happens to have *every* bad human trait, but he is also a symptom rather than the disease itself. Trump exists because we live in a world that rewards bad behavior, that offers impunity and success to people who behave like he does. If we didn't have a media that focused on spectacle rather than substance, we wouldn't have Trump. If money didn't confer the power to evade laws that ordinary people must follow, we wouldn't have Trump. If women's complaints of sexual assault were taken seriously, we wouldn't have Trump. If people didn't respect and admire those who were the most vicious, selfish, and uncharitable, we wouldn't have Trump. If the Democratic Party had a set of genuine and consistent principles, and ran candidates who didn't share half of Trump's vices, then we wouldn't have Trump. If reality television didn't exist, then we wouldn't have Trump.

In other words, Trump is only possible because we live in a world that makes and encourages Trumps. A just world, in which people who exploit, betray, and bully others are treated as socially toxic rather than handed powerful offices, is a Trumpless world. Yet a Trumpless world is not necessarily a just world. There are millions of micro-Trumps, little assholes who do whatever they please and get away with it. They must all be stopped.

This is one reason why a certain response to the "pussy tape"—that this was *not* true "locker room talk"—was ill-conceived. When Trump defended his admission of grabbing women "by the pussy" as mere laddish banter, plenty of men came out and contradicted him. They said this was *not* in fact, how men talked in locker rooms. True men were gentlemen. True men *did not* grab women by their you-know-whats. Whatever Trump was doing, he was speaking only for himself.[759]

This response was misguided, because it treated Trump as anomalous in his awfulness. In fact, the kind of behavior Trump engaged in *is* common. Trump said that because he was famous and powerful, he could do what he pleased to women and they would let him. And this *is* the sort of thing famous and powerful men do, and get away with all the time. One should not treat Trump as suffering from a *uniquely* extreme pathology; he demonstrates traits that are characteristic of many men. Trump's greed, sexual predation, and lack of empathy are shared widely among powerful males. Frequently, the difference between Trump and other 1-percenters is that Trump is far more honest about his motives. He doesn't attempt to disguise his acts beneath euphemism and decorous language. He'll tell you precisely what he does and how he does it. He'll tell you that he is out for vengeance, or that he puts his tongue down women's throats whenever he feels like it. This is, at least, blunt.

This is an extremely important point, and so it should be emphasized as much as possible: it is a mistake to see Trump as some serious departure from the ordinary. Trump may be more unhinged and dangerous than other people. But his politics are not atypical for a 21st century Republican. All the talk about building walls, the blasé attitude toward nuclear annihilation, the installation of crony billionaires in powerful positions? This is the stuff of everyday Republican politics in the Tea Party era. Same with the attitude toward workers, women, and minorities. This is what CEOs are like. They don't care about other people. That's *capitalism*, not Trump.

It would therefore be unwise to single out Trump as the sole enemy, and think that if he is driven from power, progressives have succeeded. Not so. Progressives will have succeeded when they create a humane and compassionate world, and not before. If Trump disappeared, but ended up replaced by some Republican equally indifferent to human suffering (such as Mike Pence, or Heaven forbid, Ted Cruz), humanity would be no better off.

The fight to rid ourselves of Trump is not just a fight to get rid of a single bulbous, bloviating man. It is a fight to get rid of *Trumpism*, a tendency covering all of our basest and, yes, most deplorable tendencies. Trump is a funhouse mirror caricature showing us what we will be if we give up on caring about one another.

◆   ◆   ◆   ◆

FORTUNATELY, THERE'S GOOD REASON TO BELIEVE THAT IT IS, IN FACT, possible to recover the left's fortunes and build the sort of compassionate and healthy world it aspires toward. Trump himself is more vulnerable than he looks, highly unpopular and has clear weaknesses when it comes to actually accomplishing things that will endear the public to him.[760] It might be comforting to think of Trump as a kind of tornado, a brutally destructive natural phenomenon impossible to tame. This conception absolves us of any responsibility in allowing him to come to power (a tornado is nobody's fault!). But it is also false. Trump nearly lost the election, and if the Democrats hadn't made a series of dreadful strategic mistakes, he would have been resoundingly defeated.

The first of these mistakes was to run a candidate hardly anybody liked. The second was to run on ideas nobody could understand.

That's an exaggeration, of course. Plenty of people like Hillary Clinton and whatever it is the Democratic Party stands for. But it's important to consider the downside of running someone with very high unfavorable ratings. It's also true that Democrats made a point of trying to defend Barack Obama's major policies rather than by explaining how they planned to improve these policies and eliminate their problems. Rather than acknowledge the serious deficiencies in the Affordable Care Act (it's overly complicated, difficult to deal with, and premiums were rising), Democrats pretended that nothing was wrong. Rather than admit that there were legitimate reasons why people might feel as if the Obama presidency had not been good for them personally, they suggested that all negative feelings were the product of prejudice or delusion. Rather than admit that the consequences of globalization have not been evenly distributed, they made hats reading "America Is Already Great."

Running Hillary Clinton for president at a time of anti-Establishment anger was never a very good idea. But running Clinton against Donald Trump was an *especially* bad idea, because all of Clinton's weaknesses as a candidate played to all of Trump's strengths. Clinton gave Trump precisely the kind of fodder (mini-scandals, shady dealings, etc.) on which his bombast thrives. She also happens to be a very poor campaigner, and a complacent one. The weakness was obvious even in the differing campaign slogans. "I'm With Her" is about the interests of the candidate. "Make America Great Again" is about the voters. Let's learn an important lesson here: do not run a widely despised ruling-class candidate who has open contempt for the white working class. That is a recipe for electoral catastrophe.

Yet we can also see how easy this would be to fix. Imagine having a candidate people liked, and some policies people liked. Since Democrats were close to winning without either of these, imagine the victory they could secure if they *did* provide someone likable who actually had something to offer. One could do much better electorally by being just a *little bit* better politically.

There wasn't actually any kind of "working class revolt." There was no fundamental shift in the composition of the American body politic, and the country hasn't been consumed by a tide of Trumpism. This election was more about political disillusionment generally than Trump support specifically. As usual, most people simply didn't vote to begin with. Americans are mostly just *indifferent* to politics, or disgusted by it, rather than animated by some new form of hyper-nationalist sentiment.

In fact, it's staggering just how little effort Democrats seem to have put into building support. When Hillary Clinton entered the race (not after she lifted her policy platform from Bernie Sanders), did anybody know what she intended to accomplish as President, other than to be generally competent and experienced? Asked to name a single thing Hillary Clinton planned to do as president, most voters would have literally struggled to answer. That's madness. How is it possible that the Democratic Party could so fail to communicate with voters that nobody knew anything they even wanted to do in power? But it also means that with just a small amount of effort, self-reflection, and strategy, it would be perfectly possible to reverse the recent disaster and bring the left some political power.

One thing we know is that it won't be done if we cling to the aspects of Democratic politics that are widely disliked. If the Party continues to make people like Harry Reid and Nancy Pelosi (i.e. lifeless empty shells with no ideas and zero communicative skills) into national figureheads, progressive politics will wither and die. Conversely, if it continues to rely solely on finding charismatic but ineffectual leaders like Barack Obama, it may recapture the White House but will continue its descent into oblivion at the state and local level. We need likable candidates and a serious platform that makes sense to people, and can be communicated.

Progressives are going to have to fight for their values. They are going to have to fight hard. But they are also going to have to fight *differently*. The left is fundamentally doomed if it does not seriously rethink its practices. We've just lost every branch of government, and watched the presidency be given to a misogynistic sociopathic fraudster. Clearly we have gone wrong somewhere.

The most fundamental part of a new plan is this: *do not do the same damn thing all over again and expect different results.* We need a new *kind* of left politics. We need something that truly speaks to people. We have to get back to what, despite his many flaws and general vacuity, Barack Obama *did* have: inspiration, hope. It was joked that Hillary Clinton's campaign slogan was "No you can't." That's no good. It doesn't work.

Donald Trump inspires people. He may inspire people by appealing to their nastiest, most inhuman, and un-neighborly instincts. But he inspires the nonetheless. We have to have an agenda that gets people excited. It can't be like trying to make people eat their vegetables. "You'll vote for me and you'll like it, because you have no alternative" is not an effective way to get votes.

Progressives *need* to understand how people who are different from them think. No more writing them off as racist and deplorable. Even if they *are*, what good does that do? You need to understand racists *not* so you can sympathize with them, but so you can figure out what shapes people's beliefs, and help them reach different beliefs. People on the left must reach out to people on the right. They must make their case. They must go into red states. They must take counter-arguments seriously and respond to them. It is not sufficient to have John Oliver eviscerate Trump on television and call him Drumpf. It is not sufficient to have Lena Dunham dance around in a pantsuit.[761] It is not sufficient to line up a bunch of Hollywood celebrities to tell people how to vote. When someone asks "What kind of world does the left want to build?", we need to have a vision. When someone asks "Why should I vote for you?" the answer cannot be "Because I am not Trump." After all, people *like* Trump.

The Clinton campaign was a disaster. Let's never do anything like it again. Let's never again have a campaign in which people were constantly having to defend the indefensible. Let's never again run on "experience" rather than values. Let's never again treat everything as fine when it clearly isn't.

Let's also never again underestimate Donald Trump. The man is wily. He may have never read a book in his adult life. But he knows how to win an election. Calling him stupid, or treating him as stupid, misses the point. For a "stupid" man, he sure showed the elites.

◆   ◆   ◆   ◆

EVERY SINGLE PERSON WHO OPPOSED DONALD TRUMP AND DIDN'T want him to be President of the United States should have many, many regrets. I have plenty of them myself. I regret that I didn't do more for Sanders, and then that I didn't do more for Clinton after Sanders lost. I should have been knocking doors. Instead I watched movies and wrote magazine articles and went to class. I wrote an academic article.[762] An academic article! *What on earth was I thinking?* I regret that I allowed myself to be lulled into believing everything would be alright, even though I knew deep down that there was no rational reason for feeling assuaged, and that the "experts" who were telling me Clinton would win didn't know any more than I did.

The truth is, those of us on the left were complacent asses. All of us. I wrote in February that Trump would definitely defeat Clinton,[763] and I believed that. But then I didn't *act* as if I believed it. If I'd really *felt* like I believed it, I should have been spending my every waking hour working to prevent this hideous outcome. I didn't, though. And when all of us think of how uselessly we frittered away so much of our time, how much more we could have done, we may be kicking ourselves for years. Especially if the nuclear apocalypse shows up.

But now we must fix it. There is no time to sit around in bafflement, goggle-eyed and slack-jawed. People who were not previously particularly political need to understand that if they do not get involved, not just in *talking* about politics but in taking serious political action, the consequences could well be dire. Each of us has just been handed an extraordinary amount of personal moral responsibility.

We may have thought history had ended, that nothing too terribly unexpected would ever shake us up again. But history never ends. The future could hold anything. It may hold catastrophe. But there is no time to think about that. What is needed now is a plan. In the immortal words of Joe Hill:

Don't mourn, organize!

Appendix

CURRENT AFFAIRS
ELECTION COVERAGE

At the beginning of 2016, I began running a political magazine called Current Affairs. Some people might call this a perfect time to be entering the world of political media. It didn't feel that way to me. In fact, it was a horrendous time: Trump was dominating the news, and it was very difficult to get anybody to pay attention to anything that wasn't Trump-related, a problem that will now only become more intractable. But even worse, at that time there was still a bizarre refusal to take Trump as seriously as he needed to be taken. Even as he was being obsessed over, Trump was being dismissed. It was (and still is) a paradox: people can insist that Trump is a serious threat to the future of humanity, and then treat him as if he is an amusing buffoon and we can spend our time jeering at him. People affirm that he could cause major harm to the world, but then don't seem motivated to actually think strategically about how to stop him.

In the spring and summer, I wrote a series of articles for Current Affairs making roughly the same points I do in this book: that Donald Trump should be taken far more seriously, and that Democrats will need to adjust their own course of action in order to defeat him. I reprint these articles here, because I think they hold up as pieces of political analysis, and though the events they describe are now passed and cannot be undone, I think they helpfully complement the main text of this book.

I want to stress that these pieces are not offered in order to prove that I had some superior insight at the time. In fact, I was wrong about many things (I predicted Ted Cruz would run on a third-party ticket![1]). In fact, I totally reject the idea that the points I was making required any kind of unique prescience. They were obvious, but many Democrats were caught up believing in Hillary Clinton's inevitability, and could not see the facts that contradicted their worldview. I offer these pieces as evidence against the idea that it is mere "Monday morning quarterbacking" to point out that Hillary Clinton was a poor choice as a Democratic candidate.

Unless The Democrats Nominate Sanders, A Trump Nomination Means A Trump Presidency

FEB. 23, 2016

With Donald Trump looking increasingly likely to actually be the Republican nominee for President, it's long past time for the Democrats to start working on a pragmatic strategy to defeat him. Months of complacent, wishful insistences that Trump will disappear have proven false, and with a firm commanding lead in polls and several major primary victories, predictions are increasingly favoring Trump to win the nomination. If Democrats honestly believe, as they say they do, that Trump poses a serious threat to the wellbeing of the country and the lives of minority citizens, that means doing everything possible to keep him out of office. To do that will require them to very quickly unite around a single goal, albeit a counterintuitive one: they must make absolutely sure that Bernie Sanders is the Democratic nominee for President.

The electability question should be at the center of the Democratic primary. After all, elections are about winning, and high-minded liberal principles mean nothing if one has no chance of actually triumphing in a general election. Hillary Clinton has been right to emphasize that the pragmatic achievement of goals should be the central concern of a presidential candidate, and that Bernie Sanders' supporters often behave as if this is immaterial.

Instinctively, Hillary Clinton has long seemed by far the more electable of the two Democratic candidates. She is, after all, an experienced, pragmatic moderate, whereas Sanders is a raving, arm-flapping elderly Jewish socialist from Vermont. Clinton is simply closer to the American mainstream, thus she is more attractive to a broader swath of voters. Sanders campaigners have grown used to hearing the heavy-hearted lament "I like Bernie, I just don't think he can win." And in typical previous American elections, this would be perfectly accurate.

But this is far from a typical previous American election. And recently, everything about the electability calculus has changed, due to one simple fact: Donald Trump is likely to be the Republican nominee for President. Given this reality, every Democratic strategic question must operate not on the basis of abstract electability against a hypothetical candidate, but specific electability against the actual Republican nominee, Donald Trump.

Here, a Clinton match-up is highly likely to be an unmitigated electoral disaster, whereas a Sanders candidacy stands a far better chance. Every one of Clinton's (considerable) weaknesses plays to every one of Trump's strengths, whereas every one of Trump's (few) weaknesses plays to every one of Sanders's strengths. From a purely pragmatic standpoint, running Clinton against Trump is a disastrous, suicidal proposition.

Sanders supporters have lately been arguing that their candidate is more electable than people think, and they have some support from the available polling. In a number of hypotheticals, Sanders does better than Clinton at beating Trump,[2] and his "unfavorable" ratings among voters are a good deal lower than Clinton's.[3] In response to this, however, Clinton supporters insist that polling at this stage means very little, and since Bernie is not well known and there has not been a national attack campaign directed at him from the right yet, his supporters do not account for the drop in support that will occur when voters realize he is on the fringes. Imagine, they say, how viciously the right will attack Sanders's liberal record.

Clinton's people are right to point out that these polls mean very little; after all, Sanders's entire campaign success is a caution against placing too much weight on early polling. And they are especially right to emphasize that we should visualize how the campaign by conservatives will realistically play out, rather than attempting to divine the future from highly fallible polling numbers. But it's precisely when we try to envision how the real dynamics of the campaign will transpire that we see just how disastrous a Clinton-Trump fight will be for Clinton.

Her supporters insist that she has already been "tried and tested" against all the attacks that can be thrown at her. But this is not the case; she has never been subjected to the full brunt of attacks that come in a general presidential election. Bernie Sanders has ignored most tabloid dirt, treating it as a sensationalist distraction from real issues ("Enough with the damned emails!"). But for Donald Trump, sensationalist distractions are the whole game. He will attempt to crucify her. And it is very, very likely that he will succeed.

Trump's political dominance is highly dependent on his idiosyncratic, audacious method of campaigning. He deals almost entirely in amusing, outrageous, below-the-belt personal attacks, and is skilled at turning public discussions away from the issues and toward personalities (He/she's a "loser," "phony," "nervous," "hypocrite," "incompetent.") If Trump does have to speak about the issues, he makes himself sound foolish, because he doesn't know very much. Thus he requires the media not to ask him difficult questions,[4] and depends on his opponents' having personal weaknesses and scandals that he can merrily, mercilessly exploit.

This campaigning style makes Hillary Clinton Donald Trump's dream opponent. She gives him an endless amount to work with. The emails, Benghazi, Whitewater, Iraq, the Lewinsky scandal, Chinagate,[5] Travelgate,[6] the missing law firm records,[7] Jeffrey Epstein,[8] Kissinger,[9] Marc Rich,[10] Haiti,[11] Clinton Foundation tax errors,[12] Clinton Foundation conflicts of interest,[13] "We were broke when we left the White House,"[14] Goldman Sachs[15]... There is enough material in Hillary Clinton's background for Donald Trump to run with six times over.

The defense offered by Clinton supporters is that none of these issues actually amount to anything once you look at them carefully. But this is completely irrelevant; all that matters is the fodder they would provide for the Trump machine. Who is going to be looking carefully? In the time you spend trying to clear up the basic facts of Whitewater, Trump will have made five more allegations.

Even a skilled campaigner would have a very difficult time parrying such endless attacks by Trump. Even the best campaigner would find it impossible to draw attention back to actual substantive policy issues, and would spend their every moment on the defensive. But Hillary Clinton is neither the best campaigner nor even a skilled one. In fact, she is a dreadful campaigner. She may be a skilled policymaker, but on the campaign trail she makes constant missteps and never realizes things have gone wrong until it's too late.

Everyone knows this. Even among Democratic Party operatives, she's acknowledged as "awkward and uninspiring on the stump," carrying "Bill's baggage with none of Bill's warmth."[16] *New York* magazine described her "failing to demonstrate the most elementary political skills, much less those learned at Toastmasters or Dale Carnegie."[17] Last year the White House was panicking at her levels of electoral incompetence, her questionable decision-making, and her inclination for taking sleazy shortcuts.[18] More recently, noting Sanders's catch-up in the polls, *The Washington Post*'s Jennifer Rubin said that she was a "rotten candidate" whose attacks on Sanders made no sense, and that "at some point, you cannot blame the national mood or a poor staff or a brilliant opponent for Hillary Clinton's campaign woes."[19] Yet in a race against Trump, Hillary will be handicapped not only by her feeble campaigning skills, but the fact that she will have a sour national mood, a poor staff, and a brilliant opponent.

Every Democrat should take some time to fairly, dispassionately examine Clinton's track record as a campaigner. Study how the '08 campaign was handled,[20] and how this one has gone.[21] Assess her strengths and weaknesses with as little bias or prejudice as possible. Then picture the race against Trump, and think about how it will unfold.

It's easy to see that Trump has every single advantage. Because the

Republican primary will be over, he can come at her from both right and left as he pleases. As the candidate who thundered against the Iraq War at the Republican debate,[22] he can taunt Clinton over her support for it. He will paint her as a member of the corrupt political establishment, and will even offer proof: "Well, I know you can buy politicians, because I bought Senator Clinton. I gave her money, she came to my wedding."[23] He can make it appear that Hillary Clinton can be bought, that he can't, and that he is in charge. It's also hard to defend against, because it appears to be partly true. Any denial looks like a lie, thus making Hillary's situation look even worse. And then, when she stumbles, he will mock her as incompetent.

Charges of misogyny against Trump won't work. He is going to fill the press[24] with the rape and harassment allegations against Bill Clinton and Hillary's role in discrediting the victims[25] (something that made even Lena Dunham deeply queasy[26]). He can always remind people that Hillary Clinton referred to Monica Lewinsky as a "narcissistic loony toon."[27] Furthermore, since Trump is not an anti-Planned Parenthood zealot (being the only one willing to stick up for women's health in a room full of Republicans[28]), it will be hard for Clinton to paint him as the usual anti-feminist right-winger.

Trump will capitalize on his reputation as a truth-teller, and be vicious about both Clinton's sudden changes of position (e.g. the switch on gay marriage,[29] plus the affected economic populism of her run against Sanders) and her perceived dishonesty. One can already imagine the monologue:

> *She lies so much. Everything she says is a lie. I've never seen someone who lies so much in my life. Let me tell you three lies she's told. She made up a story about how she was ducking sniper fire![30] There was no sniper fire. She made it up! How do you forget a thing like that? She said she was named after Sir Edmund Hillary, the guy*

who climbed Mount Everest.[31] He hadn't even climbed it when she was born! Total lie! She lied about the emails,[32] of course, as we all know, and is probably going to be indicted. You know she said there were weapons of mass destruction in Iraq! It was a lie! Thousands of American soldiers are dead because of her. Not only does she lie, her lies kill people. That's four lies, I said I'd give you three. You can't even count them. You want to go on PolitiFact, see how many lies she has?[33] It takes you an hour to read them all! In fact, they ask her, she doesn't even say she hasn't lied. They asked her straight up, she says she usually tries to tell the truth![34] Ooooh, she tries! Come on! This is a person, every single word out of her mouth is a lie. Nobody trusts her. Check the polls, nobody trusts her. Yuge liar.

Where does she even begin to respond to this? Some of it's true, some of it isn't, but the more she tries to defensively parse it ("There's been no suggestion I'm going to be indicted! And I didn't say I usually tried to tell the truth, I said I *always* tried and *usually* succeeded") the deeper she sinks into the hole.

Trump will bob, weave, jab, and hook. He won't let up. And because Clinton actually has lied, and actually did vote for the Iraq War, and actually is hyper-cosy with Wall Street, and actually does change her positions based on expediency, all she can do is issue further implausible denials, which will further embolden Trump. Nor does she have a single offensive weapon at her disposal, since every legitimate criticism of Trump's background (inconsistent political positions, shady financial dealings, pattern of deception) is equally applicable to Clinton, and he knows how to make such things slide off him, whereas she does not.

The whole Clinton campaign has been unraveling from its inception. It fell apart completely in 2008, and has barely held together against the longest of long shot candidates. No matter how likely she may be to win the primary, things do not bode well for a general election, whomever the nominee may be. As H.A. Goodman put it in Salon:

> *Please name the last person to win the presidency along-side an ongoing FBI investigation, negative favorability ratings, questions about character linked to continual flip-flops, a dubious money trail of donors, and the genuine contempt of the rival political party.*[35]

The "contempt" bit of this is obviously silly; we all know levels of contempt have reached their world-historic high point in the Republican attitude toward Obama. But the rest is true: it's incredibly hard to run somebody very few people like and expect to win. With the jocular, shrewd Donald Trump as an opponent, that holds true a million times over.

Nor are the demographics going to be as favorable to Clinton as she thinks. Trump's populism will have huge resonance among the white working class in both red and blue states;[36] he might even peel away her black support.[37] And Trump has already proven false the prediction that he would alienate Evangelicals through his vulgarity and his self-deification.[38] Democrats are insistently repeating their belief that a Trump nomination will mobilize liberals to head to the polls like never before, but with nobody particularly enthusiastic for Clinton's candidacy, it's not implausible that a large number of people will find both options so unappealing that they stay home.

A Clinton/Trump match should therefore not just worry Democrats. It should terrify them. They should be doing everything possible to avoid it. A Trump/Sanders contest, however, looks very different indeed.

Trump's various unique methods of attack would instantly be made far less useful in a run against Sanders. All of the most personal charges (untrustworthiness, corruption, rank hypocrisy) are much more difficult to make stick. The rich history of dubious business dealings is nonexistent. None of the sleaze in which Trump traffics can be found clinging to Bernie. Trump's standup routine just has much less obvious personal material to work with. Sanders is a fairly transparent guy; he likes the social safety net, he doesn't like oligarchy, he's a workaholic who sometimes takes a break to play basketball,[39] and that's pretty much all there is to it. Contrast that with the above-noted list of juicy Clinton tidbits.

Trump can't clown around nearly as much at a debate with Sanders, for the simple reason that Sanders is dead set on keeping every conversation about the plight of America's poor under the present economic system. If Trump tells jokes and goofs off here, he looks as if he's belittling poor people, not a magnificent idea for an Ivy League trust fund billionaire running against a working class public servant and veteran of the Civil Rights movement. Instead, Trump will be forced to do what Hillary Clinton has been forced to do during the primary, namely to make himself sound as much like Bernie Sanders as possible. For Trump, having to get serious and take the Trump Show off the air will be devastating to his unique charismatic appeal.

Against Trump, Bernie can play the same "experience" card that Hillary plays. After all, while Sanders may look like a policy amateur next to Clinton, next to Trump he looks positively statesmanlike. Sanders can point to his successful mayoralty[40] and long history as Congress's "Amendment King"[41] as evidence of his administrative bona fides. And Sanders's lack of foreign policy knowledge won't hurt him when facing someone with even less.[42] Sanders will be enough of an outsider for Trump's populist anti-Washington appeal to be powerless, but enough of an insider to appear an experienced hand at governance.

Trump is an attention-craving parasite, and such creatures are powerful only when indulged and paid attention to. Clinton will be forced to pay attention to Trump because of his constant evocation of her scandals. She will attempt to go after him.[43] She will, in other words, feed the troll. Sanders, by contrast, will almost certainly behave as if Trump isn't even there. He is unlikely to rise to Trump's bait, because Sanders doesn't even care to listen to anything that's not about saving social security or the disappearing middle class. He will almost certainly seem as if he barely knows who Trump is. Sanders's commercials will be similar to those he has run in the primary, featuring uplifting images of America,[44] aspirational sentiments about what we can be together,[45] and moving testimonies from ordinary Americans.[46] Putting such genuine dignity and good feeling against Trump's race-baiting clownishness will be like finally pouring water on the Wicked Witch. Hillary Clinton cannot do this; with her, the campaign will inevitably descend into the gutter, and the unstoppable bloated Trump menace will continue to grow ever larger.

Sanders is thus an almost perfect secret weapon against Trump. He can pull off the only maneuver that is capable of neutralizing Trump: ignoring him and actually keeping the focus on the issues. Further, Sanders will have the advantage of an enthusiastic army of young volunteers,[47] who will be strongly dedicated to the mission of stalling Trump's quest for the presidency. The Sanders team is extremely technically skilled; everything from their television commercials to their rally organizing[48] to their inspired teasing[49] is pulled off well. The Sanders team is slick and adaptable, the Clinton team is ropey and fumbling.

There's only one real way to attack Bernie Sanders, and we all know it: he's a socialist fantasist out of touch with the Realities of Economics.[50] But Trump is in the worst possible position to make this criticism. Economists have savaged Trump's own proposals as sheer lunacy,[51] using every word deployed against Bernie and then some.[52] And while from a D.C. policy veteran like Clinton, charges of a failure to understand how political decision-making works may sound reasonable, Sanders is a successful legislator who has run a city; the host of *The Apprentice* may have a more difficult time portraying a long-serving congressman as being unfamiliar with how Washington works.

Of course, the American people are still jittery about socialism. But they're less jittery than they used to be,[53] and Bernie does a good job portraying socialism as being about little more than paid family leave and sick days[54] (a debatable proposition, but one beside the point). His policies are popular and appeal to the prevailing national sentiment.[55] It's a risk, certainly. But the Soviet Union bogeyman is long gone, and everyone gets called a socialist these days no matter what their politics.[56] It's possible that swing voters dislike socialism more than they dislike Hillary Clinton, but in a time of economic discontent one probably shouldn't bet on it.

One thing that should be noted is that all of this analysis applies solely to a race against Trump; the situation changes drastically and unpredictably if Marco Rubio is the nominee or Michael Bloomberg enters the race. Yet at the moment, it doesn't look like Marco Rubio will be nominated, but that Donald Trump will be. And in that case, Clinton is toast.

Some in the media have rushed to declare Sanders's campaign moribund in the wake of his recent loss in Nevada. This is absurd; after all, out of 50 states, only three have voted, one being a tie, one being a major Sanders win, and one being a small Clinton win. The media has dishonestly pointed to Hillary Clinton's higher superdelegate count as evidence of her strong lead, despite knowing full well that superdelegates are highly unlikely to risk tearing the party apart by taking the nomination out of voters' hands, and are thus mostly a formality. The press has also crafted a narrative about Sanders "slipping behind," ignoring the fact that Sanders has been behind from the very start; not for a moment has he been in front.

But even if it was correct to say that Sanders was "starting to" lose (instead of progressively losing less and less), this should only motivate all Democrats to work harder to make sure he is nominated. One's support for Sanders should increase in direct proportion to one's fear of Trump. And if Trump is the nominee, Hillary Clinton should drop out of the race and throw her every ounce of energy into supporting Sanders. If this does not occur, the resulting consequences for Muslims and Mexican immigrants of a Trump presidency will be fully the responsibility of Clinton and the Democratic Party. To run a candidate who can't win, or who is a very high-risk proposition, is to recklessly play with the lives of millions of people. So much depends on stopping Trump; a principled defeat will mean nothing to the deported, or to those being roughed up by Trump's goon squads or executed with pigs' blood-dipped bullets.[57]

Donald Trump is one of the most formidable opponents in the history of American politics. He is sharp, shameless, and likable. If he is going to be the nominee, Democrats need to think very seriously about how to defeat him. If they don't, he will be the President of the United States, which will have disastrous repercussions for religious and racial minorities and likely for everyone else, too. Democrats should consider carefully how a Trump/Clinton matchup would develop, and how a Trump/Sanders matchup would. For their sake, hopefully they will realize that the only way to prevent a Trump presidency is the nomination of Bernie Sanders.

Democrats Should Be Very Worried About Hillary's Anti-Trump Strategy

MAY 6, 2016

On Wednesday, Hillary Clinton's campaign released two new attack ads against Donald Trump.[58] The first shows a string of prominent Republicans denouncing Trump, including Ted Cruz calling him a narcissistic bully and Marco Rubio labeling him a phony. In the second ad, Clinton simply plays a series of Trump's most controversial soundbites, from lines about anchor babies to his classic "bomb the shit out of them."

The new anti-Trump ads have been called "straight-up savage"[59] and "devastating."[60] *The Washington Post*'s Greg Sargent said that the first "brutal" ad "shows the shredding machine that awaits Trump."[61] *Slate* called the ads a "one-two punch" that seem like a "good plan."[62]

But to the contrary, these ads are a horrible plan. They're the worst possible plan. And the fact that the Clinton campaign can believe they're useful demonstrates just how minimal their understanding of voter psychology is, and reveals them to be woefully unprepared to deal with Trump in a general election. If this is the sort of material that the Hillary campaign has up its sleeve, the Democrats should be very worried indeed.

The essential problem is that, but for a few small tweaks, *the Trump campaign itself could have put out these ads.* Trump *loves* to be called names by Mitt Romney, Ted Cruz, and Lindsey Graham. He's proud of it. Stringing these clips together just showcases what Trump himself says: establishment Republican losers hate him. That ad makes him look like a rebel: stuffed shirts like Mitt Romney hate his guts. (I'm a socialist, but I literally found myself *warming to Trump* as I watched him driving these conservative blowhards apoplectic.)

The ad also erodes the coherence of Hillary's own campaign. Not only does it not hurt Trump, but it actually damages Hillary, by muddying her own politics. If she's a progressive Democrat, then why would she give any credence to what Ted Cruz thinks? Shouldn't being loathed by Ted Cruz reflect incredibly positively on someone? If the Democrats believe that conservative Republicans have policies that are essentially just as heinous as Trump's, why should Hillary believe denouncements of Trump by Republicans carry any weight? If we produced a set of clips of the numerous times that right-wing Republicans have said nasty things about Clinton, would she want us to listen to *that?* Of course not. Because nothing said by Lindsey

Graham should be given a shred of attention or credence by anyone. (And indeed, it isn't.)

One of the key flaws in these ads is that they assume the viewer already agrees with them. Anyone who supports Trump is going to already know that the rest of the party hates him; that's part of his appeal. Likewise, they're also going to know that Trump says extreme and uncouth things; that's another part of his appeal. Every single person who believes Trump was "destroyed" by this ad *hated Trump already.* This ad is about as effective as John Oliver calling Trump "Drumpf." It does absolutely nothing to persuade people who do not already dislike Trump. All it does is congratulate people who agreed from the start.

That means that Hillary Clinton is basing her anti-Trump strategy on a dangerous premise: that merely by telling people what they already know about Trump, they will be motivated to show up to vote for her. Clearly, she believes that she will forge a coalition between the Republicans who hate him for being a nihilistic showboating vulgarian, and the Democrats who hate him for being a vicious bigot and possible fascist.

At first, this may seem smart. But it's actually just complacent. It shows a failure to absorb the lessons that were learned too late by the other Republican candidates. They, too, believed that all you needed to do to turn people off of Trump was to point at him and say "Look at him, he's… well, he's TRUMP!" As if that, in itself, was sufficient. But all Trump had to do was reply "I'm Trump. So what?" and they would be left stammering. "Well, well, just *look at him!*"

This tactic relies on the voter already sharing your fixed opinion of Trump. Meanwhile, you've given nobody any actual reason why they should vote for you instead. So Hillary Clinton offers not a single argument in her own favor, she merely campaigns by holding up a picture of Donald Trump's face, hoping that will be enough. And perhaps it will be, at first. But meanwhile, Donald Trump is slowly out converting people. And every time he does so, holding up a picture of his face seems less and less effective, is met with more and more responses of "So?", and ever more resembles an advertisement for Trump rather than an attack on him.

Political causes fail when they act as if they can win simply by existing, without the need to convince the unconvinced. This is something Republicans actually discovered for themselves when they went after Bill Clinton during his presidency. Conservatives would say "But he's an adulterer!" assuming that all they needed to do was point this out, and Clinton's support would collapse. But since they had nothing prepared to answer the follow-up question "And why should that matter to me?", and he himself remained charming and kept his cool, the attacks ended up boosting Clinton further. This is also one of the reasons liberals often lose political arguments. They believe that to point out that something is offensive is sufficient to convince people that it is bad. But they end up unable to deal with the person who simply replies "Well, what's wrong with a thing being offensive?"

If Hillary Clinton's entire case is going to be "I'm not Trump," she's going to have a hard time knowing what to do when he comes back with "Well, I *am* Trump. And Trump is great." She'll have no agenda of her own; in fact, she *can't* have one if she hopes to say that supporters of Ted Cruz and Bernie Sanders alike should rally behind her. All she can do is pray very hard that Trump's unfavorable ratings don't begin to erode, taking her entire argument with them.

I've previously written about the unique disadvantages that Clinton faces in a race against Trump. She has a tendency to flounder when attacks begin, and her background provides perfect fodder for his brand of primetime sleaze-slinging. She is also not well-positioned to criticize Trump on a number of his most important weaknesses, like shady business dealings; for every dubious quid-pro-quo of his, he'll bring up nine of hers. One can already see her heading for charges of hypocrisy: in the second of the new ads, Trump is depicted as crazy for refusing to take the nuclear option "off the table", but Clinton herself is notorious for having refused to take "any option off the table"[63] in regard to Iran. Half the things Clinton will say of Trump (evasive, narcissistic, opportunistic) are equally true of Clinton herself; the difference is that Trump owns these qualities and is proud of them. He'll get points for honesty, despite being one of the most prolific liars in the country.

The one strategy that might work against Trump is an attempt to neutralize his attention-seeking through the promotion of a positive agenda. This is why I've argued before that Bernie Sanders may have been the more effective candidate against Trump; if you can focus single-mindedly on your principles, and avoid being dragged down to Trump's level, you may stand a chance of forcing him to get serious (and therefore lose his schtick, which is the basis of his appeal). But if you get down in the gutter with him, as Marco Rubio found out, you're toast. If you start bashing him, he will bash you back, and he will be funnier and more shameless than you are. Trump will always win a battle conducted on Trump turf. If Hillary Clinton is committed to pursuing the "You're a racist and Republicans hate you" line, instead of working to appear stately and above the fray, she might be walking directly into Trump's gaping trap.[64]

Already, liberals are beginning to count their chickens and confidently predict a Clinton victory. One might expect more humility given how many pundits were just humiliated over their certain predictions that Trump would lose the primary.[65] But this is especially dicey given how vulnerable and clueless the Clinton campaign is now hinting it will be. If these ads are any indication, Clinton, like so many poor souls before her, has no idea how to stop Trump.

The Democrats Are Making a Suicidal Mistake
MAY 26, 2016

Somewhat predictably, Hillary Clinton's campaign has become a sinking ship. All of the lessons that should have been learned after her 2008 run failed so badly (that voters' trust in her diminishes with each word she speaks, that her campaigns are woefully poorly run,[66] that Bill is a liability[67]) have been ignored, as the Democrats press forward with what looks like a doomed strategy.

Things were already looking bad when new polling showed that Trump had drawn even with Clinton,[68] or was actually beating her (something Democrats have insisted is impossible[69]). Now, the Inspector General for the State Department has released a report that contradicts large parts of Clinton's story about her email server, which was already a highly troublesome and persistent issue.[70]

The report hands the Trump campaign a powerful issue to deploy against Clinton. As the *New York Times* reported, it has numerous damning portions:

> *The inspector general found that Mrs. Clinton "had an obligation to discuss using her personal email account to conduct official business" with department officials but that, contrary to her claims that the department "allowed" the arrangement, there was "no evidence" she had requested or received approval for it... Department officials told the inspector general's office that "Secretary Clinton never demonstrated to them that her private server or mobile device met minimum information security requirements," the report said. The report also criticized Mrs. Clinton for not adhering to the department's rules for handling records under the Federal Records Act once she stepped down in January 2013... The rules gov-*

erning emails under previous secretaries were, the report said, "very fluid." By the time Mrs. Clinton came to office, however, they were "considerably more detailed and sophisticated," spelling out the "obligation to use department systems in most circumstances and identifying the risks of not doing so."[71]

The Clinton campaign quickly released a statement arguing that the report had in fact exonerated her of wrongdoing. But even the *Times*, whose Clinton coverage is generally extremely sympathetic (they are the paper, after all, that went back and re-edited a news piece about Bernie Sanders to avoid making it seem too complimentary[72]), seemed unable to stomach this attempt to twist the report's findings. The *Times* makes clear that the Clinton campaign's response to the report ranges from distortion and omission to at least one outright lie. Clinton's statement insists that "As this report makes clear, Hillary Clinton's use of personal email was not unique." But as the *Times* replies, the report actually indicates that "Mrs. Clinton's use of a private email and server stored in her home was, in fact, unique."[73] Thus the Clinton campaign has responded to the report by simply pretending it says something other than what it actually says.

This is a useful exemplification of a disturbing recurrent Clinton trait: responding to criticisms that she has lied by telling... even more lies, thus causing the whole thing to degenerate further down into disaster. It's the same tactic Clinton thought would work when she was called out on her claim about ducking sniper fire in Bosnia. There, Clinton said that she remembered "landing under sniper fire"; "There was supposed to be some kind of a greeting ceremony at the airport," Clinton said, "but instead we just ran with our heads down to get into the vehicles to get to our base."[74] "There was no greeting ceremony," she later repeated. *CBS News* then pointed out that this was false, and that the footage contradicted Clinton's statement. The *Philadelphia*

Daily News then asked Clinton why, if there was no greeting ceremony, there was footage of her calmly meeting a little girl on the tarmac. Clinton replied "I was told that the greeting ceremony had been moved away from the tarmac, but that there *was* this eight-year-old girl, so I can't rush by her, I've got to at least greet her. So I greeted her, I took her stuff, and I left."[75] *CBS* then reported that *once again,* Clinton was lying. In fact, she lingered for ages on the tarmac in a highly elaborate greeting ceremony, not only meeting the little girl, but shaking hands with a large group of military officials individually, taking photos, and staging a group picture with an entire class of 7th graders.

The lie about ducking sniper fire is the one most often discussed, but it was actually the *second* lie (the lie *about* the lie) that was far worse. Asked why she greeted a little girl if there was sniper fire, Clinton simply *made up a story* about how she didn't want to break the little girl's heart by fleeing from the danger, even though there was no danger and she did much more than greet the girl and run off. This was much, much more egregious than the initial lie, because it was a deliberate fabrication rather than a false memory. After she had been caught, telling the truth would have been fine. She could have simply said that our minds often tell us stories that aren't true, we think of ourselves as braver than we actually were, and things we hear about others doing become misremembered as things we ourselves did. Yet rather than do that, Clinton became defensive, and created a whole new falsehood in which she bravely refused to rush away from the tarmac so that a little girl could meet her.

The sniper fire story itself is trivial. But her response to it suggested that whenever Clinton is caught out, she will simply become even more shameless, hoping that at some point people give up and stop pressing her. This dynamic is, of course, familiar to all children who have attempted to pile untruths on top of untruths in the desperate hope that a certain number of lies will eventually cancel each other out. But as every child learns, this only ever leads to further trouble and, sooner or later, you just have to come clean and admit that you've been dishonest.

But it's quite clear that Clinton will never, ever do this. Even now that the State Department's Inspector General has released a report explaining in detail why Clinton's claims about her emails are false, she has responded by doubling down with even more implausible statements.

This does not augur well for the remainder of the campaign. It means that Hillary Clinton has what might be termed a "trust death spiral." She begins by having the public think she is untrustworthy. Then, in response to accusations that she is untrustworthy, she says things that make her sound *even more untrustworthy*.[76] Because there's no point at which she'll simply break free and come clean, things can only ever get worse for Hillary Clinton. If you point out that her positions have changed (making her somewhat untrustworthy), she responds by insisting that they *haven't* changed[77] (making her *even more* untrustworthy). If a report says she is misrepresenting the situation with her email, she will then *misrepresent the report itself*.[78]

This is a problem not just because it decreases public trust; it also treats voters like they must be *incredibly stupid*. It's brazenly insulting to people's intelligence to simply deny that a report says what it says. And because people *are* more intelligent than that, they don't like it when you try to pull tricks like this.

That fatal flaw means that Clinton is in terrible trouble. As this publication has explained in detail before, Clinton suffers from the fact that her weaknesses are those that Donald Trump is well-positioned to exploit. Trump is uniquely strong against Clinton, and Clinton is uniquely weak against Trump. One core problem is that nobody ever seems to go from disliking Clinton to liking her, while plenty of people seem to go from disliking Trump to liking Trump.

Meanwhile, desperate liberals are falling back on some of their worst arguments yet in an attempt to convince people that the obvious is in fact the impossible. New methods of explaining away the facts include: "The election is still many months away, it's too early to tell anything"[79] (Right, but unless people start liking Hillary Clinton *more* with each additional disaster, things will only get worse); "Sanders backers will come around and realize Clinton is the better of the two options"[80] (Sure, but *how are you going to get them to physically go to the polls to support someone they still can't stand?*); and "Obama's approval ratings have been going up, which will favor Democrats in the fall"[81] (they are almost certainly going up because everyone despises Clinton and Trump so much that Obama now looks positively spectacular by comparison).

Liberal pundits have also already begun preparing their excuses for a Clinton loss in November. It will all be Bernie's fault. After all, "if Bernie splinters the left and erodes Clinton's support among voters, the consequences for our country could be even more dire than another Bush administration."[82] I am not the first to point out that Democrats seem to have a more developed strategy for blaming Sanders for Clinton's loss to Trump than they have for *actually defeating Trump*. Their plan, should they lose, is not to concede that they ran a disastrous candidate from the beginning and ignored all of the warning signs, but to simply spend four years shouting the word "Nader" at every progressive who cares to point out what a blunder Clinton's nomination was. In this way, just as Democrats after 2000 learned no lessons (perhaps you should have nominated someone who wouldn't cause people to vote for Nader?), Democrats after 2016 will similarly remain smugly convinced that Clinton was the best choice, no matter how much the vast majority of Americans may disagree.

Watching this mistake play out in slow-motion is painful. As Clinton continues to tank, and continues to delude herself as to why she is tanking, and thereby cause herself to tank further, Sanders supporters will have to watch in exasperation watching their predictions all come true before their eyes. Even the satisfaction of an "I told you so" will be robbed thanks to the liberals' insistence on calling them Naderites.

Meanwhile, a monstrosity named Trump continues his unstoppable ascendance. Of course, there's a simple way to solve the problem and salvage the party's chances of winning the election.[83] Yet some Democrats continue to prefer the unrealistic candidate over the pragmatic one, and insist on nominating Clinton.

Democrats Need To Stop Pretending That Everything Is Going Well

JULY 23, 2016

Among members of the liberal press, the reaction to Donald Trump's RNC acceptance speech has been almost unanimous. It was, they say, "grim,"[84] "angry,"[85] and "dark."[86] Trump painted a "Mad Max" picture of the United States,[87] as a nation in crisis, beset by crime, terrorism, unemployment, and despair.

This picture, say the commentators, is false.[88] Trump exaggerated crime rates, which are actually going down rather than up.[89] He scare-mongered about immigrants and terrorism, creating threats where there are none. And he suggested that the world is going to hell in a handbasket, when it is not. As Ezra Klein put it in a blog post for his website,[90] Trump had to convince people that "things are really, really bad" when things are *not* "really, really bad."

This has been a consistent thread in the liberal reply to Trump's rhetoric. Trump casts America as a broken land in need of fixing. Democrats respond that America is doing just fine,[91] and that everyone is better off than they have been in years. They highlight the achievements of the Obama administration in bringing healthcare to millions[92] and reducing unemployment.[93] In response to Trump's bright-red "Make America Great Again" baseball caps, the Democratic Party attempted to popularize its own brand of "America Is Already Great" hats.[94] (They did not take off.[95])

All of this is a peculiar role reversal. Ordinarily, conservatives are the ones defending the status quo, while the left tries to rouse public interest in various pressing social problems. Now, Trump is the one speaking of the decline of the country's fortunes, while liberals have become the new cheerleaders for America-as-it-is.

Of course, Trump is hardly a leftist in his diagnosis of the cause of the present troubles. In his speech, Trump displayed a downright Nixonian view of the country's cities, as hotbeds of murder and social dysfunction. Naturally, the immigrant hordes and Muslim menace are looming over us, threatening to kill our police officers, take our jobs, and convert our children to Islam.

But some of Trump's populist rhetoric *is* distinctly leftist in its tone, and there were portions of the speech that could have come straight from the mouth of Big Bill Haywood or Eugene V. Debs:

> *I have visited the laid-off factory workers, and the communities crushed by our horrible and unfair trade deals. These are the forgotten men and women of our country. People who work hard but no longer have a voice.*[96]

That posture presents a formidable challenge for the Democrats. Trump is positioning himself to the left of Hillary Clinton on many economic issues, decrying the influence of big business and the "disaster" of NAFTA. In doing so, he could well appeal to the millions of people who were drawn to Bernie Sanders because of Sanders' willingness to fight for the working class.

Yet the response among Democratic commentators has not been to explain why Democratic policies will better serve laid-off factory workers. Instead, they have tried to downplay the very *existence* of laid-off factory workers, with article[97] after article[98] explaining that Trump has overlooked the positive. The press has even taken Trump to task for overstating how many young African Americans are unemployed, pointing out that actually, it's only ⅓ rather than ½ (though it does rise to ½ if you count the underemployed).[99] But it's odd to go after Trump for pointing out how hard African Americans have it, considering that the facts on black wealth[100] and unemployment[101] are indeed disturbing.

Pointing out Trump's statistical errors does not provide an effective counter-narrative, and it threatens to make the Democrats seem totally out of touch with people's concerns. When people working cushy media jobs tell working class Americans that they're better off than they think they are, one can almost hear a variant on the myth of Pauline Kael's puzzlement that Nixon could have won the election when nobody she knew voted for him: "I can't understand what this whole 'widespread despair' business is all about. Nobody I know is in despair."

The vision of America as profoundly broken is not some delusion. Things might not be "really, really bad" for Ezra Klein, but they are for many others. Liberals may point to the low unemployment rate as proof that the Obama economy is rebounding. But those numbers conceal important truths about the state of the country. For example, look at the vast rates of consumer debt, with credit card debt alone reaching $1 trillion.[102] Even if access to credit has positive overall effects, debt creates nightmares for people.

Consider what happened to Kevin Evans.[103] After 25 years at his job, Evans was laid off during the recession. He was forced to sell his home, and reduced to mere subsistence. Whenever he could, he worked low-wage jobs at lumberyards and the like. At the same time, Evans build up $7,000 in credit card debt trying to pay for his daughters' college education. In the past few years, Evans' employment position has improved as the economy has grown; he's back to a better-paying full-time job. But now, CapitalOne is garnishing his wages, taking 25% of everything he earns in order to pay back his outstanding debt. He continues to live in constant economic uncertainty.

The important thing about Evans' story is that it shows how recovery can exist on paper while a person's level of financial stress remains high. If we look solely at employment, Evans is a success. But in reality, he's still struggling, a huge chunk of his wages disappearing to pay off debts. Stories like Evans' are perfectly consistent with economic recovery, buried beneath ostensibly encouraging statistics. In other areas, too, the actual factors creating despair are overlooked. For example, as Matthew Desmond has recently pointed out, many people's lives are now dominated by the threat of eviction from their homes.

Actually, these truths aren't really any kind of a secret; the facts are well-known and frequently discussed. Whole areas of the country are "dying of despair."[104] In West Virginia, "the economy is declining along with the coal industry, towns are hollowed out as people flee, and communities are scarred by family dissolution, prescription drug abuse and a high rate of imprisonment."[105] The suicide rate is the highest it has been in 30 years.[106] Life expectancy is actually diminishing among poor whites.[107] Rising levels of alcoholism are destroying countless lives,[108] with the result that the white working class holds "a shockingly dismal view of what the future holds for them."[109]

These facts shouldn't have to be reiterated. It's been explained repeatedly, by everyone from the *National Review* to Noam Chomsky,[110] that Donald Trump's success emerges from working-class anxiety over these real social problems. As writer J.D. Vance tells it:

> *These people—my people—are really struggling, and there hasn't been a single political candidate who speaks to those struggles in a long time. Donald Trump at least tries. What many don't understand is how truly desperate these places are, and we're not talking about small enclaves or a few towns—we're talking about multiple states where a significant chunk of the white working class struggles to get by.*[111]

And yet right after Trump's speech, instead of focusing on her own solutions to America's problems, Hillary Clinton remarked that "the last thing we need is somebody running for president who talks trash about America."[112] That sounds like something George W. Bush would have said about John Kerry. And it's hard to think who such a line will persuade. The despairing, angry mass of Trump supporters is hardly likely to buy into the theory that its grievances are "unpatriotic," and people on the left are supposed to reject the idea that criticisms of social problems constitute "trashing America."

But, we might say, economic anxiety is one thing, racially-charged national security anxiety is quite another. What about the fear-mongering on immigration, crime, and terrorism? Surely Trump's apocalyptic image of the country's security needs to be rebutted. Trump has explicitly tried to insist that crime is rising, when has been going down steadily for the last 20 years. And the number of Americans killed in terror attacks is minuscule.[113]

Here again though, we see the weakness of the Democrats' approach to countering Trump. Trump's rhetoric is certainly ominous and paranoid, pretending that enemies lurk around every corner, that immigrants, criminals, and terrorists are tearing apart the country they love. That's not the case. But in order to *persuade* people that that's not the case, you need more than a graph of crime rates. You need a compelling alternate explanation for what is going wrong in people's lives.

It's somewhat important to point out that nearly everything Trump says is a transparent falsehood. But it's also true that while Trump may lie a lot, he's not *always* lying. When Trump talks about abandoned factories and bodies in the streets of Chicago, he's not making *those* things up.[114] (Nor, despite misstating his own previous positions, is he wrong about Clinton's "failed policy of nation building and regime change … in Iraq, Libya, Egypt and Syria."[115])

It's also important to understand *why* it's easy to create an imaginary crime wave, namely that when people feel a generalized and nameless sense of fear and hopelessness, they grasp at myths that help explain their feelings. Take the Brexit crisis in the U.K., which was an instructive lesson in what can happen when the working class feels excluded and angry.[116] The consensus among elites is that Brexit voters were driven by racism and the fear of immigrants. And it's true that, *were it not for fear of immigration*, the Brexit vote would likely have gone the other way.[117]

However, in terms of a political strategy, it is pointless to simply scoff at pro-Leave voters for being racists. If people are *blaming immigrants for their problems*, the correct strategic response is to build a platform that shows people what the actual source of their problems is, and proposes a means of solving them. By simply lobbing charges of xenophobia, one denies that any of the underlying anxieties fueling anti-immigrant sentiment (as opposed to the sentiment itself) are real and legitimate. If you don't have a compelling alternate vision and program, then of course people will be susceptible to demagoguery about crime and immigration. Trump and Nigel Farage may have a racist and delusional explanation for the cause of the world's troubles, but *they have an explanation*.

Creating a successful competing political philosophy isn't just a matter of making those communities understand that immigration benefits them. (Actually, among low-wage workers, immigration may well slightly increase competition for jobs, a fact that needs to be acknowledged and dealt with.)[118] It's also a matter of actually proposing ways of better redistributing the economic benefits of globalization. As Fredrik deBoer pointed out [in *Current Affairs*] recently, we know where the economic gains have gone; they're certainly not evenly shared across society.[119] Global inequality has risen to the point that nearly all wealth is controlled by a tiny minority of the super-rich,[120] and labor power is in decline.[121] It might be wise for the left to have something to say about this.

So far, centrist Democrats have been miserably bad at generating that kind of meaningful alternative (possibly because they are, themselves, largely the beneficiaries of inequality). In fact, by dismissing the concerns of working-class voters, and gushing about the Obama administration's wonderful policy achievements, liberals almost seem to be mocking and taunting their working-class constituents. (Clinton's missteps, like telling coal country voters that she would put miners out of business, have also been unhelpful.) As Emmett Rensin has written, elite liberalism has become characterized by a "smug style" that simply shouts "idiots!" at the "stupid hicks" who are getting "conned by right-wingers."[122] Rensin says that liberalism has come to believe in "the politics of smart people in command of Good Facts," which has "no moral convictions, only charts."

One could see that after Trump's speech. The most common response to Trump among liberal commentators seems to be the relentless fact-checking of his statements, rather than any attempt to articulate a comprehensive alternate political worldview. Barack Obama himself, in addition to adopting the "America is already great" mantra,[123] has decided that the best way to defend his health care policy to the public is through writing a heavily-footnoted academic article for a scholarly journal.[124]

Clinton supporters can often seem stunningly oblivious. Pundit Andrew Sullivan (who believes that the rise of Trump proves that people are too stupid to be entrusted with democratic decision-making[125]) responded to Trump's criticism of Obamacare by saying that "I'm on Obamacare and I picked my own doctor."[126] Well, bully for Andrew Sullivan. But not everybody shares in his good fortune,[127] and it's both arrogant and useless to explain why Democratic policies look great from where *you're* sitting. Such people *fundamentally do not seem to understand what it feels like* to live outside of the coastal elite bubble. Prominent liberal writers like Ezra Klein, who help shape policy priorities and set agendas, are totally uninterested in the way other types of people's lives are actually *lived*. Their view of the working-class experience comes entirely from Bureau of Labor Statistics reports. Thus they don't understand the things that make people unhappy, stressed out, hopeless, and frightened.

One person who *did* appear to understand these things was Bernie Sanders. This was clear from his interactions with voters,[128] and it's why tens of thousands of people showed up at his rallies. It's why he was able to rival Trump in the enthusiasm of his voters. He went from being a fringe candidate to a serious contender for the nomination, by tapping into an important part of the national mood. The fact that Sanders took off so unexpectedly, despite his total lack of traditional political charisma and a disorganized campaign apparatus, should have been a lesson.

Democrats need to pay attention to the Sanders model if they want to generate any enthusiasm or make any inroads with new groups of voters. Instead of telling people that everything is alright, they need to acknowledge that for many, many people things aren't alright at all. Then, instead of offering terrifying doomsaying like Trump, they need to inspire people to believe things can get better. They need to run a campaign of hope rather than a campaign of complacency. If they want to successfully win Trump's voters over, they will need to stop treating such people as nothing more than delusional racists. Yet, worryingly, many Democrats don't actually seem to be committed to the task of winning people over. They seem to believe that Trump supporters are, indeed, just "dumb hicks" who can't be reasoned with.

This is a fatal position to take. So long as Democrats are trying to retain support instead of grow it, Trump will continue to lure new voters while Clinton's voter base will either remain stagnant or shrink. In order to win, you've simply got to persuade people. Internet theorist and perennial TED talker Clay Shirky recognizes the wonk problem, and tells Democrats that they have wrongly "brought fact-checkers to a culture war."[129] That's true as an assessment of the problem, but the question is how Democrats intend to *win* that culture war. Do they intend to win it by trying to get people who already agree with them to half-heartedly drag themselves to the polls, and by portraying Trump's working class constituency as the enemy? Or do they intend to win it by offering an actual principled contrast that deals with the real problems that people have?

The selection of Tim Kaine as Clinton's running mate is not a good sign here. Kaine has no potential whatsoever to craft the kind of inspiring alternative platform that Democrats need. Hillary Clinton has not just admitted Kaine is boring, but says that she "love[s] that about him" because he fits her "fondness for wonks."[130] But wonks are precisely the problem; they are incapable of understanding voters' emotions. Such people will puzzle over why Americans are "stubbornly negative" about the economy,[131] failing to even recognize that large parts of the country are characterized by massive inequality[132] and poverty.[133]

Kaine certainly doesn't help with the Democrats' need to reclaim a progressive populism, since he infamously tried to help banks evade consumer protection regulations.[134] Trump will (accurately) seize on this as a reflection of Democratic obliviousness. Indeed, just hours after the pick was announced, the Republican National Committee sent out a statement pointing out that "Kaine has castigated opponents of free-trade agreements as 'losers' and strongly supported the War in Iraq."[135] By selecting Kaine, Clinton shows that she has no intention of trying to rechannel the working class anxiety fueling the Trump campaign into something positive. Instead, she's simply hoping that people will be so afraid of Trump that they have no choice but to join her. Perhaps they will be. But consider: Trump tells people he will keep them safe from joblessness, terrorism, and crime. Clinton tells people that joblessness, terrorism, and crime aren't problems, and that she'll keep them safe from Trump. Which scare tactic is more compelling?

In an age where millions of people are looking for explanations and solutions for their despair, it might be unwise to count on fear of Trump as one's sole campaign message. So long as Democrats stick with the mantra that everything is fine and Obama is fantastic, not only will they come across as smug, not only will what they are saying be false, but it's hard to see how they will win a presidential election.

On the whole, I stand by most of what I wrote in these columns. I should note, however, that what I said in February was not exactly correct: a Trump nomination did not have to mean a Trump presidency. The election was winnable. But winning it would have required the Democrats to do some serious introspection, and to recognize that Trump's threat needed to be countered with a clear message that spoke to voters. Instead, there was little more than the constant drumbeat of Clinton's inevitability. It drowned everything else out.

In fact, despite having held such a dire perspective throughout the spring and summer, I began to change my own mind come the fall, when the sexual assault revelations threatened to doom Trump. Caught up in the prevailing atmosphere, I wrote a cautious piece proclaiming his vanquishment that turned out to be spectacularly wrong. In the spirit of accountability, and to show just how profoundly affected even the most cynical people were by the near-universal certainty that Trump was doomed, I reprint the first paragraphs here.

Good Riddance To A Revolting Monster
Oct. 8, 2016

It is always unwise to be complacent, especially when it comes to Donald Trump. A hundred scandals that would destroy an ordinary man have failed to undo him. But with Trump having now proudly admitted to groping multiple women (you "grab them by the pussy"), and his behavior graphically confirmed by a victim, perhaps it will at last be possible to declare truthfully (instead of wishfully) that Trump's campaign is over. Our long national nightmare may finally be at an end.

Again, caution is warranted. Like shell-shocked townspeople emerging from a bomb shelter, we should make sure the threat is truly vanquished before celebrating. But something feels qualitatively different about this most recent Trump scandal. Trump's racism, militarism, and misogyny were on open display before. But electing racists is certainly not without precedent in United States presidential history, and threatening to bomb helpless non-white people if elected is almost a job requirement. Handing the presidency to a man who openly brags of committing serial sexual assault, however, would be a dramatic new kind of low.... [But] Trump will be back. Not the man himself, perhaps, but the dark and menacing tendencies he represents. [...] A serious left alternative, one with a platform beyond "We're not them," needs to be readied. The next monster may be even deadlier.

Indeed, Trump would be back. I should have realized that the sexual assault allegations would have had less of an impact than expected, precisely because those who intended to vote for Trump were already committing themselves to overlooking a series of horrific character flaws. But the other part of this remains true: unless the left offers a credible alternative, Trump and Trumpism cannot be gotten rid of. We must save our final "Good Riddances" until then...

SOURCES

1   Quoted in Marie Brenner, "After the Gold Rush," *Vanity Fair* (May 1990).

2   A sample of the major Trump Studies literature:

   • Wayne Barrett, *Trump: The Greatest Show On Earth* (Regan Arts, 2016).
   • Timothy L. O'Brien, *TrumpNation: The Art of Being the Donald* (Grand Central Publishing, 2007).
   • Gwenda Blair, *The Trumps: Three Gene=rations of Builders and a Presidential Candidate* (Simon & Schuster, 2001).
   • John R. O'Donnell, *Trumped!: The Inside Story of the Real Donald Trump-His Cunning Rise and Spectacular Fall* (Simon & Schuster, 1991).
   • David Cay Johnson, *The Making of Donald Trump* (Melville House, 2016).
   • Harry Hurt III, *Lost Tycoon: The Many Lives of Donald Trump* (Echo Point Books, 2016).
   • Michael Kranish and Marc Fisher, *Trump Revealed: An American Journey of Ambition, Ego, Money, and Power* (Scribner 2016).
   • Michael D'Antonio, *The Truth About Trump* (Thomas Dunne, 2016).

3   See, e.g. Dan McLaughlin, "How The White House Correspondents' Dinner Gave Us The Trump Campaign," *National Review* (July 19, 2016) and Michael Isikoff, "The birth of a candidacy: Did the president's mockery propel Trump into the race?" *Yahoo News* (Sept. 22, 2016).

4   See Michelle Dean, "Making the man: to understand Trump, look at his relationship with his dad," *The Guardian* (March 26, 2016).

5   I am, however, also no mindless partisan for the existing Democratic Party (of which I am not a member). Human loyalties should be toward principles rather than parties.

6   See "Bad Ways to Criticize Trump," Part IV, p. 229.

7   See William J. Broad and David E. Sanger, "Debate Over Trump's Fitness Raises Issue of Checks on Nuclear Power," *The New York Times* (Aug. 4, 2016). ("Is there any check on a president's power to launch nuclear arms that could destroy entire cities or nations? The short answer is no…")

8   The O'Jays, "For the Love of Money," Philadelphia International Records (1973).

9   Maggie Severns, "Tales from the Trump University legal vault, *Politico* (Mar. 3, 2016).

10   "Trump University 2010 Playbook." Available at *Politico*. The internal manual is worth reviewing, because it makes clear that the "university's" priorities were almost entirely toward driving sales.

11   John Cassidy, "Trump University: It's Worse Than You Think," *The New York* (June 2, 2016).

12   Tom McNichol, "The Art of the Upsell: How Donald Trump Profits From 'Free' Seminars," *The Atlantic* (Mar. 17, 2014).

13   *Id.*

14   Quoted from Cassidy, *supra*. Original statement: Declaration of Ronald Schnackenburg in Support of Plaintiffs' Motion for Class Certification, McKaeff et. al. v. Trump University LLC, United States District Court for the Southern District of California, Case No. 3:10-CV-00940-CAB(WVG).

15   Jim Zarroli, "Trump University Customer: 'Gold Elite' Program Nothing But Fool's Gold," *NPR* (June 6, 2016). 76-year-old Bob Guillo said of his experience getting ripped off: "At first it was embarrassing…Then I became very, very angry that the man that scammed me out of all that money had the audacity to run for president. And I'm still angry."

16   Johnston, *supra* note 2, 120-121.

17   *Id.*

18   *Id.*

19   Complaint, Cohen v. Trump, United States Court for the Southern District of California, Case No. '13CV2519

DMS RBB, at 14.

20   *Id.*

21   Michael Garofalo, "Trump University was a 'scam from beginning to end': The most damning allegations against the "school,'" *Salon* (June 3, 2016).

22   "Playbook," *supra*, at 45.

23   *Id.*, at 46.

24   *Id.*

25   Johnston, *supra*, at 121.

26   "Playbook," *supra*, 113-114.

27   *Id.*, at 113.

28   *Id.*

29   *Id.*, at 110.

30   *Id.*, at 111.

31   *Id.*, at 139.

32   *Id.*, at 99.

33   Elliot Spagat, "Documents show aggressive sales tactics at Trump University," *Associated Press* (May 21, 2016).

34   *Id.*

35   "Playbook," *supra*, at 114.

36   *Id.*, at 113.

37   Cassidy, *supra*.

38   D'Antonio, *supra*, at 283.

39   Cassidy, *supra*.

40   Michael Biesecker and Paul J. Weber, "Texas regulator: Trump U preyed on 'novice' investors," *Associated Press* (June 7, 2016).

41   Steve Eder, "Donald Trump Agrees to Pay $25 million in Trump University Settlement," *The New York Times* (Nov. 18, 2016).

42   Glenn Kessler, "A Trio of Truthful Attack Ads About Trump University," *The Washington Post* (Feb. 29, 2016).

43   Paul Singer and David McKay Wilson, "Trump U. made 'impossible' promises,," *USA Today* (June 2, 2016).

44   D'Angelo Gore, "Trump's Defense of His 'University,'" *Fact-Check.org* (March 1, 2016).

45 Brandy Zadronsky, "Trump University's Star Student: 'It Was a Con," *The Daily Beast* (June 2, 2016).

46 *Id.*

47 Michael Barbaro and Steve Eder, "At Trump University, Students Recall Pressure to Give Positive Reviews," *The New York Times* (March 11, 2016).

48 *Id.*

49 *Id.*

50 *Id.*

51 *Id.*

52 *Id.*

53 See "Trump & Women," p. 34.

54 Considering some of the ghouls and rogues who have been successful politicians, though, this term could be seen as unfair. Depending on your level of cynicism about government, Trump may be a perfect fit for office.

55 For a comprehensive compilation of Trump's epithets, see Jasmine C. Lee and Kevin Quealy, "The 289 People, Places, and Things Donald Trump Has Insulted On Twitter: A Complete List," *The New York Times* (Dec. 6, 2016).

56 Robert Mendick, "Donald Trump profile: How a ravenous desire for money, power and women was forged even before the president was born," *The Telegraph* (Nov. 9, 2016). Mendick points out that during his childhood Donald's share of the family trust fund was around $12,000 per year, meaning that "even as a baby, Trump enjoyed an income four times [that] of a typical family."

57 Ryan Grenoble, "This Photo Of A Trump Billboard In Mumbai Is Real, And So Is The Dark Irony," *The Huffington Post* (Dec. 31, 2016).

58 Maureen Dowd, "Liberties; Trump Shrugged," *The New York Times* (Nov. 28, 1999).

59 "Trump: The Least Charitable Billionaire," *The Smoking Gun* (April 12, 2011).

60 Quoted in David A. Fahrenthold, "Trump boasts about his philanthropy. But his giving falls short of his words," *The Washington Post* (Oct. 29, 2016).

61 *Id.*

62   David A. Fahrenthold, "Trump used $258,000 from his charity to settle legal problems," *The Washington Post* (Sept. 20, 2016).

63   Fahrenthold, *supra* note 60.

64   *Id.*

65   *Id.*

66   *Id.*

67   *Id.*

68   *Id.*

69   *Id.*

70   *Id.*

71   Brenner, *supra.*

72   Hurt, *supra*, at 18. See also Michael Kruse, "Donald Trump's Shortest Attribute Isn't His Fingers," *Politico* (Sept. 8, 2016).

73   Jane Mayer, "Donald Trump's Ghostwriter Tells All," *The New Yorker* (July 25, 2016).

74   Jonathan Chait, "Donald Trump Is A Lazy Idiot, Trump Campaign Tell New York *Times*," *New York* (Sept. 23, 2016).

75   Bob Cesca, "No, Mitch McConnell, we're not going to 'get past' it — the president your voters elected is a dangerous idiot," *Salon* (Jan 10, 2017).

76   E.g. Monica Potts, "Donald Trump's boorish behavior is bad for all women, even if some don't mind it," *The Washington Post* (May 18, 2016).

77   E.g. Jessica Samakow, "50 Ways Donald Trump Is Every Obnoxious Guy You've Ever Met," *The Huffington Post* (Oct. 3, 2016).

78   E.g. Colin Gorenstein, "Jon Stewart completely decimates Donald Trump: 'A rich, crazy, egotistical monster,'" *Salon* (July 21, 2015).

79   E.g. Jennifer Rubin, "Trump reminds us that he is a crude, mean boor," *The Washington Post* (Oct. 21, 2016).

80   E.g. Jesse Singal, "An Expert on Bullying Explains Donald Trump's Mean, Consequence-Free Rise," *New York* (Sept. 10, 2015).

81   E.g. Carlos Lozada, "Donald Trump: vain, greedy, and all-American," *The Washington Post* (Sept. 11, 2015).

82   E.g. Taylor Dibbert, "Donald Trump: Megalomaniac in Chief," *The Huffington Post* (Apr. 2, 2016).

83   E.g. Rupert Cornwell, "Donald Trump? The unlikely President whose ignorance is only outstripped by his arrogance," *The Independent* (Nov. 9, 2016).

84   Gwenda Blair, *Donald Trump: The Candidate* (Simon & Schuster, 2016), p. 89.

85   Quoted in Susan B. Glasser and Michael Kruse, "Trumpology: A Master Class," *Politico Magazine* (May/June 2016).

86   Look up the photo. It's absurd.

87   Maxwell Tani, "Trump: I'm a 'smart person,' don't need intelligence briefings every single day," *Business Insider* (Dec. 11, 2016).

88   Gideon Resnick, "Trump Won't Prove He Was a 'Super Genius' at Wharton," *The Daily Beast* (Sept. 21, 2015).

89   Quoted in Paul Schwartzman and Michael E. Miller, "Confident. Incorrigible. Bully. Little Donny was a lot like candidate Donald Trump," *The Washington Post* (June 22, 2016)/

90   *Id.*

91   *Id.*

92   Brenner, *supra* note 1. See also "Donald Trump was a horrible child who threw cake at birthday parties," *The Week* (Mar. 24, 2016).

93   Schwartzman and Miller, *supra*.

94   Nicole Brown, "Donald Trump's New York: From the president-elect's Queens roots to Manhattan legacy," *AMNewYork* (Nov. 28, 2016).

95   Marilyn Bender, "The Empire and Ego of Donald Trump," *The New York Times* (Aug. 7, 1983).

96   Nicholas Kristof, "The Black Eyes in Donald Trump's Life," *The New York Times* (Sept. 8, 2016).

97   James B. Stewart, "'Never Enough: Donald Trump and the Pursuit of Success,' by Michael D'Antonio," *The New York Times* (Sept. 10, 2015).

98   Schwartzman and Miller, *supra* note 89.

99   Hurt, *supra*, at 78.

100   Alisa Chang, "This Is Where Donald Trump Played By The Rules And Learned To Beat The Game," *NPR* (Nov. 10,

2015).

101   Lozada, *supra* note 81.

102   Glasser and Kruse, *supra* note 85.

103   Johnston, *supra* note 2, at 11.

104   Glasser and Kruse, *supra* note 85.

105   Brown, *supra* note 94.

106   "Meet young Donald Trump, a 'pioneer of self-promotion,'" *PBS NewsHour* (July 17, 2016).

107   Schwartzman and Miller, *supra* note 89.

108   *Id.*

109   *Id.*

110   Brenner, *supra* note 1.

111   *Id.*

112   Hurt, *supra*.

113   *Id.*, at 14.

114   Brenner, *supra* note 1.

115   Glasser and Kruse, *supra* note 85.

116   Kranish and Fisher, *supra* note 2, at 93.

117   Morris Kaplan, "Major Landlord Accused of Antiblack Bias in City," *The New York Times* (Oct. 16, 1973).

118   Lisa Belkin, "Be a killer, be a king: The education of Donald Trump," *Yahoo News* (July 16, 2016).

119   Lois Romano, "Donald Trump, Holding All The Cards," *The Washington Post* (Nov. 15, 1984).

120   *Id.*

121   Alexandra Berzon and Richard Rubin, "Trump's Father Helped GOP Candidate With Numerous Loans," *Wall Street Journal* (Sept. 23, 2016). The journal's report contradicts Trump's frequent claim that he only got $1 million from his father; in fact, Fred, Sr. was a source of considerably more financial support.

122   Charles V. Bagli, "A Trump Empire Built on Inside Connections and $885 Million in Tax Breaks," *The New York Times* (Sept. 17, 2016). Bagli also documents Donald Trump's relentless use of political connections to secure tax breaks for his properties, quoting New York's deputy mayor as saying "Donald Trump is probably worse than any other developer

in his relentless pursuit of every single dime of taxpayer sub-
sidies he can get his paws on."

123   Quoted in Glasser and Kruse, *supra*.

124   Allan Sloan, "From Father Fred to the Donald: Cashing
in Chips off the Old Block," *The Washington Post* (Jan. 29,
1991).

125   Max J. Rosenthal, "The Trump Files: The Shady Way Fred
Trump Tried to Save His Son's Casino," *Mother Jones* (Sept.
26, 2016).

126   Quoted in Glasser and Kruse, *supra*.

127   Thomas Kaplan, "Woody Guthrie Wrote of His Contempt
For His Landlord, Donald Trump's Father," *The New York
Times* (Jan. 25, 2016). Guthrie *really* hated Trump and wrote
multiple sets of lyrics about him. Another song contained
the line: "Well, well, Trump, you made a tramp out of me,
You charge me so much it just ain't human…" In a letter to
a friend, Guthrie wrote: "In addition to not being able to
enjoy one single day of normal or natural life in Mr. Trump's
project of buildings here on [account] of about ninety and
nine clauses in his damnable old tenant's contract, I find out
that I'm dwelling in the deadly center of a Jim Crow town
where no negroid families yet are allowed to move in and
to live freelike." Guthrie's words simultaneously support the
federal government's position that the Trumps deliberately
excluded blacks from renting their units *and* also suggest that
Fred Trump was one of the world's worst landlords. (And the
world is full of bad landlords.) See "Woody Guthrie Whacks
'Old Man Trump' Again In Another Recently-Discovered
Song," *Raw Story* (Sept. 6, 2016).

128   Nicholas Kristof, "Is Donald Trump A Racist?" *The New York
Times* (July 23, 2016).

129   *Id.*

130   *Id.*

131   Lozada, *supra*.

132   Sydney H. Schanberg, "New York: Doer and Slumlord Both,"
The New York Times (Mar. 9, 1985).

133   Jonathan Mahler, "Tenants Thwarted Donald Trump's Central Park Real Estate Ambitions," *The New York Times* (April
18, 2016).

134   Kranish and Fisher, *supra*, at 91.

135 Tony Schwartz, "A Different Kind of Donald Trump Story," *New York* (Feb. 11, 1985).

136 Mahler, *supra*.

137 Steven Wishnia, "How Rent-Stabilized Tenants Foiled Donald Trump," Metropolitan Council on Housing (April 2016).

138 Brenner, *supra*.

139 Blair, *supra,* at 312.

140 D'Antonio, *supra*, at 151.

141 Lozada, *supra*.

142 Selwyn Raab, "After 15 Years in Court, Workers' Lawsuit Against Trump Faces Yet Another Delay," *The New York Times* (June 14, 1998).

143 Brenner, *supra*.

144 Wayne Barrett, quoted in Glasser and Kruse, *supra* note 85.

145 David Cay Johnston, "Just What Were Donald Trump's Ties to the Mob," *Politico Magazine* (May 22, 2016).

146 Hurt, *supra* note 2, at 233.

147 Brenner, *supra*.

148 Mark Bowden, "Donald Trump Really Doesn't Want Me To Tell You This, But…" *Vanity Fair* (Dec. 10, 2015).

149 Quoted in Glasser and Kruse, *supra* note 85.

150 Laura Bult, "Remembering the failed 'wealth porn' Trump Magazine," *New York Daily News* (Feb. 11, 2016).

151 Max Abelson, "On the Rocks: The Story of Trump Vodka," *Bloomberg Businessweek* (Apr. 20, 2016).

152 Robert Frank, "Trump's product claims more sizzle than steak," *CNBC* (Mar. 9, 2016).

153 For a totally superfluous comprehensive history of the Trump Steaks venture, see Natasha Geiling, "A Definitive History of Trump Steaks™" *Think Progress* (Mar. 4, 2016).

154 Quoted in Glasser and Kruse, *supra* note 85.

155 See Ross Beuettner and Charles V. Bagli, "How Donald Trump Bankrupted His Atlantic City Casinos, but Still Earned Millions," *The New York Times* (June 11, 2016). For a report on how the casino bankruptcies hurt Trump's employees as Trump himself prospered from them, see Patrick Caldwell, "How Trump's Casino Bankruptcies Screwed His Work-

ers out of Millions in Retirement Savings," *Mother Jones* (Oct. 17, 2016).

156   Comedian Louis C.K. poignantly recalls an encounter with Trump at one of Trump's casinos, where C.K. observed that even though scores of people came to hand over their money to Trump, he showed no sign of joy or gratitude: "… Buses were showing up from all over the country with little old ladies…They take what little they have…They take that nothing, the little tiny scraps, and they turn it into chips and they pour buckets of money into his machines… He didn't say 'thank you' to anybody, he just walked around… and when I was in the elevator with him I just looked in his face, and he was just miserable looking. And everybody was so excited to see him, and they're giving him everything." Quoted in Amy Zimmerman, "Louis C.K. on the Time He Met the 'Real Trump': A 'Miserable,' Money-Grubbing Narcissist," *The Daily Beast* (Oct. 8, 2016).

157   Deborah Friedell, "Tycooniest," *The London Review of Books* (Oct. 22, 2015).

158   Donald J. Trump and Tony Schwartz, *The Art of the Deal* (Random House, 1987), p. 3.

159   Quoted in Christopher Howard, *Turning Passions Into Profits: Three Steps to Wealth and Power* (Wiley, 2005), p. 116.

160   Quoted in Glasser and Kruse, *supra* note 85.

161   Lozada, *supra*.

162   Michael Barbaro, "Pithy, Mean and Powerful: How Donald Trump Mastered Twitter for 2016," *The New York Times* (Oct. 5, 2015).

163   Andy Cush, "Remember Donald Trump's Freakish Obsession With Robert Pattinson and Kristen Stewart?" *Gawker* (July 14, 2016).

164   Daniella Diaz, "Trump defends tweet on military sexual assault," *CNN* (Sept. 8, 2016). Trump's professed concern with sexual assault is ironic. See next chapter.

165   "Donald Trump's most outrageous quotes," *The Week* (Aug. 18, 2016).

166   Pamela Engel, "Donald Trump taunts Jeb Bush for ditching his glasses in favor of contacts," *Business Insider* (Feb. 17, 2016).

167   Erin Carlson, "Donald Trump Calls Arianna Huffington

'Unattractive' in Twitter Rant," *The Hollywood Reporter* (Aug. 28, 2012).

168 "Cher mocks Donald Trump's hair, he disses her plastic surgery," *NBC News* (Nov. 14, 2012).

169 Barbaro, *supra* note 162.

170 *Id.*

171 Abby Ohlheiser, "A look at the 170 times Donald Trump has tweeted about the 'losers,'" *The Washington Post* (Sept. 22, 2016).

172 *Id.*

173 Eddie Scarry, "Donald Trump Addresses His 'Haters': 'They Were Born F*cked Up!'" *Mediaite* (Sept. 29, 2014).

174 Michael Barbaro, "Donald Trump Clung to 'Birther' Lie for Years, and Still Isn't Apologetic," *The New York Times* (Sept. 16, 2016).

175 Gregory Krieg, "14 of Trump's most outrageous 'birther' claims – half from after 2011," *CNN* (Sept. 16, 2016).

176 *Id.*

177 *Id.*

178 *Id.*

179 *Id.*

180 *Id.*

181 Kevin Cirilli, "Trump: Hack Obama's birth records," *The Hill* (Sept. 6, 2014).

182 Beth Fouhy, "Trump: Obama a 'Terrible Student' Not Good Enough for Harvard," *NBC News New York* (April 25, 2011).

183 Robert Farley, "Donald Trump says people who went to school with Obama never saw him," *PolitiFact* (Feb. 14, 2011).

184 Stephen Collinson and Jeremy Diamond, "Trump finally admits it: 'President Barack Obama was born in the United States,'" *CNN* (Sept. 16, 2016).

185 Quoted in Julie Baumgold, "Fighting Back: Trump Scrambles off the Canvas," *New York* (Nov. 9, 1992).

186 Tim Mak and Brandy Zadrozny, "Ex-Wife: Donald Trump Made Me Feel 'Violated' During Sex," *The Daily Beast* (July 27, 2015).

187   Michael Daly, "Why Was Marital Rape Legal in New York State Until 1984?" *The Daily Beast* (July 29, 2015).

188   Mak and Zadrozny, *supra* note 186. It is worth noting that Ivana Trump was bound by a confidentiality agreement signed as part of the divorce settlement, which prohibited her from speaking about her marriage to Donald, with immediate termination of her payments and benefits if she violated the highly restrictive gag order. See Rachel Stockman, "Donald Trump Even Made His Ex-Wife Ivana Sign Confidentiality Agreement, *LawNewz* (June 30, 2016). Donald's other ex-wife, Marla Maples, is bound by a similar agreement. In 1999, when Donald was considering a run for President, Maples told the press that "If he is really serious about being president and runs in the general election next year, I will not be silent… I will feel it is my duty as an American citizen to tell the people what he is really like." Trump's reaction, according to *BuzzFeed*, was "swift and brutal." Trump promised to take "very strong measures," since Maples was "not allowed to talk" per her agreement. He skipped an alimony payment and launched an assault on Maples in the press, intending to "send a message," maligning her intelligence and insisting that Maples was just looking for her "day in the sun." Trump's lawyer characterized Maples as a "woman scorned" and suggested her limited "mental capacity" made her inferior to Ivana. See Andrew Kaczynski, "Trump Withheld Alimony From Marla Maples When She Threatened His Presidential Ambitions," *BuzzFeed* (May 27, 2016).

189   Mak and Zadrozny, *supra* note 186.

190   *Id.*

191   Emily Crockett, "Donald Trump in 1994: I tell my friends to 'be rougher' with their wives," *Vox* (Oct. 14, 2016).

192   *Id.*

193   Brenner, *supra.*

194   *Id.*

195   *Id.*

196   Baumgold, *supra.*

197   "Transcript: Trump's Taped Comments About Women," *The New York Times* (Oct. 8, 2016).

198   Sarah K. Burris, "'He was relentless': Former business partner tells horrific story about Trump's attempt to rape her," *Raw Story* (Oct. 8, 2016).

199   *Id.*

200   Nicholas Kristof, "Donald Trump: Groper in Chief," *The New York Times* (Oct. 7, 2016).

201   *Id.*

202   *Id.*

203   Megan Twohey and Michael Barbaro, "Two Women Say Donald Trump Touched Them Inappropriately, *The New York Times* (Oct. 12, 2016).

204   Molly Redden, "Donald Trump 'grabbed me and went for the lips', says new accuser," *The Guardian* (Oct. 16, 2016).

205   Hallie Jackson and Alex Johnson, "Miss USA Contestant Details Unwanted Encounters With Trump," *NBC News* (Oct. 13, 2016).

206   Molly Redden, "Tenth woman accuses Donald Trump of sexual misconduct," *The Guardian* (Oct. 20, 2016).

207   Karen Tumulty, "Woman says Trump reached under her skirt and groped her in early 1990s," *The Washington Post* (Oct. 14, 2016).

208   Joe Capozzi, "Palm Beach Post exclusive: Local woman says Trump groped her," *The Palm Beach Post* (Oct. 12, 2016).

209   Natasha Stoynoff, "Physically Attacked by Donald Trump: A *People* Writer's Own Harrowing Story," *People* (Oct. 12, 2016).

210   Stephanie Petit, "Revealed: 6 People Who Corroborate Natasha Stoynoff's Story of Being Attacked by Donald Trump," *People* (Oct. 19, 2016).

211   "Ex-Miss Finland Accuses Trump of Groping Her in 2006," *The Daily Beast* (Oct. 27, 2016).

212   Tessa Stuart, "A Timeline of Donald Trump's Creepiness While He Owned Miss Universe," *Rolling Stone* (Oct. 12, 2016).

213   Quoted in Susan B. Glasser and Michael Kruse, "'I think He's a Very Dangerous Man for the Next Three or Four Weeks,'" *Politico Magazine* (Oct. 12, 2016).

214   Brandy Zadrozny and Tim Mak, "Trump Lawyer Bragged: I 'Destroyed a Beauty Queen's Life," *The Daily Beast* (July 31, 2015).

215   See "Revenge," p. 80.

216   Philip Bump, "Contrary to what Trump claims, none of his

accusers have been proved to be lying," *The Washington Post* (Oct. 24, 2016).

217   Jeremy Diamond and Daniella Diaz, "Trump on sex assault allegations: 'I am a victim,'" *CNN* (Oct. 15, 2016).

218   David A. Fahrenthold, "Trump recorded having extremely lewd conversation about women in 2005," *The Washington Post* (Oct. 8, 2016).

219   "Transcript: Trump's Taped Comments About Women," *The New York Times* (Oct. 8, 2016).

220   Trump laughably attempted to defend the tape as mere "locker room talk," leading scores of sanctimonious men to declare that nothing so dreadful would ever be overheard in *their* locker rooms. But even if America's locker-rooms do overflow with rapist braggadocio, this is an indictment of locker room culture rather than an exoneration of Trump. However widespread such practices may or may not be, Trump remains an unconvicted sex offender.

221   Michael Barbaro and Megan Twohey, "Crossing the Line: How Donald Trump Behaved With Women in Private," *The New York Times* (May 14, 2016).

222   Graydon Carter, "Donald Trump: The Ugly American," *Vanity Fair* (Nov. 2016).

223   *Id.*

224   David A. Fahrenthold, "New clips show Trump talking about sex, rating women's bodies, reminiscing about infidelity on Howard Stern's show," *The Washington Post* (Oct. 14, 2016).

225   Andrew Kaczynski, "Trump Weighing In On Kim Kardashian in 2013: Does She Have a Fat Ass? Absolutely," *BuzzFeed* (Nov. 30, 2015).

226   Tom Sykes, "Trump: 'I Could Have 'Nailed' Princess Diana,'" *The Daily Beast* (Feb. 26, 2016).

227   Kranish and Fisher, *supra* note 1, at 167.

228   Gwenda Blair, "Why Trump Survives," *Politico Magazine* (Aug. 10, 2015).

229   Neetzan Zimmerman, "Trump mocks Fiorina's physical appearance: 'Look at that face!'" *The Hill* (Sept. 9, 2015).

230   Mark Singer, *Trump and Me* (Tim Duggan Books, 2016), p. 69.

231   Theresa Avila, "Donald Trump Once Saw a 10-Year-Old and

Joked That He'd Be 'Dating Her in 10 Years,'" *New York* (Oct. 12, 2016).

232   Seema Mehta, "Tribune archive: Trump told 14-year-old girls, 'In a couple of years, I'll be dating you,'" *The Chicago Tribune* (Oct. 14, 2016).

233   Barbaro and Twohey, *supra*.

234   Adam Withnall, "Donald Trump's unsettling record of comments about his daughter," *The Independent* (Oct. 10, 2016).

235   Helin Jung, "Donald Trump Once Allegedly Asked If It Was 'Wrong' to be 'Sexually Attracted' to Ivanka," *Cosmopolitan* (Nov. 22, 2016).

236   Mitchel Maddux, "Fired losers lash 'sexist' Trump," *The New York Post* (Nov. 2, 2010).

237   Garance Burke, "'Apprentice' cast and crew say Trump was lewd and sexist," *Associated Press* (Oct. 3, 2016).

238   *Id.*

239   Seth Stevenson, "He's Obsessed With Menstruation: Former *Apprentice* crew members on their old boss, Donald Trump," *Slate* (June 16, 2016).

240   *Id.*

241   Maddux, *supra* note 236.

242   *Id.*

243   Tom Boggioni, "Penn Jilette: 'The way Trump talked about African-Americans on Celebrity Apprentice was 'distasteful,'" *RawStory* (Oct. 17, 2016).

244   Carlos Lozada, "Donald Trump on women, sex, marriage, and feminism," *The Washington Post* (Aug. 5, 2015).

245   Anna Silman, "Donald Trump Reportedly Sexually Harassed Female Cast and Crew on *The Apprentice*," *New York* (Oct. 3, 2016).

246   "A Timeline of Donald Trump's Creepiness While He Owned Miss Universe," *Rolling Stone* (Oct. 12, 2016).

247   Alex Heigl, "A Brief History of Donald Trump's *Letterman* Appearances, After the Retired Host Calls Him 'Damaged,'" *People* (Oct. 7, 2016).

248   Andrew Kaczynski and Nathan McDermott, "Donald Trump Said A Lot of Gross Things About Women on Howard Stern," *BuzzFeed* (Feb. 24, 2016).

249   Jessica Testa, Jessica Garrison, and Kendall Taggart, "Fifth Teen Beauty Queen Says Trump Visited Dressing Room," *BuzzFeed* (Oct. 13, 2016). 0

250   Yaron Steinbuch, "Former teen beauty queens: Trump barged in on us changing," *The New York Post* Oct. 12, 2016).

251   Claire Landsbaum, "'Don't Worry Ladies, I've Seen It All Before': Teen Pageant Contestants Say Donald Trump Walked In On Them Changing," *New York* (Oct.13, 2016).

252   Kendall Taggart, Jessica Garrison, and Jessica Testa, "Teen Beauty Queens Say Trump Walked In On Them Changing," *BuzzFeed* (Oct. 12, 2016).

253   *Id.* Ivanka has been criticized for adopting a public position as a feminist role model while providing cover for and implicitly endorsing/exonerating her father's behavior and policies.

254   Fred Barbash, "Former Miss Arizona: Trump 'just came strolling right in' on naked contestants," *The Washington Post* (Oct. 12, 2016).

255   Testa et al, *supra*.

256   Asawin Suebsaeng, "Donald Trump Told Miss Universe Alicia Machado: Do Sit-Ups Or You're Fired," *The Daily Beast* (Sept. 27, 2016).

257   Eliza Collins, "Donald Trump: It's fine to describe ex-Miss Universe as 'Miss Piggy,'" *USA Today* (Sept. 27, 2016).

258   Barbaro and Twohey, *supra*.

259   Ali Gharib, "In 1998, Trump said his record with 'the women' was too 'controversial' to run for president," *Fusion* (Oct. 13, 2016).

260   Steven Zeitchik, "Trump's 'Lady' comes to Fox," *Variety* (June 12, 2007).

261   Janell Ross, "So which women has Donald Trump called 'dogs' and 'fat pigs'?" *The Washington Post* (Aug. 8, 2015).

262   Daniel Politi, "Trump is OK With Calling Ivanka a 'Piece of Ass' and Other Horrible Things He Told Howard Stern," *Slate* (Oct. 8, 2016).

263   "Transcript: Trump's Taped Comments About Women," *The New York Times* (Oct. 8, 2016).

264   Ian Tuttle, "The Playboy Bully of the Western World," *National Review* (Feb. 22, 2016).

265   Jenna Johnson, "Trump's top example of foreign experience:

A Scottish golf course losing millions," *The Washington Post* (June 22, 2016). The quotation is Johnson's characterization of what Trump said at a news conference, not a direct report of Trump's exact wording from the news conference.

266   *Id.*

267   *Id.*

268   "Town Oks Trump golf resort in bird habitat," *Associated Press* (Nov. 21, 20017).

269   Peter Popham, "Tee'd off: The residents of Foveran Links speak out about Donald Trump's golf project," *The Independent* (July 14, 2012).

270   *Id.*

271   James Greenwood, "Trump Gives Scotland The Bird By Tearing Up Environmental Agreement," *GolfPunk* (Dec. 13, 2016).

272   *Id.*

273   Jamie Ross, "Watch How Donald Trump Treats People Who Work For Him," *BuzzFeed News* (Nov. 27, 2016).

274   Katrin Bennhold, "In Scotland, Trump Built a Wall. Then He Sent Residents the Bill," *The New York Times* (Nov. 25, 2016).

275   Anthony Baxter, "Donald Trump Deserves His Frosty Reception In Scotland," *The Guardian* (June 24, 2016).

276   Jen Yamato, "Meet a 92-Year-Old Woman Whose Life Was Ruined By Donald Trump," *The Daily Beast* (Oct. 26, 2016).

277   *Id.*

278   *Id.*

279   Anthony Baxter, "Why did it take Alex Salmond so long to turn on Donald Trump?" *The Guardian* (Dec. 20, 2015).

280   Yamato, *supra.*

281   Manuel Roig-Franzi, "The time Donald Trump's empire took on a stubborn widow – and lost," *The Washington Post* (Sept. 9, 2015).

282   John McCormack, "Trump: I Tried But Failed To Bulldoze Elderly Widow's Home for My Casino Parking Lot," *The Weekly Standard* (Jan. 24, 2016).

283   Baxter, *supra.*

284   Johnson, *supra.*

285   "Donald Trump: Robert Gordon University strips honorary degree," *BBC News* (Dec. 9, 2015).

286   Fraser McAlpine, "Donald Trump's Nemesis Michael Forbes Wins 'Scotsman of the Year,' *BBC America* (Dec. 2012).

287   Severin Carrell, "Mexican flags raised in view of Donald Trump's Scotland golf course," *The Guardian* (June 21, 2016).

288   Francesca Gillett, "Scottish MP Alex Salmond: Donald Trump 'showed sociopathic behavior when I met him,'" *Evening Standard* (Feb. 11, 2016). Trump and Salmond came into conflict over Trump's efforts to prevent a wind farm from being constructed near the golf course.

289   Stephanie Baker, "Trump Will Face Scottish Scorn on His Golf Trip," *Bloomberg* (June 22, 2016).

290   "Anthony Baxter on Donald Trump's Callous Capitalism," *BillMoyers.com* (Aug. 3, 2012). This is the Moyers show's summary of Baxter's characterization, not a direct quotation from Baxter himself.

291   Johnson, *supra*.

292   Popham, *supra*.

293   Yamato, *supra*.

294   Johnson, *supra*.

295   Jason M. Breslow, "The Frontline Interview: Tony Schwartz," *PBS Frontline* (Sept. 27, 2016).

296   Donald J. Trump with Meredith McIver, *How to Get Rich* (Random House, 2004), p. 35. Of course, since this is from one of Trump's books, one cannot assume that the words are actually his own. But he *did* read and approve them, presumably. Again, it's not clear what you can get from the books.

297   The brooch can be seen on the cover of: Ann Conover Heller, *Ayn Rand and the World She Made* (Anchor, 2010).

298   Max J. Rosenthal, "The Trump Files: Why Donald Called His 4-Year-Old Son a 'Loser,'" *Mother Jones* (Sept. 1, 2016).

299   Dylan Matthews, "Zero-sum Trump," *Vox* (July 7, 2016).

300   Trump and McIver, *supra* note 296, at 97. The actual quotation from the book is "Show me someone with no ego and I'll show you a big loser," but Trump himself quoted the above variation on Twitter.

301   Hurt, *supra* note 2, at 42.

302   *Id.*

303 *Id.* See also Seth Abramson, "Did Trump Lie About The Heli-copter Death of a Mormon Executive?" *The Huffington Post* (Nov. 2, 2016). Abramson points out that multiple biographers have investigated the helicopter story, each concluding that Trump did not have the near-death experience that he claimed to have had.

304 Max J. Rosenthal, "The Trump Files: Donald's Near-Death Experience (That He Invented)," *Mother Jones* (July 15, 2016).

305 Michael Kruse, "What Trump and Clinton Did on 9/11," *Politico Magazine* (Sept. 10, 2016).

306 *Id.*

307 O'Donnell, *supra*, at 200.

308 *Id.*

309 Blair, *supra*, at 455. Blair writes that "At his own father's funeral, he did not stop patting himself on the back and promoting himself. The first-person singular pronouns, the I and me and my, eclipsed the he and his."

310 D'Antonio, *supra,* at 204.

311 Baumgold, *supra.*

312 Donald J. Trump with Bill Zanker, *Think Big: Make It Happen In Business and Life* (HarperBusiness, 2008), p. 183.

313 David Corn, "Donald Trump Is Completely Obsessed With Revenge," *Mother Jones* (Oct. 19, 2016).

314 *Id.*

315 Alexander Burns, "Ignoring Advice, Donald Trump Presses Attack on Khan Family and G.O.P. Leaders," *The New York Times* (Aug. 2, 2016).

316 Trump and Zanker, *supra*, at 166.

317 Richard Branson, "Meeting Donald Trump," *Virgin.com* (Oct. 21, 2016).

318 *Id.*

319 Daniel Politi, "Salma Hayek Rejected Trump; He Planted a Story About Her in the *National Enquirer*," *Slate* (Oct. 22, 2016).

320 Heidi Evans, "Inside Trumps' Bitter Battle: Nephew's Ailing Baby Caught In The Middle," *The New York Daily News* (Dec. 19, 2000).

321 *Id.*

322   Ed Mazza, "Omarosa Manigault: 'Every Critic, Every Detractor, Will Have To Bow Down To President Trump,'" *The Huffington Post* (Sept. 22, 2016).

323   Quoted in O'Donnell, *supra* note 2. Trump later told *Playboy* that "The stuff O'Donnell wrote about me is probably true," before denying issue the remark two years later. See Glenn Kessler, "Did Donald Trump really say those things?" *The Washington Post* (July 25, 2016).

324   Scott Alexander, "You Are Still Crying Wolf," *SlateStarCodex* (Nov. 16, 2016).

325   Glasser and Kruse, *supra.*

326   Otto Friedrich, "Flashy Symbol of an Acquisitive Age: Donald Trump," *TIME* (Jan. 16, 1989).

327   Nick Paumgarten, "The Death and Life of Atlantic City," *The New Yorker* (Sept. 7, 2015).

328   Michael Kranish, "Trump's courtship of black voters hampered by decades of race controversies," *The Washington Post* (July 20, 2016).

329   Nicholas Kristof, "Is Donald Trump A Racist?" *The New York Times* (July 23, 2016).

330   O'Donnell, *supra.*

331   Erin Gloria Ryan, "Only Black Apprentice Winner: Trump Has Learned Nothing," *The Daily Beast* (Oct. 14, 2016).

332   Boggioni, *supra* note 243.

333   Asawin Suebsaeng, "Donald Trump Kept Calling Lil Jon an 'Uncle Tom' on Celebrity Apprentice," *The Daily Beaast* (Oct 14, 2016).

334   D. Watkins, "Original 'Apprentice' Star Kwame Jackson Says Donald Trump Is 'At His Core Racist,'" *Salon* (Oct. 12, 2016).

335   Sarah Burns, "Why Trump Doubled Down on the Central Park Five," *The New York Times* (Oct. 17th, 2016).

336   Jim Dwyer, "Telling Fact From Fiction in Campaign Rhetoric Fueled by Race," *The New York Times* (Mar. 8, 2016).

337   Joseph Tanfani, "Trump was once so involved in trying to block an Indian casino that he secretly approved attack ads," *The Los Angeles Times* (June 30, 2016).

338   Michael Saul, "Trump Faking Remorse on Ads: Town," *New York Daily News* (Dec. 23, 2000).

339   *Id.*

340   *Id.*

341   Tal Kopan, "What Donald Trump has said about Mexico and vice versa," *CNN* (Aug. 31, 2016).

342   Bianca E. Bersani and Alex R. Piquero, "Immigrants don't commit more crimes. Why does the myth persist?" *The Los Angeles Times* (Sept. 6, 2016). See also Bianca E. Bersani, "An Examination of First and Second Generation Immigrant Offending Trajectories," *Justice Quarterly*, (Vol. 31, Issue 2 (2014).

343   Brent Kendall, "Trump Says Judge's Mexican Heritage Presents 'Absolute Conflict,'" *The Wall Street Journal* (June 3, 2016).

344   Rachael Revesz, "Donald Trump still wants to ban Muslims from U.S. and build 'registry' despite backtracking after election," *The Independent* (Dec. 22, 2016).

345   Lozada, *supra.*

346   Brenner, *supra.*

347   William E. Geist, "The Expanding Empire of Donald Trump," *The New York Times* (Apr. 8, 1984).

348   Hurt, *supra,* at 103.

349   Trump and Schwartz, *supra,* at 58.

350   Harry G. Frankfurt, *On Bullshit* (Princeton University Press, 2005).

351   Daniel Dale and Tanya Talaga, "Donald Trump: The unauthorized database of false things," *The Toronto Star* (Nov. 4, 2016).

352   Brenner, *supra.*

353   Jay Hathaway, "Donald Trump's Grossly Exaggerated Net Worth: A Timeline," *Gawker* (June 18, 2015).

354   Dale and Talaga, *supra.*

355   *Id.*

356   *Id.*

357   Tal Kopan, "Donald Trump: I meant that Obama founded ISIS, literally," *CNN* (Aug. 12, 2016).

358   Brenner, *supra*.

359   *Id.*

360   Brenner, *supra*.

361   Eliza Collins, "Les Moonves: Trump's run is 'damn good for CBS,'" *Politico* (Feb. 29, 2016).

362   Christopher Lehmann-Haupt, "Books of the Times: The Art of the Deal," *The New York Times* (Dec. 7, 1987).

363   Quoted in Hurt, *supra* note 2, at 138.

364   Judy Klemsrud, "Donald Trump, Real Estate Promoter, Builds Image as he Buys Buildings," *The New York Times* (Nov. 1, 1976).

365   Quoted in Hurt, *supra*, at 136.

366   Klemsrud, *supra*.

367   Glenn Plaskin, "The Playboy Interview: Donald Trump," *Playboy* (1990).

368   *Id.*

369   Stewart, *supra*.

370   Yes, the same dynamic plagues this book. Yes, it is inevitable to some degree, and happens even if one tries to account for it consciously. No, I am not suggesting nobody ever write about Trump. However, I do think there are better and worse ways to cover him, and that some forms of criticism serve his interests.

371   Jane Mayer, "Donald Trump's Ghostwriter Tells All," *The New Yorker* (July 25, 2016).

372   Jim Rutenberg, "Megyn Kelly's Cautionary Tale of Crossing Donald Trump," *The New York Times* (Nov. 22, 2016).

373   See Chris Kelly, "What Donald Trump learned about politics from pro wrestling," *The Washington Post* (Nov. 11, 2016).

374   David Folkenflik, "Decades Later, 'Spy' Magazine Founders Continue to Torment Trump," *NPR Morning Edition* (March 7, 2016). See also Bruce Feirstein, "Trump's War on 'Losers': The Early Years," *Vanity Fair* (Aug. 12, 2015).

375   Hurt, *supra*, at 148.

376   By the way, the *Times* review of *The Art of the Deal* was not wrong that Trump exemplifies the American Dream. But it is not because Trump is a "Gatsby without flaws." It is, rather, because Trump's career, like the American Dream, is a swin-

dle, convincing people to believe in something that doesn't actually exist.

377   Friedell, *supra.*

378   *Id.*

379   Barrett, *supra,* at 9.

380   Friedell, *supra.*

381   Quoted in Glasser and Kruse, *supra.*

382   Stevenson, *supra.*

383   Marc Fisher and Will Hobson, "Donald Trump masqueraded as publicist to brag about himself," *The Washington Post* (May 13, 2016).

384   See, e.g. Gregory Krieg "Trump's still going wrong on Twitter," *CNN* (Dec. 21, 2016).

385   Michael O'Connell, "Jeff Zucker Talks Trump TV and CNN's Ratings Hot Streak: We've 'Outshined Everybody,'" *The Hollywood Reporter* (Oct. 27, 2016).

386   Hadas Gold, "Jeff Zucker has no regrets," *Politico* (Oct. 14, 2016).

387   *Id.*

388   Collins, *supra.*

389   McKay Coppins, "36 Hours on the Fake Campaign Trail With Donald Trump," *BuzzFeed* (Feb. 13, 2014).

390   *Id.*

391   D'Antonio, *supra*, at 343.

392   Olivia Nuzzi, "Trump to U.S.: 'I Am Rich,' Hire Me," *The Daily Beast* (June 16, 2015).

393   "Full text: Donald Trump announces a presidential bid," *The Washington Post* (June 16, 2015).

394   Igor Bobic, "Donald Trump Is Actually Running For President. God Help Us All." *The Huffington Post* (June 16, 2015).

395   Annie Karni and Adam B. Lerner, "Trump says he's running for president, really," *Politico* (June 16, 2015).

396   Andrew Ross Sorkin, "Trump's a Businessman, Where's His Business Backing," *The New York Times* (Sept. 26, 2016).

397   Mark Leibovich, "Donald Trump Is Not Going Anywhere," *The New York Times* (Sept. 29, 2015).

398   Ryan Grim, "A Note About Our Coverage of Donald Trump's

'Campaign,'" *The Huffington Post* (July 17, 2015).

399 John Cassidy, "Trump's Circus Will Damage the GOP," *The New Yorker* (June 17, 2015).

400 Jonathan Topaz and Daniel Strauss, "Trump bump terrifies GOP," *Politico* (June 26, 2015).

401 *Id.*

402 Jordan Chariton, "Donald Trump's 'Godly' Presidential Announcement Sparks Media Circus," *SFGate* (June 17, 2015).

403 "Clown Runs for Prez," *New York Daily News* (June 17, 2015).

404 Michael Reagan, "In the end, the joke will be on Trump," *The Athens Banner-Herald* (June 24, 2015).

405 Nate Silver, "Donald Trump's Six Stages of Doom," *FiveThirtyEight* (Aug. 6, 2015).

406 James Fallows, "3 Truths About Trump," *The Atlantic* (July 13, 2015).

407 John DiStaso, "WMUR/CNN Poll: Trump moves to within striking distance of GOP leader Bush," *WMUR* (June 25, 2015).

408 Heather Digby Parton, "We Must Take Donald Trump Seriously: Enough of the 'Fuckface von ClownStick,'" *Salon* (June 18, 2015).

409 Ben Schreckinger, "Trump Attacks McCain: 'I Like People Who Weren't Captured,'" *Politico* (July 18, 2015).

410 Conor Kelly, "What John McCain Went Through as a POW," *ABC News* (July 20, 2015).

411 Ashley Killough, "Trump: No regret over questioning McCain's heroism," *CNN* (May 11, 2016).

412 Michael Barbaro, Nate Cohn, and Jeremy Peters, "Why Trump Won't Fold," *The New York Times* (Aug. 23, 2015).

413 Nick Gass, "Study: Trump boosted, Clinton hurt by primary media coverage," *Politico* (June 14, 2016).

414 Thomas E. Patterson, "Pre-Primary News Coverage of the 2016 Presidential Race: Trump's Rise, Sanders' Emergence, Clinton's Struggle," Shorenstein Center on Media, Politics, and Public Policy, Harvard Kennedy School (June 13, 2016).

415 Caitlin MacNeal, "Donald Trump Compares Ben Carson to a 'Child Molester,'" *Talking Points Memo* (Nov. 13, 2015).

416 Nolan D. McCaskill, "Trump: Lindsey Graham a 'disgrace,' 'nut job,' 'one of the dumbest human beings,'" *Politico* (Feb. 17, 2016).

417 "Trump: Bush is 'poor, pathetic, low-energy guy,'" *The Washington Post* (Jan. 21, 2016).

418 Jacob Koffler, "Donald Trump Tweets Racially Charged Jab at Jeb Bush's Wife," *TIME* (July 6, 2015).

419 Alexis Levinson, "Jeb Bush Slams Trump: 'This Hurts the Republican Party,'" *National Review* (Aug. 8, 2015).

420 Nicholas Confessore and Sarah Cohen, "How Jeb Bush Spent $130 Million Running for President With Nothing to Show for It," *The New York Times* (Feb. 22, 2016).

421 Incidentally, it is well-remembered that Trump bragged about the size of his penis during a debate. Less noted is the fact that Marco Rubio was the one who put Trump's penis at issue, by making a joke about how men with "small hands" probably have other small features. The other candidates willingly played Trump's game, debasing themselves in the process and failing to do anything to undermine him.

422 Theodore Schleifer and Julia Manchester, "Donald Trump makes wild threat to 'spill the beans' on Ted Cruz's wife," *CNN* (Mar. 24, 2016).

423 "Trump: Rick Perry 'Put On Glasses So People Think He's Smart,'" *CBS DC* (July 22, 2015).

424 Will Doran, "Donald Trump set the record for the most GOP primary votes ever. But that's not his only record." *PolitiFact* (July 8th, 2016).

425 Bernie Sanders Interview, *The Charlie Rose Show* (Nov. 2016).

426 Marty Cohen, et al., *The Party Decides: Presidential Nominations Before and After Reform* (University of Chicago Press, 2008).

427 Julia Ioffe, "On the Lonely Island of 'Never Trump,'" *Politico Magazine* (May 17, 2016).

428 Tim Hains, "Trump's Updated ISIS Plan: 'Bomb the Shit Out of Them,' Send in Exxon to Rebuild," *RealClearPolitics* (Nov. 13, 2015).

429 "Lindsey Graham: Donald Trump is a 'race-baiting, xenophobic religious bigot,'" *The Week* (Dec. 8, 2015).

430 Arlette Saenz, "Rick Perry's Debate Lapse: 'Oops' – Can't Remember Department of Energy," *ABC News* (Nov. 9, 2011). Rick Perry would go on to become Secretary of the

very department whose name slipped his mind.

431   As a young man, Trump's family pastor was Norman Vincent Peale, the man who pioneered the "positive thinking" doctrine and was the progenitor of the "prosperity gospel." There is some good reason to believe that Peale contributed to Trump's adoption of the idea that if you wish for something hard enough and insist on its truth, it becomes true. Incidentally, Peale once hilariously described Trump as having "a profound streak of honest humility." See Marilyn Bender, "The Empire and Ego of Donald Trump," *The New York Times* (Aug. 7, 1983).

432   Matthews, *supra*.

433   Kelly Weill, "Everything Donald Trump Has Plagiarized," *The Daily Beast* (July 19, 2016).

434   "Jim Messina backs Hillary Clinton for 2016," Ronan Farrow Daily, *MSNBC* (Feb. 2, 2016).

435   "Hillary Racks up endorsements for 2016," *The Hill* (Apr. 15, 2015).

436   Chris Cillizza and Sean Sullivan, "Hillary Clinton is the biggest frontrunner for the Democratic presidential nomination ever. Yes, ever." *The Washington Post* (Jan. 30, 2014).

437   Justin Beach, "The Presidential Election Will Be Hillary's Coronation," *The Huffington Post* (Apr. 4, 2014).

438   Dana Milbank, "Democrats are not so fired up about Hillary Clinton," *The Washington Post* (Mar. 9, 2015).

439   *Id.*

440   Evan Halper, "Why Is Hillary Clinton Running For President? She'll Answer That At A New York Rally," *The Los Angeles Times* (June 11, 2015).

441   John Cassidy, "Bernie Sanders: A Man With A Cause," *The New Yorker* (June 1, 2015).

442   Michael A. Cohen, "Bernie Sanders will learn: Candor and winning campaigns don't mix," *The Boston Globe* (May 28. 2015).

443   Matthew Yglesias, "7 Reasons the Democratic Coalition is More Unified Than Ever," *Vox* (June 14, 2014).

444   Donald J. Trump, *Crippled America: How To Make America Great Again* (Threshold Editions, 2015).

445   Peter W. Stevenson, "A brief history of the 'Lock her up!'

chant by Trump supporters against Clinton," *The Washington Post* (Nov. 22, 2016).

446   Matt Taibbi, "The Fury and Failure of Donald Trump," *Rolling Stone* (Oct. 14, 2016).

447   See Isaac Arnsdorf, Josh Dawsey, and Daniel Lippman, "Will 'drain the swamp' be Trump's first broken promise?" *Politico* (Dec. 22, 2016).

448   Aaron Blake, "Newt Gingrich says Trump is done with 'drain the swamp,'" *The Washington Post* (Dec. 21, 2016). Trump soon chastised Gingrich for his disclosure, and Gingrich got back in line, posting a video to Twitter insisting: "I made a big boo-boo… [President-elect Trump] reminded me he likes draining the swamp… He intends to drain the swamp." (It

449   Rich Lowry, "No, the Swamp Won't Be Drained," *Politico Magazine* (Dec. 1, 2016).

450   Bruce Y. Lee, "Donald Trump's Sniffling Continues: Here Are The Possible Causes," *Forbes* (Oct. 9, 2016).

451   Liz Plank, "'Nasty Woman' becomes the feminist rallying cry Hillary Clinton was waiting for," *Vox* (Oct. 20, 2016).

452   Including me. See Appendix.

453   Nicholas Loffredo, "'SNL' Welcomes 'President Clinton' to 'Worst-Ever Presidential Debate,'" *Newsweek* (Oct. 15, 2016).

454   Pamela Engel, "New poll shows we're 'starting to there the faint rumblings of a Hillary Clinton landslide,'" *Business Insider* (Aug. 25, 2016).

455   Steven Shepard, "Democratic insiders near-certain of Clinton win," *Politico* (Nov. 8, 2016).

456   Harry Enten, "About A Third Of Bernie Sanders's Supporters Still Aren't Backing Hillary Clinton," *FiveThirtyEight* (Aug. 8, 2016).

457   Actually, since we know that Clinton's team did make nearly every decision on the basis of an algorithm, this is not as outlandishly implausible a scenario as it seems.

458   Jonathan Easley and Amie Parnes, "Hillary Clinton faces dilemma following 'deplorables' remark," *The Hill* (Sept. 15, 2016). Polling showed that voters had a *strong* negative reaction to the "deplorables" approach, with 2/3 of voters generally and even 47% of Democrats describing it as "unfair" to label a "large portion of Trump's supporters as prejudiced against women and minorities." See Aaron Blake, "Vot-

ers strongly reject Hillary Clinton's 'basket of deplorables' approach," *The Washington Post* (Sept. 26, 2016). Clinton told an adviser afterward that she knew she had "just stepped in it" by making the remark. Quoted in Amy Chozick, "Hillary Clinton's Expectations, and Her Ultimate Campaign Missteps," *The New York Times* (Nov. 9, 2016).

459   Chris Cillizza, "Why Mitt Romney's '47%' Comment Was So Bad," *The Washington Post* (Mar. 4, 2013).

460   "Full Text of James Comey's Letter On The New Clinton Emails," *USA Today* (Nov. 6, 2016). See also Bill Chappell, "FBI Affirms July Decision Not To Charge Clinton, After Review of Weiner Emails," *NPR* (Nov. 6, 2016).

461   Matt Flegenheimer, "Clinton to Ring in Election Under a Real 'Glass Ceiling': Manhattan's Javits Center," *The New York Times* (Oct. 26, 2016).

462   Not that these are mutually exclusive categories.

463   Brenner, *supra*. For more on Trump's performance at the dinner, see Sam Sanders, "At Al Smith Dinner, Donald Trump Turns Friendly Roast Into 3-Alarm Fire," *NPR* (Oct. 21, 2016).

464   Olivia Becker, "Bad at jokes: Trump somehow bombed at charity dinner," *Vice* (Oct. 21, 2016); Michael Daly, "Donald Trump, Son of a Catholic Hater, Disgraces Al Smith Dinner," *The Daily Beast* (Oct. 21, 2016). But see how it could appear to Trump supporters: Charlie Spiering, "Wealthy New York Elite Boo Donald Trump At Al Smith Dinner," *Breitbart* (Oct. 21, 2016).

465   Adam Edelman, "Rubio teases Trump about spray-tan, size of his hands," *New York Daily News* (Feb. 29, 2016).

466   A.J. Vicens, "Trump on His Penis: 'I Guarantee You There's No Problem,'" *Mother Jones* (Mar. 3, 2016).

467   Jessie Hellmann, "Rubio apologized to Trump for 'small hands' crack," *The Hill* (May 29, 2016).

468   Will Wilkinson, "Because You'd Be In Jail," *The New York Times* (Oct. 9, 2016).

469   "Watch: Megyn Kelly Challenges Trump on Derogatory Comments About Women," *Fox News* (Aug. 6, 2015).

470   Grace Guarnieri, "Donald Trump downplays leaked audio clip about women: 'Bill Clinton has said far worse,'" *Salon* (Oct. 7, 2016).

471   Daniella Diaz and Jeff Zeleny, "Trump appears with Bill Clinton accusers before debate," *CNN* (Oct. 10, 2016).

472   Eric Posner, "Trump, the Great Communicator." *EricPosner. com* (Dec. 6., 2016).

473   Ben Dolnick, "No One Understands Trump Like The Horny Narcissist Who Created *Dilbert*," *Slate* (Sept. 30, 2016).

474   Donald J. Trump, "Remarks on the Clinton Campaign of Destruction, " West Palm Beach, (Oct. 13, 2016).

475   These are paraphrased summaries of the respective candidates' philosophies, not direct quotations.

476   See Brendan O'Connor, "How the DNC Decided on 'Dangerous Donald,'" *Gawker* (July 25, 2016). *Gawker's* Alex Pareene pointed out how unwise this form of messaging was: *"Did they try testing 'Sexy Donald' first? 'Leather Jacket Donald'?... The problem with that line of argument is that it's Donald Trump's argument for his candidacy: Conventional politicians and conventional politics haven't worked—so take a gamble on the ultimate outsider... They're going to build Trump up as a reckless and virile force of nature—and a true outsider—rather than expose him as a pitiful clown and an obvious fraud. This is completely backwards. As any writer who's ever received an angry personal response from Trump can tell you, you get under his skin by mocking and emasculating him, not by feeding the myth of his power and strength."*

477   Donald J. Trump, "Remarks on the Clinton Campaign of Destruction, " West Palm Beach, (Oct. 13, 2016).

478   Callum Borchers, "Donna Brazile is totally not sorry for leaking CNN debate questions to Hillary Clinton," *The Washington Post* (Nov. 7, 2016).

479   Donald J. Trump, "Remarks on the Clinton Campaign of Destruction, " West Palm Beach, (Oct. 13, 2016).

480   For example: Hillary Clinton's speeches included the line "we send a clear message: America is better than this. America is better than Donald Trump." A word of wisdom: never declare "We're better than this." If you're at the point where you have to make the plea, then we probably aren't, in fact, better than this.

481   Mathew Ingram, "How Donald Trump Took Advantage of a Broken Media Landscape," *Fortune* (Nov. 7, 2016).

482   Louis Nelson, "Conway: Judge Trump by what's in his heart, not what comes out of his mouth," *Politico* (Jan. 9, 2017).

483   Brenner, *supra*.

484   Sean McElwee, Matt McDermott, and Will Jordan, "4 pieces of evidence showing FBI Director James Comey cost Clinton the election," *Vox* (Jan 11, 2017). Note that the authors make the same logical error as those blaming Nader for Bush: they prove that a factor made enough of a difference in the outcome to have changed it, and then conclude that it was the factor that caused the outcome. In doing so, they do not make a case for why we should focus on this *single* factor among the many similar single factors that also made the difference. For example, if we can equally well make the case that Comey's letter *and* Hillary Clinton's strategic mistakes made decisive differences in the outcome, we need a theory for why we are going to focus on the Comey letter as "the" cause. Democrats consistently choose the but-for causes they *want* to blame, rather than accepting the full range of but-for causes and focusing on the ones that they had control over.

485   Chris Cillizza, "In an alternate universe, this Obamacare news is absolutely devastating for Hillary Clinton," *The Washington Post* (Oct. 25, 2016).

486   There are more reasons to believe that it was not wholly Comey's letter that caused the late switch to Trump. Rather than simply relying on numbers, *The Huffington Post* actually (gasp!) talked to some voters, in order to found out what they were thinking in breaking for Trump at the last minute. The *Post* did not find the Comey letter to be the dominant reason people gave. In fact, to the extent that it was a factor, some even suggested that it was the Democrats' outraged *response* to the letter that made Clinton look worse than the letter itself. As one reported: "The letter itself didn't phase me or move me either way on Clinton. But her reaction to it kind of solidified it... If I wanted to say when I knew for sure, it was when they started attacking Comey for doing his job in the weekend prior to the election." Sam Stein, "Did James Comey Cost Hillary Clinton the Election? We Asked the Late-Deciding Voters," *The Huffington Post* (Dec. 27, 2016).

487   For this perspective, see for example, *The Nation*'s Joan Walsh, who wrote: "It's been two months since the election. If you're still fighting the Democratic primary from either side you're part of the problem." Quoted in Michael Tracey, "Actually Yes, Let's Keep Litigating the Democratic Primary," *Medium* (Jan. 8, 2017).

488   Amy Chozick and Jonathan Martin, "Where Has Hillary

Clinton Been? Ask The Ultrarich," *The New York Times* (Sept. 3, 2016).

489   "Hillary Clinton speaks to estimated crowd of 10,000," *The Arizona Republic* (Nov. 2, 2016). The paper called Clinton "the first Democratic presidential nominee to run competitively in Arizona in 20 years." Certainly, Clinton was the first Democrat in 20 years to be deluded enough to think that Arizona was worth campaigning in for any reason (after all, if Arizona was competitive enough to where she could win it, then she would already have won the election).

490   Michael Squires, "Tim Kaine to rally Hillary Clinton Supporters in Tuscon, Phoenix on Thursday," *The Arizona Republic* (Oct. 30, 2016).

491   Pamela Engel, "Clinton never set foot in Wisconsin – then she lost it, and it helped cost her the presidency," *Business Insider* (Nov. 9, 2016).

492   Edward-Isaac Dovere, "How Clinton lost Michigan—and blew the election," *Politico* (Dec. 14, 2016).

493   *Id.*

494   Jim Tankersley, "The advertising decisions that helped doom Hillary Clinton," *The Washington Post* (Nov. 12, 2016).

495   Dovere, *supra.*

496   *Id.*

497   *Id.*

498   *Id.*

499   *Id.*

500   See Jessica Arp, "Why Hasn't Clinton come to Wisconsin? Here are some theories," *WISC News 3 Madison* (Oct. 31, 2016). There were plans to hold a joint event with Clinton and Barack Obama in Green Bay during June, but after the mass shooting in Orlando the event was "postponed," never to be rescheduled. Katie Delong, "Campaign event involving Hillary Clinton, Pres. Obama in Green Bay postponed," *Fox 6 Now* (June 12, 2016).

501   Also, why the *hell* did the HQ have to be in in Brooklyn of all places to begin with?

502   Asawin Suebsaeng, "Team Bernie: Hillary 'F*cking Ignored' Us in Swing States," *The Daily Beast* (Dec. 20, 2016).

503   *Id.*

504   Michael Moore, "5 Reasons Why Trump Will Win," *Michael-Moore.com* (July 21, 2016).

505   *Id.*

506   Shane Goldmacher, "Hillary Clinton's 'Invisible Guiding Hand,'" *Politico Magazine* (Sept. 7, 2016).

507   *Id.*

508   *Id.*

509   *Id.*

510   John Wagner, "Clinton's data-driven campaign relied heavily on an algorithm named Ada. What didn't she see?" *The Washington Post* (Nov. 9, 2016).

511   Ricky Kreitner, "Wall Street Responsible For One-Third of Obama's Campaign Funds," *Business Insider* (July 22, 2011); John Carney and Anupreeta Das, "Hedge Fund Money Has Vastly Favored Clinton Over Trump," *The Wall Street Journal* (July 29, 2016).

512   Daniel Strauss, "Clinton haunted by coal country comment," *Politico* (May 10, 2016). Strauss reports that "When officials in Logan, West Virginia, were contacted last week about hosting Hillary Clinton for a local rally, it didn't take long for them to respond with an answer: Hell no." The officials wrote a letter saying that "Mrs. Clinton's anti-coal messages are the last thing our suffering town needs at this point. The policies that have been championed by people like Mrs. Clinton have all but devastated our fair town."

513   Lindsey Cook, "Here's Who Paid Hillary Clinton $22 Million in Speaking Fees," *U.S. News & World Report* (Apr. 22, 2016); Robert Yoon and Dan Merica, "Clintons earned more than $6.7 million from paid speeches in 2015," *CNN* (May 18, 2016).

514   Jacob Sullum, "Clinton Lies About Lying About Her Lies," *Reason* (Nov. 2, 2016).

515   Jonah Walters, "Can They Count?" *Jacobin* (Nov. 29, 2016).

516   "Election 2016 Results," *The Guardian* (Nov. 8, 2016).

517   Jeffrey M. Jones, "The Nader Factor," *Gallup* (Feb. 26, 2004).

518   Paul Krugman, "Our Unknown Country," *The New York Times* (Nov. 8, 2016).

519   It is also an extremely discouraging story, because it suggests that the majority of voters are bad, nasty, *deplorable* people, totally beyond salvation.

520   David Masciotra, "White flight from reality: Inside the racist panic that fueled Donald Trump's victory," *Salon* (Nov. 12, 2016).

521   Sean McElwee, "Yep, race really did Trump economics: A data dive on his supporters reveals deep racial animosity," *Salon* (Nov. 13, 2016).

522   For another example, see Carol Anderson, "Donald Trump Is The Result of White Rage, Not Economic Anxiety," *TIME* (Nov. 16, 2016).

523   Jed Kolko, "Trump Was Stronger Where The Economy Is Weaker," *FiveThirtyEight* (Nov. 10, 2016).

524   Ben Casselman, "Stop Saying Trump's Win Had Nothing To Do With Economics," *FiveThirtyEight* (Jan. 9, 2017).

525   Susan Chira, "'You Focus On The Good': Women Who Voted for Trump, in Their Own Words," *The New York Times* (Jan. 14, 2017).

526   Note that the voter draws a distinction between Clinton and Sanders in this respect. Another small piece of evidence that Bernie would have won.

527   Jamelle Bouie, "There's No Such Thing As A Good Trump Voter," *Slate* (Nov. 15, 2016).

528   Fredrik deBoer, "Ok, Let's Get Constructive," *FredrikdeBoer. com* (Jan. 10, 2017). Unfortunately, this kind of universal empathy often proves difficult for Democrats. A particularly horrifying example came from Markos Moulitsas, founder of the progressive *Daily Kos* blog. After the election, he wrote an article on why Democrats should celebrate people losing their health insurance under Trump, since the poor whites who stood to lose insurance probably voted Republican. Being pleased by the suffering of others, no matter how foolish or prejudiced you think they are, should never be considered "progressive." Markos Moulitsas, "Be happy for coal miners losing their health insurance. They're getting exactly what they voted for," *Daily Kos* (Dec. 12, 2016).

529   This is not to say that there are not plenty of Democrats who *do* know lots of Trump voters. America is a big place, and every generalization and its opposite are usually true to one degree or another.

530   Christine Wang, "Michael Moore says Trump is a 'human Molotov cocktail' supporters get to throw," *CNBC* (Nov. 4, 2016).

531   See Mona Chalabi, "Young women are feminists – but that doesn't mean they'll vote Hillary Clinton," *The Guardian* (Feb. 8, 2016). Chalabi pointed out that some millennial women are actually put off by appeals to vote based on gender, seeing it as patronizing. This was especially seen in the backlash that occurred when Clinton supporter Madeleine Albright said there was a "special place in hell" for women who didn't support women, and Gloria Steinem suggested that young women who supported Bernie Sanders were doing so because they were trying to impress boys.

532   Elizabeth Preza, "'Trump That Bitch' Takes Over as a Favorite Slogan of the Trump Hordes," *AlterNet* (Apr. 26, 2016); Claire Landsbaum, "The Most Misogynistic Gear Spotted at Trump Rallies," *New York* (Oct. 12, 2016). Some of the slogans worn were truly appalling, including "She's a cunt, vote for Trump" and "Hillary Couldn't Satisfy Her Husband, She Can't Satisfy Us" (the latter being worn by a *female* Trump supporter).

533   Lucy Clarke-Billings, "Hillary Clinton's Voter Gender Gap Largest Since Exit Poll Surveys Began," *Newsweek* (Nov. 10, 2016).

534   "Letters: As the Democrats Lick Their Wounds," *The New York Times* (Nov. 14, 2016).

535   "Wisconsin primary results," *The Guardian* (April 5, 2016).

536   Another "pragmatic" argument made against Sanders is that his agenda was "too extreme" for the mainstream of American voters to accept. Kevin Drum of *Mother Jones* makes this argument, suggesting that Sanders would have lost "in a landslide" because he is far too the left of the Democratic candidates who have been successful in previous election. The idea here is that only moderates win elections. This argument is a curious one, coming as it does immediately after the election of one of the *least mainstream* presidents in American history; if you need to be moderate to be successful, it's difficult to explain the success of Donald J. Trump.

537   Jim Geraghty, "Chuck Schumer: Democrats Will Lose Blue-Collar Whites But Gain in the Suburbs," *National Review* (July 28, 2016).

538   Quoted in Amy Chozick, "Hillary Clinton's Expectations, and Her Ultimate Campaign Missteps," *The New York Times*

(Nov. 9, 2016).

539   What of Theda Skocpol's other charge? That Sanders damaged Clinton, and in doing so bore responsibility for her loss in the general election. We do know that the Democratic primary was highly contentious, and that Sanders vigorously criticized Clinton for her Wall Street ties, Iraq War vote, friendship with Henry Kissinger, and support of the Trans-Pacific Partnership. Surely, goes this argument, by attacking Clinton on these issues for month after month, Sanders eroded support that would otherwise have gone to her, and in doing so made her a weaker general election candidate than she otherwise would have been. This may actually be factually true, insofar as *if* Sanders had never run, Clinton may have coasted to victory easily in the primary, and been better position for the general election (which was, of course, close, meaning that small things mattered). But recognize what this belief means: it means that there should *not* have been an opportunity for progressive Democrats to bring up issues like the social welfare system, economic inequality, Iraq, and Wall Street. There were, as Jeff Stein writes, "huge and obvious gaps between the candidates over taxes, foreign policy, healthcare, and a host of other critical policy issues." Jeff Stein, "The DNC race has become another fight over Bernie Sanders when Dems need it least," *Vox* (Dec. 30, 2016). If we believe Sanders shouldn't have run, we believe that these matters should never have been given a public airing, that people who do not share Hillary Clinton's politics should not have gotten to vote for a candidate whose politics they do share, and that the Democratic party should be free of *any* input through the voting process into what values it should represent. In the event, Sanders' candidacy forced Hillary Clinton to adopt far more progressive positions than she otherwise would have had (including advocating minimum wage increases and a free college proposal). Without Sanders, those in the progressive wing of the Democratic Party would have no voice in what the party stood for.

540   Debbie Dingell, "I said Clinton was in trouble with the voters I represent. Democrats didn't listen." *The Washington Post* (Nov. 10, 2016). Dingell also gave further credence to the "economic anxiety" theory. She says she repeatedly tried to warn national Democrats that the voters in her district were hurting and would resent attempts to treat them as if they didn't matter or could be taken for granted. But she says that there was a reluctance to listen. Dingell told President

Obama: "Mr. President, with all due respect, many of these workers don't translate what you have done to them. They don't feel better off. Their real wages have not risen in decades, and in fact for many it has dropped. They have less purchasing power; their health insurance costs more; they don't trust their pensions to be there; and because we are a cyclical industry, they are frightened that something bad could happen at any time. Add to that, trade deals that they view as shipping jobs overseas and threatening the ones they have here. Top it off with fear about national security and potential threats at workplaces or movie theaters and you have workers who are scared, worried and concerned in their hearts and souls."

541   Rachel Larimore, "Note to Democrats: Don't Run The Candidate Whose Turn It Is," *Slate* (Nov. 11, 2016).

542   Because she isn't.

543   "Economic Report of the President Together With The Annual Report of the Council of Economic Advisers" (Feb. 2016).

544   Stephen Grocer, "Stock Market Rallied in 2016, IPO Market Didn't," *The Wall Street Journal* (Dec. 27, 2016).

545   Matthew Friedman, Ames Grawert, and James Cullen, "Crime in 2016: A Preliminary Analysis," Brennan Center for Law and Justice (Sept. 19, 2016).

546   Dan Mangan, "Record number of Obamacare sign-ups on HealthCare.gov for 2017 health insurance coverage," *CNBC* (Dec. 21, 2016).

547   Lawrence F. Katz and Alan B. Kreuger, "The Rise and Nature of Alternative Work Arrangements in the United States, 1995-2015" (2016).

548   "The State of Housing in Black America," National Association of Real Estate Brokers (2013).

549   Sarah Burd-Sharps and Rebecca Rasch, "Impact of the US Housing Crisis on the Racial Wealth Gap Across Generations," Social Science Research Council (2015).

550   Rakesh Kochhar and Richard Fry, "Wealth inequality has widened along racial, ethnic lines since end of Great Recession," *Pew Research Center* (Dec. 12, 2014).

551   Jeff Guo, "America has locked up so many black people it has warped our sense of reality," *The Washington Post* (Feb. 26, 2016).

552   Annamaria Lusardi, "The Alarming Facts About Millennials

and Debt," *The Wall Street Journal* (Oct. 5, 2015).

553   Jessica Dickler, "US Households now have over $16,000 in credit card debt," *CNNC* (Dec. 13, 2016).

554   Taylor Tepper, "Americans Are Sinking Further Into Credit Card Debt," *TIME* (Dec. 9, 2015).

555   Federica Cocco, "Most US manufacturing jobs lost due to technology, not trade," *The Financial Times* (Dec. 2, 2016).

556   Alana Semuels, "Ghost Towns of the 21st Century," *The Atlantic* (Oct. 21, 2015).

557   Chris McGreal, "Financial despair, addiction, and the rise of suicide in white America," *The Guardian* (Feb. 7, 2016).

558   Dan Keating and Kennedy Elliott, "Why death rates for white women in rural America are spiking," *The Washington Post* (Apr. 9, 2016); Janet Adamy, "Rising Death Rates for Middle-Aged White Americans Are Forcing a Policy Rethink," *The Wall Street Journal* (June 30, 2016).

559   Adam Gaffney, "How Class Kills," *Jacobin* (Nov. 8, 2015).

560   "Inside a Killer Drug Epidemic: A Look At America's Opioid Crisis," *The New York Times* (Jan. 6, 2017).

561   Sabrina Tavernise, "U.S. Suicide Rate Surges to a 30-Year High," *The New York Times* (Apr. 22, 2016). For more on the link between economics and suicide, see Nathan J. Robinson, "Suicide and the American Dream," *Current Affairs* (July/Aug. 2016).

562   Dan O'Sullivan, "Vengeance is Mine," *Jacobin* (Nov. 18, 2016).

563   Hibah Yousuf, "Obama admits 95% of income gains gone to top 1%," *CNN* (Sept. 15, 2013).

564   Bourree Lam, "The Recovery's Geographic Disparities," *The Atlantic* (Feb. 26, 2016).

565   *Id.*

566   Zac Auter, "Americans Continue to Cite the Economy as Top Problem," *Gallup* (Oct. 14, 2016).

567   Bruce Drake, "Public opinion on the economy and Obama's handling of it," *Pew Research Center* (Jan. 20, 2015).

568   Jeff Guo, "Death Predicts Whether People Vote For Donald Trump," *The New York Times* (Mar. 4, 2016).

569   Eduardo Porter, "Where Were Trump's Votes? Where The Jobs Weren't" *The New York Times* (Dec. 13, 2016).

570   See Stephen Wolf, "Republicans now dominate state government, with 32 legislatures and 33 governors," *DailyKos* (Nov. 14, 2016). Wolf points out that Republicans now "have total control over 25 states outright and another two where they can override a Democratic governor's veto." Democrats, on the other hand, have control over only 8 states. That means Republicans have control in states containing 56 percent of the population, while Democrats have control of states containing 19 percent of the population. See also Kyle Cheney and Ben Schreckinger, "Diminishing Democratic governors look for answers," *Politico* (Feb. 22, 2015). Cheney and Schreckinger talk to the remaining Democratic governors, asking them why they feel their party is losing. Notably, the governors blame "bad luck, bad timing, and an unpopular president." However, "none of [their theories] are about the substance of the party's policies." The governors' assessments are worrying, because they suggest that there is no inclination whatsoever on the part of Democrats to look inward and see if they ought to be doing things differently. Rather, they are waiting for "timing" to shift and for a Republican president against whom Democrats can rally.

571   James Oliphant, "Democrats search for answers to stem a spreading Republican," *Reuters* (Nov. 23, 2016).

572   Nicole Narea and Alex Shephard, "The Democrats' Biggest Disaster," *The New Republic* (Nov. 22, 2016). Incidentally, the last time Republicans controlled both houses of the U.S. Congress and the Presidency was 1928, a fact Ann Coulter excitedly noted on Election Night without pausing to recall what proceeded to happen one year later in 1929.

573   Matthew Yglesias, "Democrats are in denial. Their party is actually in deep trouble." *Vox* (Oct. 19, 2015). For more on the steadily unfolding calamity, see Mara Liasson, "The Democratic Party Got Crushed During the Obama Presidency. Here's Why," *NPR* (March 4,2016); Jamelle Bouie, "Down and Out: The Democratic Party's losses at the state level are almost unprecedented, and could cripple it for a long time to come," *Slate* (Dec. 11, 2014).

574   Chris Cillizza, "President Obama may not have destroyed the Democratic Party. But he hurt it real bad." *The Washington Post* (Dec. 29, 2016).

575   Tim Hains, "Sam Stein: Obama Oversaw The Destruction Of The Democratic Party," *RealClearPolitics* (Dec. 29, 2016).

576   Quoted in Narea and Shephard, *supra*.

577   Michael Grunwald, "The Nation He Built," *Politico* (Jan. 7, 2016).

578   *Id.*

579   Sean McElwee, "Obama-to-Trump voters are not a myth—but they're also not the real story," *Salon* (Nov. 27, 2016).

580   *Id.*

581   Hal Walker, "The Front of the Classroom," *Medium* (Dec. 17, 2016).

582   Thomas Frank, *Listen Liberal* (Metropolitan Books, 2016).

583   For more on how Democrats since the 1970s have consciously abandoned traditional anti-monopolist and populist policies, see Matthew Stoller, "How The Democrats Killed Their Populist Soul," *The Atlantic* (Oct. 24, 2016).

584   Tim Dickinson, "No We Can't," *Rolling Stone* (Feb. 2, 2010).

585   Nicholas Fandos, "Hillary Clinton Speaks Favorably About $12 Minimum Wage," *The New York Times* (July 30, 2015).

586   Bryce Covert, "Hillary Clinton Widens Her Embrace Of A $15 Minimum Wage," *ThinkProgress* (Apr. 15, 2016).

587   Jason Delisle and Rooney Columbus, "Working for Free College," *U.S. News & World Report* (Sept. 13, 2016). See also: Nick Gass, "Clinton knocks Sanders' College plan: Trump's kids shouldn't get free ride," *Politico* (Oct. 5, 2015).

588   Stephanie Saul and Matt Flegenheimer, "Hillary Clinton Embraces Ideas From Bernie Sanders's College Tuition Plan," *The New York Times* (July 6, 2016).

589   "Interview with Doug Henwood," *The Katie Halper Show* (Jan. 7, 2017).

590   Daniella Silva, "Dakota Access Pipeline: More Than 100 Arrested as Protesters Ousted From Camp," *NBC News* (Oct. 28, 2016).

591   Bill McKibben on Twitter https://twitter.com/billmckibben/status/791821838708072448

592   Clare Foran, "Hillary Clinton's Intersectional Politics," *The Atlantic* (Mar. 9, 2016). See also Kali Holloway, "Hillary Clinton Tries To Grasp 'Intersectionality' to Understand the Mix of Race, Gender, and Class – Does She Get It?" *AlterNet* (Mar. 14, 2016).

593   Kevin Liptak, "Biden: Clinton never figured out why she was running," *CNN* (Dec. 23, 2016). Barack Obama, too,

has issued veiled criticisms of Clinton's campaign in the days after the election, especially focusing on the failure to take seriously the need to persuade voters in rural areas. Obama has pointed out that unlike Clinton, he "won Iowa… not because the demographics dictated that I would win Iowa. It was because I spent 87 days going to every small town and fair and fish fry and VFW Hall…" Aaron Blake, "Did President Obama Just Dis Hillary Clinton's Campaign?" *The Washington Post* (Nov. 15, 2016).

594   Brooke Seipel, "Anthony Bourdain on Trump win: People were sick of 'privileged' liberals," *The Hill* (Dec. 31, 2016).

595   Hal Walker, "The Front of the Classroom," *Medium* (Dec. 17, 2016). Walker's article is worth reading in its entirety; he explains concisely how Democrats have come to adopt variations on Republican meritocratic mythology, and become a party of A-students who believes that everyone else should be an A-student as well. As Walker concludes: *"Education is presented as a solution to every problem. Breaking down barriers to the top of the ladder of success becomes the primary civil rights issue. Women and minorities who are not striving for elite positions do not merit so much consideration… [And] what should be a progressive politics becomes just another version of the bootstraps myth, with grades and scholarships standing in for sweat and prudent personal budgeting."*

596   Sabrina Tavernise, "Many in Milwaukee Neighborhood Didn't Vote – And Don't Regret It," *The New York Times* (Nov. 20, 2016).

597   Carly Mallenbaum, "Not-so-famous celebrities speak at Trump convention," *USA Today* (July 19, 2016); Marlow Stern, "Scott Baio Hand-Picked by a Desperate Trump to Speak at His D-List RNC," *The Daily Beast* (July 17, 2016).

598   Daniella Diaz, "*West Wing* Cast To Campaign for Clinton," *CNN* (Sept. 21, 2016).

599   The racial diversity of the ads' participants is important. The criticism here is *not* that the campaign against Trump failed to appeal to the *white* working class specifically, but to workers *generally*. In fact, that is the problem with *so* much of the public response to Trump's remarks on Mexicans. How much of it has come from Mexican immigrants themselves, rather than rich people offended on their behalf? Democrats should have flooded the airwaves with videos of immigrant families talking about their lives and struggles. Now, I don't want to have to say this, but Bernie Sanders prepared almost *exactly* this kind of ad in the primary…

600   The original advertisement is now unavailable but was previously found at this YouTube address: https://www.youtube.com/watch?v=niUXUx1hD4E

601   Ben Shapiro, "Celebrities Cut Anti-Trump Ad to 'Stop Orange Muppet Hitler," *The Daily Wire* (Sept. 21, 2016).

602   Jack Holmes, "Robert De Niro Might Not Punch Donald Trump In The Face After All," *Esquire* (Nov. 23, 2016). He could at least have followed through!

603   Dan Merica, "Lena Dunham to campaign for Hillary Clinton in North Carolina," *CNN* (Oct. 29, 2016).

604   "Lena Dunham faces criticism after posting 'sexist' and 'racist' video on Twitter," *The New York Times* (Nov. 4, 2016).

605   Jon Hendren on Twitter, https://twitter.com/fart/status/796371826549014528 Yes, this man's Twitter handle is "@fart." No, I do not think this invalidates the wisdom of his observation.

606   See Alex Nichols, "You Should Be Terrified That People Who Like *Hamilton* Run This Country," *Current Affairs* (July/August 2016).

607   Kirsten West Savali, "For the Record: 'Superpredators' Is Absolutely a Racist Term," *The Root* (Sept. 30, 2016).

608   Dahleen Glanton, "Hillary Clinton Isn't Afraid to Say Black Lives Matter," *The Chicago Tribune* (July 27, 2016).

609   Tobita Chow, "Thomas Frank on How the Democrats Went from Being the Party of the People to the Party of Rich Elites," *In These Times* (Apr. 26, 2016). Robert Reich reports on a phone call he had with a "Washington friend" who captured the total certainty Frank describes. Reich's friend "breathless[ly]" insisted that "Hillary's going to win in places we haven't won in years – Georgia, Nevada, Arizona. She'll take the entire West, the whole East Coast. Trump is sinking like a stone." Robert Reich, "A landslide election?" *The Christian Science Monitor* (Aug. 28, 2016).

610   Lena Dunham, "Don't Agonize, Organize," *Lenny Letter* (Nov. 11, 2016).

611   Tim Hains, "Pelosi on Future of Democratic Party: 'I Don't Think People Want a New Direction,'" *RealClearPolitics* (Dec. 4, 2016).

612   Frank Bruni, "Rumors of Hillary Clinton's Comeback," *The New York Times* (Jan. 6, 2017).

613   Virginia Heffernan, "Hillary Clinton is More Than a Presi-
      dent." *Lenny* (Nov. 15, 2016). It is certainly true that Hillary
      Clinton is no less worthy a candidate for having an airport
      named for her than any other figure. After all, there's a Trent
      Lott Airport in Pascagoula, and Palestine has its Yasser Arafat
      International. All kinds of murderous political ghouls have
      airports. Nobody should deny Hillary hers.

614   See Jonathan Katz, "The King and Queen of Haiti," *Polit-
      ico* (May 4, 2015). See also Nathan J. Robinson, "What The
      Clintons Did to Haiti," *Current Affairs* (Nov. 2, 2016).

615   See Jo Becker and Scott Shane, "Hillary Clinton, 'Smart
      Power,' and a Dictator's Fall," *The New York Times* (Feb. 27,
      2016).

616   See Stephen Zunes, "Clinton's Iraq War Vote Still Appalls,"
      The Progressive (April 14, 2016).

617   See William D. Cohan, "Why Wall Street Loves Hillary,"
      Politico (Nov. 11, 2014).

618   Christie D'Zurilla and Jessica Roy, "Meryl Streep: Without
      'vilified' Hollywood, there'd be nothing but football and
      MMA," *The Los Angeles Times* (Jan. 8, 2017).

619   Not only that, but it really is entirely hypocritical of Holly-
      wood to be delivering a righteous message on behalf of the
      excluded; there is as much racial and gender bias in casting
      as in the hiring practices of any other industry, and rich Hol-
      lywood liberalism survives on the back of hundreds of thou-
      sands of poorly-paid Hispanic immigrants.

620   Louis Nelson, "Trump slams Meryl Streep as over-rated 'Hil-
      lary flunky,'" *Politico* (Jan. 9, 2017).

621   Donald J. Trump on Twitter (Jan. 9, 2017), https://twitter.
      com/realDonaldTrump/status/818460862675558400

622   Isaac Chotiner, "Donald Trump could have been president.
      Don't forget it." *Slate* (Oct. 8, 2016). We definitely won't for-
      get it, Isaac.

623   Bouie later wrote a column entitled "Donald Trump Isn't
      Going to Be President" listing the many reasons why the
      demographics proved that Trump was incapable of winning.

624   Klein also crowed that Clinton had "left the Trump cam-
      paign in ruins," and that "Hillary Clinton destroyed him."
      Ezra Klein, "Hillary Clinton's 3 debate performances left the
      Trump campaign in ruins," *Vox* (Oct. 19, 2016). Here, Klein
      illustrates one of the central fallacies of elite liberal logic:

that politics is about how many points you score in a debate, rather than whether you actually build movements. It's very telling that Klein thinks that a "debate performance" can kill a "campaign." In fact, campaigns are about mobilizing voters, and they are won or lost based on who actually turns up at the polls.

625   Joseph Crespino, "Why Hillary Clinton Might Win Georgia," *The New York Times* (Aug. 22, 2016).

626   Matthew Yglesias, "Why I think Nate Silver's model underrates Clinton's odds," *Vox* (Nov. 7, 2016).

627   Nate Silver, "The Six Stages of Donald Trump's Doom," *FiveThirtyEight* (Aug. 6, 2015).

628   Nate Silver on Twitter (Nov. 23, 2015), https://twitter.com/natesilver538/status/668837011499954176 For more on Silver's performance in the election, see Nathan J. Robinson, "Why You Should Never, Ever Listen to Nate Silver," *Current Affairs* (Jan./Feb. 2017).

629   Jonathan Chait, "Why Liberals Should Support a Trump Republican Nomination," *New York* (Feb. 5, 2016).

630   See Ian Jack, "In this Brexit vote, the poor turned on an elite who ignored them," *The Guardian* (June 25, 2016); Glenn Greenwald, "Brexit is Only The Latest Proof of the Insularity and Failure of Western Establishment Institutions," *The Intercept* (June 25, 2016).

631   George Saunders, "Who Are All These Trump Supporters?" *The New Yorker* (July 11, 2016).

632   See James Wolcott, "The Fraudulent Factoid That Refuses to Die," *Vanity Fair* (Oct. 23, 2012).

633   Michael Tracey on Twitter (Nov. 15, 2016), https://twitter.com/mtracey/status/798936797938089984

634   James Hohmann interview, "Podcast: What Lessons Should Political Journalists Learn From 2016?" *The Federalist* (Nov. 15, 2016).

635   Chris Arnade, "What do Donald Trump voters really crave? Respect," *The Guardian* (July 20, 2016).

636   Chris Arnade, "Divided by Meaning," *Medium* (Oct. 9, 2016). As Arnade summarizes his perspective: "Kids are growing up in towns where by six, or seven, or eleven, they are doomed to be viewed as second class. They feel unvalued. They feel stuck. They are mocked. And there is nothing

they feel they can do about it. When they turn to religion for worth, they are seen by the elites as uneducated, irrational, clowns. When they turn to identity through race they are racists. Regardless of their color. The only thing they can do, faced with that, is break the fucking system. And they are going to try. Either by Trump or by some other way." See Chris Arnade, "Why Trump voters are not 'complete idiots,'" *Medium* (May 30, 2016).

637   Adam Wren, "Trump County, USA," *Politico Magazine* (Dec. 4, 2015).

638   Paul Solotaroff, "Trump Seriously: On the Trail With the GOP's Tough Guy," *Rolling Stone* (Sept. 9, 2015).

639   James Downie, "Why Donald Trump Won't Be Elected President," *The Washington Post* (Mar. 2. 2016).

640   Matt Taibbi reflects on the insularity of his colleagues in political journalism: *"Whenever we sought insight into the motives and tendencies of this elusive creature [the Trump voter], our first calls were always to other eggheads like ourselves. We talked to pollsters, think-tankers, academics, former campaign strategists, party spokes-hacks, even other journalists. Day after day, our political talk shows consisted of one geek in a suit interviewing another geek in a suit about the behaviors of pipe fitters and store clerks and cops in Florida, Wisconsin, Ohio and West Virginia. We'd stand over glitzy video maps and discuss demographic data points like we were trying to determine the location of a downed jetliner... We journalists made the same mistake the Republicans made, the same mistake the Democrats made. We were too sure of our own influence, too lazy to bother hearing things firsthand, and too in love with ourselves to imagine that so many people could hate and distrust us as much as they apparently do."* Matt Taibbi, "President Trump: How America Got It So Wrong," *Rolling Stone* (Nov. 10, 2016).

641   Chris Hanretty, "Here's why pollsters and pundits got Brexit wrong," *The Washington Post* (June 24, 2016).

642   Bernie Sanders, *Our Revolution: A Future to Believe In* (Thomas Dunne Books, 2016), p. 421.

643   Thomas E. Patterson, "News Coverage of the 2016 Presidential Primaries: Horse Race Reporting Has Consequences," Shorenstein Center on Media, Politics, and Public Policy, Harvard Kennedy School (July 11, 2016).

644   See "The Biological Threat," Nuclear Threat Initative (Dec. 30, 2015); Steven Block, "The Growing Threat of Biological

Weapons," *American Scientist* (Jan./Feb. 2001).

645   Katie Valentine, "Broadcast News Stations Covered Trump and Tom Brady Last Year More Than They Covered Climate Change," *ThinkProgress* (Mar. 8, 2016).

646   Paulina Firozi, "CNN President: Airing so many full Trump rallies was a 'mistake,'" *The Hill* (Oct. 14, 2016).

647   Kevin Drum, "Donald Trump Is Lying About His Weight," *Mother Jones* (Dec. 27, 2016).

648   Laurie Penny, "Yes, you should care about Donald Trump attacking 'Hamilton,'" *The New Statesman* (Nov. 21, 2016). Penny says that while there are "perhaps" more important stories, the *Hamilton* Twitter war has implications for "the freedom of oppressed people to stand up and ask for their fundamental rights to be respected." (It does not.)

649   Jeremy Stahl, "Why The Press Is Right To Freak Out Over Trump Sneaking to a Steakhouse," *Slate* (Nov. 16, 2016). Another example of useless post-election non-journalism from the same website: L.V. Anderson, "Liberals, Don't Let Donald Trump Tarnish L.L. Bean's Sterling Brand Reputation," *Slate* (Jan. 12, 2017).

650   For more on problems with contemporary political media, see Nathan J. Robinson, "The Necessity of Credibility," *Current Affairs* (Dec. 6, 2016). There, I insist on the importance of being fundamentally fair and honest in reporting about Donald Trump, *even* when this means admitting that Donald Trump is right about certain things. I show how opinion can slip into "fact-checking," thereby reducing people's trust in media. I conclude that: *For progressives, having a reliable and trustworthy media means not being afraid of uncomfortable truths. The truth is a precious thing, and it should never, ever be distorted for partisan reasons. Being credible means being self-critical, and trying to build a press that people can depend on to help them sort truth from lies. Having a media people can actually trust should be a fundamental goal of Trump opponents. Currently, people don't trust the mainstream media. And the first thing the media must do is acknowledge that part of that mistrust is entirely rational and reasonable. After that, building true credibility will at the very least require a major rethink of how ordinary political media do business. They will have to interrogate their assumptions more, defend or revise their work in response to criticisms, and get serious about truth, fairness, and accountability. They will need to abandon the assumption, commonly held, that if people on "both sides" are mad at you, you must be doing your job well. And they will need to be extremely cautious in their factual assertions. If I go around asserting that Trump's attitude*

toward polls is "post-truth," then report that Trump is a possible Russian spy, I will have few grounds to complain when Trump's supporters decide to get their news from alt-right conspiracy websites instead.

651   Jane Mayer, "Donald Trump's Ghostwriter Tells All," *The New Yorker* (July 25, 2016).

652   Damn you, Ginsburg! Damn you, Breyer! Why didn't you fools *retire* when you had the chance?

653   James Risen, "If Donald Trump Targets Journalists, Thank Obama," *The New York Times* (Dec. 30, 2016).

654   William J. Broad and David E. Sanger, "Debate Over Trump's Fitness Raises Issue of Checks on Nuclear Power," *The New York Times* (Aug. 4, 2016). Bruce Blair of the Program on Science and Global Security at Princeton University writes that "Under the Constitution, no one could veto a bad call by a President Trump. The 90 launch officers who are always on duty in the Great Plains, along with their counterparts in submarines patrolling the oceans, would have no choice but to execute the most morally reprehensible order ever issued in the history of warfare." Bruce G. Blair, "Trump and the Nuclear Keys," *The New York Times* (Oct. 12, 2016).

655   Rachel Becker, "What's standing between Donald Trump and nuclear war?" *The Verge* (Dec. 22, 2016).

656   James Bamford, "Donald Trump Has the Keys to the Most Invasive Surveillance State in History, *Foreign Policy* (Jan. 6, 2017).

657   Ian Cobain, "Obama's secret kill list – the disposition matrix," *The Guardian* (July 14, 2013).

658   Conor Friedersdorf, "How Team Obama Justifies The Killing of a 16-year-old American," *The Atlantic* (Oct. 24, 2012). Former White House Press Secretary and senior Obama reelection adviser Robert Gibbs said that the teenaged al-Awlaki should have "had a more responsible father" if he hadn't wanted to be killed by a drone.

659   Nick Gass, "Trump on Russia hack: 'I wish I had that power,'" *Politico* (July 27, 2016).

660   Jeremy Diamond, "Trump doubles down on calls for mosque surveillance," *CNN* (June 15, 2016).

661   Cheryl K. Chumley, "Donald Trump on Edward Snowden: Kill the 'traitor,'" *The Washington Times* (July 2, 2013).

662   Readers will note that I do not much discuss the "alt-right" in this book. This is because I don't tend to believe that they

are a particularly salient factor in Trump's rise, and think that they are more successful at making themselves seem like an actual political movement than at actually becoming one. For discussions of the alt-right, however, see Brianna Rennix, "The New Alternative Right (And How To Get Rid of Them Quickly)," *Current Affairs* (Nov. 9, 2016); Angela Nagle, "What the Alt-right is really all about," *The Irish Times* (Jan. 6, 2017).

663   Jason Howerton, "Keith Olbermann Absolutely Melts Down Over 'Russian Coup' and Trump – It's Truly a Sight to Behold" *Independent Journal Review* Dec. 12, 2016). Olbermann post for a photograph wrapped in the country's flag, ostensibly signifying defiance but looking for all the world like he was huddling desperately under a blanket.

664   Quoted in Oliver Laughland and Mae Ryan, "Workers fight for dignity in Trump's Las Vegas hotel: 'You don't talk to the boss,'" *The Guardian* (May 2, 2016).

665   Steve Reilly, "Hundreds allege Donald Trump doesn't pay his bills," *USA Today* (June 9, 2016).

666   *Id.*

667   *Id.*

668   *Id.*

669   Michael Tanenbaum, "Report: Trump once drove Philly cabinetry company out of business," *The Philly Voice* (June 12, 2016).

670   J. Michael Diehl, "I sold Trump $100,000 worth of pianos. Then he stiffed me." *The Washington Post* (Sept. 28, 2016).

671   Reilly, *supra.*

672   Carey Purcell, "I Survived 'Trump' Magazine—Barely," *Politico Magazine* (Aug. 14, 2016).

673   Reddit, https://www.reddit.com/r/politics/comments/54x-m65/i_sold_trump_100000_worth_of_pianos_then_he/

674   Lucy Klebanow, "My awful date with Donald Trump: The real story of a nightmare evening with a callow but cashless heir," *Salon* (Mar. 23, 2016). "Heir" is a word not often used in describing Donald Trump, despite its accuracy. "Real estate heir Donald Trump" should probably be used instead of terms like "mogul."

675   Laura Dolan and Jessica Schneider, "The small business owners Trump never paid in full," *CNN* (Sept. 14, 2016).

676   Ross Beuttner and Charles V. Bagli, "How Donald Trump Bankrupted His Atlantic City Casinos, but Still Earned Millions," *The New York Times* (June 11, 2016).

677   David Brooks, "Donald Trump's Sad, Lonely Life," *The New York Times* (Oct. 11, 2016).

678   Still, keep in mind: Trump isn't a unique monster. He's the monster within. To the extent that we focus on Trump, we should keep in mind that he is a convenient symbol of what is wrong with humanity, not the main thing wrong with humanity. The real task is for humanity itself to become more decent and sensitive, to eliminate every last trace of its own Trumpishness.

679   "Did Trump really mock reporter's disability? Videos could back him up," *Fox News* (Sept. 14, 2016). Conservatives have insisted that Trump did *not* attempt to mock the reporter's disability, but that he was performing a series of gestures that he has used to make fun of other, non-disabled people. The point here, however, is that this issue is *less relevant* than the lives of the disabled worldwide.

680   See "Prejudice," p. 83.

681   See "Trump and Women," p. 53.

682   See Michael Rothfeld and Alexandra Berzon, "Donald Trump and the Mob," *The Wall Street Journal* (Sept. 1, 2016).

683   See "Introduction: Trump U," p. 19.

684   See Josh Marshall, "Top 10 Reasons to Doubt Trump Is Even A Billionaire," *TalkingPointsMemo* (June 2, 2016).

685   See Glenn Kessler, "All of Donald Trump's Four-Pinocchio ratings, in one place," *The Washington Post* (Mar. 22, 2016); Daniel Dale and Tanya Talaga, "Donald Trump: The unauthorized database of false things," *The Toronto Star* (Nov. 4, 2016). Note: I disagree with the classification of some of these things as "lies," as I indicate elsewhere. Nevertheless, there are many lies to be found in here.

686   See Tina Nguyen, "All The Campaign Promises Donald Trump Has Broken in the Last 24 Hours," *Vanity Fair* (Nov. 23, 2016).

687   See Jane Mayer, "Donald Trump's Ghostwriter Tells All," *The New Yorker* (July 25, 2016).

688   See Zeke J. Miller, "Donald Trump Stumbles on Foreign Policy Knowledge in New Interview," *TIME* (Sept. 4, 2015); Fred

Kaplan, "Donald Trump Once Again Revealed His Stunning Ignorance on Foreign Policy," *Slate* (Sept. 27, 2016); Michael Weiss, "Everything Donald Trump Says About Syria is Crazy, Wrong, or Both," *The Daily Beast* (Oct. 10, 2016).

689   See Charles Krauthammer, "Donald Trump's childish tantrums threaten to derail his presidency before it has even begun," *The Telegraph* (Jan. 13, 2017).

690   See "Donald Trump, bully in chief," *The Washington Post* (May 31, 2016).

691   See Josh Barro, "It Matters That Donald Trump Is Very Vulgar," *Business Insider* (July 18, 2016).

692   See, once again, "Trump and Women," p. 53.

693   Holly Yan, "Donald Trump's 'blood' comment about Megyn Kelly draws outrage," *CNN* (Aug. 8, 2015).

694   David A. Graham, "The Many Scandals of Donald Trump: A Cheat Sheet," *The Atlantic* (Nov. 22, 2016).

695   Natasha Geiling, "A Definitive History of Trump Steaks,™" *ThinkProgress* (Mar. 4, 2016); Ian Millhiser, "Memo to Donald Trump: Here's What The Law Actually Says About Raping Your Spouse," *ThinkProgress* (July 28, 2015).

696   Max J. Rosenthal, "The Trump Files: Donald Thinks Exercising Might Kill You," *Mother Jones* (Sept. 19, 2016).

697   Ivylise Simones, "The Trump Files: Donald Filmed A Music Video. It Didn't Go Well," *Mother Jones* (Sept. 8, 2016).

698   Ivylise Simones, "The Trump Files: How Donald Screwed Over New York City on His Tax Bill," *Mother Jones* (Oct. 24, 2016). The article covers the Trump Hyatt's "aberrant and distortive" accounting practices (according to the New York auditor general) and its "detailed failures in basic bookkeeping" and "efforts to stymie officials," with Trump having owed the city millions in back taxes even after securing massive tax breaks.

699   Max J. Rosenthal, "The Trump Files: How Donald Made a Fortune by Dumping His Debt on Other People," *Mother Jones* (Sept. 30, 2016).

700   Max J. Rosenthal, "The Trump Files: Watch a Clip of the Awful TV Show Trump Wanted to Make About Himself," *Mother Jones* (Aug. 29, 2016). See also Max J. Rosenthal, "The Trump Files: Trump Wanted a TV Show of Him Ogling Women," *Mother Jones* (Oct. 31, 2016).

701   Pema Levy, "The Trump Files: When a Sleazy Hot-Tub Salesman Tried to Take Donald Trump's Name," *Mother Jones*
(Nov. 3, 2016). Since this concerns something a hot tub salesman in Oregon did (namely, try to boost sales and fool credi-
tors by calling himself Donald Trump), it's unclear what possible relevance a progressive magazine could have thought the
story had to the presidential campaign. In fact, *Mother Jones*
magazine, named for the great labor organizer and radical,
has become Exhibit A in How Not To Produce Effective Progressive Journalism. See Naomi LaChance, "Mother Jones'
Legacy Is Haunting *Mother Jones* as the Magazine Embraces
Neoliberalism," *Paste Magazine* (Dec. 21, 2016).

702   Max J. Rosenthal, "The Trump Files: Donald Couldn't Name
Any of His 'Handpicked' Trump U Professors," *Mother Jones*
(Aug. 26, 2016).

703   Jasmine C. Lee and Kevin Queely, "The 289 People, Places,
and Things Donald Trump Has Insulted on Twitter: A Complete List," *The New York Times* (Dec. 6, 2016).

704   Michael Tracey, "Tips for Dealing With Trump's Tweets,"
Medium (Nov. 29, 2016).

705   *Id.*

706   See, e.g. Stephanie Mencimer, "We May Have Unlocked
the Mystery of Trump's Orange Skin," *Mother Jones* (Nov. 4,
2016).

707   See, e.g. Shahidha Bari, "Trump is the very definition of 'vulgar,'" *Times Higher Education* (Nov. 3, 2016).

708   See, e.g. Cody Cain, "Stupid and contagious: What if Donald
Trump is not 'dumbing down' and actually is this dumb?"
Salon (Oct. 9, 2016).

709   See, e.g., *Gawker*'s extensive investigation into the secrets
of Trump's hair: Ashley Feinberg, "Is Donald Trump's Hair
a $60,000 Weave? A *Gawker* Investigation," *Gawker* (May
24, 2016). For a particularly piece of hair-based clickbait, see
Marissa Wenzke, "The *New York Times* font looks like Trump's
hair and you'll never see it the same way again," *Mashable*
(Dec. 12, 2016). And the prize for least-serious headline to
come out of an ostensibly serious media outlet goes to: A.J.
Willingham, "Haha guys, this bird looks like Donald Trump,"
CNN Politics (Nov. 18, 2016). The bird does, in fact, look like
Donald Trump. But it is worth asking whether this ought
necessarily to be on *CNN*.

710   "Exposed! Naked Donald Trump Statues Pop Up in Cities Across U.S." *NBC News* (Aug. 19, 2016).

711   Meghna Sridhar, "PSA: Your Transphobia and Body Shaming Isn't Radical," *Feministing* (Aug. 19, 2016).

712   See, e.g., Raul A. Reyes, "Melania Trump, undocumented immigrant?" *The Hill* (Nov. 7, 2016).

713   See, e.g., Jonathan Merritt, "Trump's Bible Fail," *The Atlantic* (Apr. 15, 2016).

714   See, e.g., Aaron Barlow, "Donald Trump is a chicken-hawk and a hypocrite: The real story about Vietnam and the draft," *Salon* (June 4, 2016).

715   Julia Zorthian, "John Oliver's 'Donald Drumpf' Segment Broke HBO Viewing Records," *TIME* (Mar. 31, 2016).

716   Amber A'Lee Frost, "The Necessity of Political Vulgarity," *Current Affairs* (May/June 2016).

717   David A. Fahrenthold, "Trump recorded having extremely lewd conversation about women in 2005," *The Washington Post* (Oct. 8, 2016). The correct headline is "Trump recorded confessing to sexual assault in 2005."

718   Inae Oh, "Hot Mic Catches Donald Trump Saying Vulgar Things About Women," *Mother Jones* (Oct. 7, 2016). The correct headline is "Hot Mic Catches Donald Trump Confessing to Sexual Asssault."

719   Ben Craw, "Donald Trump Says 'China,'" *The Huffington Post* (Aug. 28, 2015).

720   Tim Stanley, "Donald Trump for president: *Idiocracy* is coming true," *The Telegraph* (Nov. 9, 2016).

721   Jack Shafer, "Donald Trump Talks Like a Third-Grader," *Politico Magazine* (Aug. 13, 2015).

722   Cody Cain, "It takes a village idiot: Thanks to Donald Trump, the president may be chosen by a fourth-grade mentality," *Salon* (Oct. 30, 3016).

723   Steve Benen, "As Trump skips intel briefings, questions intensify," *MSNBC* (Dec. 9, 2016).

724   Laura Bradley, "Donald Trump Is Still Executive Producer on *Celebrity Apprentice*," *Vanity Fair* (Dec. 8, 2016).

725   Noam Chomsky, *Understanding Power* (The New Press, 2002), p. 399.

726   Nelson D. Schwartz, "Trump Cites Progress in Keeping Car-

rier Air Conditioning Plant in Indiana," *The New York Times* (Nov. 24, 2016).

727   Ana Swanson, "The true size of Trump's Carrier win," *The Washington Post* (Dec. 1, 2016); Issie Lapowsky, "The Carrier Deal Is Great—But Trump Hasn't Saved Manufacturing Yet," *Wired* (Nov. 30, 2016).

728   See Michael Kinnucan, "Trump Gives Tax Cut To Company For Sending 1000 Jobs To Mexico," *Current Affairs* (Dec. 2, 2016).

729   Bernie Sanders, "Carrier just showed corporations how to beat Donald Trump," *The Washington Post* (Dec. 1, 2016).

730   Emma Stefansky, "This Is Why Trump's Taiwan Call Was Truly Bizarre," *Vanity Fair* (Dec. 3, 2016).

731   Many people insist on a distinction between "equality of opportunity" and "equality of outcome." This distinction cannot be maintained. There can never be such a thing as equality of opportunity, because of differing human capacities and family backgrounds. See Christopher Jencks, *Inequality: A Reassessment of the Effect of Family and Schooling in America* (1972). It should also be remembered that "equality of opportunity" ideas, if they are our *primary* objective, implicitly reject what should be a core left goal: improving actual wellbeing rather than just possible wellbeing. Equality of opportunity *accepts* that some people will work crappy jobs with poor benefits, and suggests that the solution to this is to make sure these people can go to college and get better jobs if they want, rather than to make the jobs themselves better. If we aim to provide mere opportunity, without caring about outcome, we risk blaming people for their struggles (by insisting we gave them the opportunity to end them) without actually eliminating those struggles. Never should a serious left define itself by its commitment to "opportunity," because opportunity is not actuality.

732   Likewise, if the left is about "ending oppression," the quickest way to end all oppression is to destroy all of civilization. No more oppression.

733   See Rod Nordland, "Lional Shriver's Address on Cultural Appropriation Roils a Writers Festival," *The New York Times* (Sept. 12, 2016).

734   See Maureen Sullivan, "Provocateur Milo Yiannopoulos Was The Speaker Most Likely To Be Disinvited To Colleges In 2016," *Forbes* (Dec. 30, 2016).

735   George Ciccariello-Maher, "The Dialectics of Standing One's Ground," *Theory & Event*, Vol. 15, Issue 3 (2012).

736   Browse for yourself: http://everydayfeminism.com/?s=privilege

737   For more on the subject of "privilege," and an evaluation of the concept's usefulness, see Z.W. Rochefort, "The Pathologies of Privilege," *Current Affairs* (Aug. 18, 2016).

738   Cody Charles, "The Everyday Comments Revealing Classism in Activist Communities," *Everyday Feminism* (Dec. 29, 2016).

739   Those who would dismiss transgender bathroom access as a significant issue are making an error. The right of transgender people to use the facilities of their choice is a matter of significant concern for their safety and dignity. And anyone who thinks bathroom access is an issue without significant rights implications should talk to the veterans of a certain earlier Civil Rights struggle.

740   "Trump berates his 'Apprentice' replacement Schwarzanegger," *Politico* (Jan. 6, 2017).

741   Patrick Healy, "'Hamilton' Cast's Appeal to Pence Ignites Showdown With Trump," *The New York Times* (Nov. 19, 2016).

742   Ashe McGovern, "Bathroom Bills, Selfies, and the Erasure of Nonbinary Trans People," *The Advocate* (April 1, 2016).

743   Maria Godoy and Kat Chow, "When Chefs Become Famous Cooking Other Cultures' Food," *NPR* (Mar. 22, 2016).

744   Pierre Macherey, "Althusser and the Young Marx," *Viewpoint Magazine* (July 18, 2016).

745   Julia Carrie Wong, "Asian Americans decry 'whitewashed' Great Wall film starring Matt Damon," *The Guardian* (July 29, 2016).

746   In referring to political progressives, I use the word "we" a lot, even though this captures a highly disparate group of people. I believe there are values shared in common among progressives, to where using this word makes sense as a way of speaking to this group of people specifically. But for a critique of this tendency to write using "we," see Nathan J. Robinson "*We* Do Not Feel That Way, Thank You Very Much," *Current Affairs* (Sept. 18., 2016).

747   Hopefully, a serious interrogation of values will also lead to a greater consistency in the application of our principles. If we are honestly committed to certain simple principles, then

we will not adopt double standards for ourselves versus the other side. We will not, for example, defend Democrats who commit acts that we would condemn if done by Republicans.

748   See William Morris, *News From Nowhere* (1890) and Edward Bellamy, *Looking Backward* (1888).

749   Janet I. Tu, "Starbucks CEO Howard Schultz Reportedly Was Hillary Clinton's Pick For Labor Secretary," *The Seattle Times* (Jan. 10, 2017).

750   For more on the Democratic Party's love affairs with supposedly "progressive" billionaires, see Nathan J. Robinson, "The Good Billionaires," *Current Affairs* (Aug. 3, 2016).

751   Dani McClain, "How the Moral Mondays 'Fusion Coalition' Is Taking North Carolina Back," *The Nation* (July 21, 2014); Dahlia Lithwick, "The Left Fights Back," *Slate* (Feb. 10, 2014). See also Rev. Dr. William J. Barber II, *The Third Reconstruction: Moral Mondays, Fusion Politics, and the Rise of a New Justice Movement* (Beacon Press, 2016).

752   And if we believe we cannot do this, we have Daryl Davis to answer to. Davis is the African American blues musician who has spent decades meeting members of the Klan, steadily persuading them one by one to turn in their hoods and abandon racial extremism. Davis' thankless work involves a superhuman amount of courage and patience. If he can sit down with the Klan, we too can try persuasion. See Conor Friedersdorf, "The Audacity of Talking About Race With the Ku Klux Klan," *The Atlantic* (Mar. 27, 2015).

753   For example: I have been quite positive about Bernie Sanders in the foregoing text. But I will freely admit that I thought he handled outreach to black voters badly, and should have listened earlier to demands to make it clear that racism is more than simply an aspect of economic inequality.

754   The interests of corporations and their workers, for example, will forever be in opposition, because at a certain point profit must be given priority over increased compensation for employees.

755   Melissa Quinn, "Inside the Comic Book Jonathan Gruber Wrote to Sell Obamacare to America," *The Daily Signal* (Nov. 17, 2014).

756   See Nathan J. Robinson, *Superpredator: Bill Clinton's Use and Abuse of Black America* (Current Affairs Press, 2016).

757   Bexology on Twitter (Nov. 17, 2016), https://twitter.com/

bexology_/status/799365255608565760

758   I am aware that this famous leftist quotation is overused to the point of having lost all meaning. However, some clichés are clichés because they are true and meaningful. This is one of them.

759   See Max Blau, "Not 'locker room' talk: Athletes push back against Trump's remark," *CNN* (Oct. 10. 2016).

760   Trump's unpopularity is hard to overstate. He is the most unpopular incoming president in the history of polling, with low approval and very high disapproval. See Steven Shepard, "Trump's Unpopularity Threatens to Hobble His Presidency," *Politico* (Dec. 24, 2016); Aaron Black, "This New Poll Has All Kinds of Bad News for Trump," *The Washington Post* (Jan. 10, 2016). Of course, many things labeled "bad news for Trump" have failed to undo him. But it should be remembered that Trump does *not* have much popular support. He has no mandate…yet.

761   Brittany Spanos, "Watch Lena Dunham Rap in 'Sensual Pantsuit' for Hillary Clinton PSA," *Rolling Stone* (Nov. 3, 2016).

762   Nathan J. Robinson, "The Necessity of Social Philosophy" (2016). Available at SSRN.

763   See Appendix.

APPENDIX SOURCES

1   Nathan J. Robinson, "Here Comes Ted Cruz's Third-Party Candidacy," *Current Affairs* (April 30, 2016). For more on Cruz, see Nathan J. Robinson, "The Political Sociopath," *Current Affairs* (May/June 2016).

2   Brent Budowsky, "In blockbuster poll, Sanders destroys Trump by 13 points," *The Hill* (Dec. 22, 2015).

3   Nate Silver, "Donald Trump Is Really Unpopular With General Election Voters," *FiveThirtyEight* (Jan. 18, 2016).

4   Dylan Byers, "Morning Joe hosts hot mic chatter fuels favoritism," *CNN* (Feb. 22, 2016).

5   Brian Ross, Rhonda Schwartz, and Alex Hosenball, "FBI Arrests Chinese Millionaire Once Tied to Clinton $$ Scandal," *ABC News* (Sept. 24, 2015).

6   Megan Carpentier, "Travelgate to Furnituregate: a guide to the

Clinton scandals of the 90s," *The Guardian* (May 27, 2016).

7   Ben Shapiro, "Hillary Clinton's Long History of Hiding Documents," *Breitbart* (Mar. 4, 2015). I do not cite *Breitbart* for its accuracy, but to demonstrate the ease of spinning the Clintons' past into fodder for right-wing news sites.

8   Ken Silverstein, "The Jeffrey Epstein Affair Imperils Hillary Clinton's Presidential Prospects," *Observer* (Mar. 25, 2015).

9   David Corn, "Hillary Clinton and Henry Kissinger: It's Personal. Very Personal." *Mother Jones* (Feb. 12, 2016).

10   James Herron, John Letzing, and Alex Macdonald, "Notorious Oil Trader, Pardoned by Clinton," *The Wall Street Journal* (June 26, 2013).

11   Jonathan M. Katz, "The Clintons' Haiti Screw-Up, As Told By Hillary's Emails," *Politico Magazine* (Sept. 2, 2015).

12   Robert W. Wood, "Clinton Foundation Admits Speech Fees Are Not Donations. Will Hillary Amend Her Own Taxes Too?" *Forbes* (Nov. 21, 2015).

13   David A. Graham, "Hillary's Campaign Is Built on a Shaky Foundation," *The Atlantic* (Mar. 20, 2015).

14   Emily Thomas, "Hillary Clinton: We Were 'Dead Broke' Upon Leaving White House," *The Huffington Post* (Jun. 10, 2014).

15   Simon Head, "Clinton and Goldman: Why It Matters," *The New York Review of Books* (Apr. 12, 2016).

16   Chris Cillizza, "Maybe Hillary Clinton Just Isn't A Very Good Candidate," *The Washington Post* (Aug. 18, 2015).

17   Jason Zengerle, "Is Hillary Clinton Any Good at Running for President?" *New York* (Apr. 5, 2015).

18   Edward-Isaac Dovere, "White House frets return of 'Clinton way,'" *Politico* (Mar. 12, 2015).

19   Jennifer Rubin, "Hillary Clinton's latest attack on Bernie Sanders shows she's a rotten candidate," *The Washington Post* (Jan. 14, 2016).

20   See, e.g. Rebecca Sinderbrand, "Analysis: Why Clinton's bid failed," *CNN* (June 6, 2008).

21   Lisa Lerer and Ken Thomas, "Is Hillary Clinton In Trouble?" *U.S. News & World Report* (Jan. 21, 2016).

22   Mollie Reilly, "Military Voters Sided With Donald Trump After He Condemned the Iraq War," *The Huffington Post* (Feb. 20, 2016).

23   Taylor Berman, "Donald Trump: I Paid Hillary Clinton to Attend My Wedding," *Gawker* (Aug. 8, 2015).

24   Jonathan Mann, "Donald Trump uses Bill Clinton's past to haunt Hillary," *CNN* (Jan. 18, 2016).

25   Steven A. Holmes and Lisa Rose, "Reality Check: Did Hillary Clinton attack her husband's accusers?" *CNN* (Oct. 12, 2016). This charge against Clinton was unfair and mostly unsubstantiated, but the point is that it doesn't matter.

26   Amy Chozick, "'90s Scandals Threaten to Erode Hillary Clinton's Strength With Women," *The New York Times* (Jan. 20, 2016).

27   Rebecca Kaplan, "Hillary Clinton: Monica Lewinsky a 'narcissistic loony toon," *CBS News* (Feb. 10, 2014).

28   Ken Shepherd, "MSNBC's Kornacki: Trump May Be 'Electable' Because of His Planned Parenthood Position," *Media Research Center* (Feb. 22, 2016).

29   Amy Sherman, "Hillary Clinton's changing position on same-sex marriage," *PolitiFact* (June 17, 2015).

30   Angie Drobnic Holan, "Video shows tarmac welcome, no snipers," *PolitiFact* (Mar. 25, 2008).

31   Michael Walsh, "Hillary Clinton's million little lies," *The New York Post* (Nov. 28, 2015).

32   "Hillary Clinton's five email lies," *The New York Post* (Aug. 16, 2015).

33   "All false statements involving Hillary Clinton," *PolitiFact.*

34   Chris Cillizza," Hillary Clinton's terrible, horrible, no good, very bad answer on whether she's ever lied," *The Washington Post* (Feb. 19, 2016).

35   H.A. Goodman, "Hillary Clinton just can't win: Democrats need to accept that only Bernie Sanders can defeat the GOP," *Salon* (Feb. 19, 2016). Generally speaking, Goodman was one of the most unreliable pundits of the entire election cycle, infamously insisting Bernie Sanders was poised for victory long after Sanders' loss was mathematically assured. But an accurate piece of analysis is an accurate piece of analysis.

36   Mike Flynn, "Working-Class Hero: Trump Expands to 20-Point Lead Among White Blue-Collars Vs. Hillary Clinton," *Breitbart* (Jan. 10, 2016).

37   Ben Schreckinger, "How Donald Trump defeats Hillary Clinton," *Politico* (Jan. 19, 2016).

38   Farai Chideya, "Trump's South Carolina Win Shows Evangelicals Aren't Necessarily Voting on their Faith," *FiveThirtyEight* (Feb. 22, 2016).

39   See "Megyn Kelly Impressed With Bernie Sanders' Basketball Skills," available on Youtube: https://www.youtube.com/watch?v=C2Xojil-P6o

40   Katharine Q. Seelye, "As Mayor, Bernie Sanders Was More Pragmatist Than Socialist," *The New York Times* (Nov. 25, 2016).

41   Zaid Jilani, "Bernie Gets It Done: Sanders' Record of Pushing Through Major Reforms Will Surprise you," *AlterNet* (Oct. 17, 2015).

42   Nick Gass, "Donald Trump's 11 worst foreign policy gaffes," *Politico* (Sept. 4, 2015).

43   Brent Budowsky, "As Sanders soars, Clinton goes negative – bad move," *The Hill* (Jan. 22, 2016).

44   Lynn Vavreck, "The Ad That Moved People the Most: Bernie Sanders's 'America,'" *The New York Times* (Dec. 30, 2016). This ad has literally made me cry before.

45   "Watch: New Bernie Sanders Ad Will Make You Feel Warm And Intersectional," *The Advocate* (Feb. 11, 2016).

46   Daniel Marans, "Erica Garner's Daughter Hails Bernie Sanders' Activism in Powerful New Campaign Ad," *The Huffington Post* (Feb. 12, 2016).

47   Zaid Jilani, "Bernie Sanders Draws Army of 100,000 Volunteers to First Nationwide Organizing Event," *AlterNet* (July 30, 2015).

48   Ed O'Keefe and John Wagner, "100,000 people have come to recent Bernie Sanders rallies. How does he do it?" *The Washington Post* (Aug. 11, 2015).

49   BerniesTranscripts.com. This was a website offering a downloadable PDF transcript of "every paid speech" Bernie Sanders had ever made to "private interests on Wall Street." The joke, of course, was that the PDF was blank.

50   See, e.g., A. Barton Hinkle, "The Foolish Socialism of Bernie Sanders," *Reason* (June 8, 2015).

51   Ben White, "Economists savage Trump's economic agenda," *Politico* (Jan. 11, 2016).

52   "Trumponomics: Donald Trump's tax plan is a fantasy," *The Economist* (Sept. 28, 2015).

53   Catherine Rampell, "Millennials have a higher opinion of socialism than of capitalism," *The Washington Post* (Feb. 5, 2016).

54   "Sanders Announces Family Values Agenda," Bernie Sanders, U.S. Senator (June 11, 2015).

55   Sarah Ferris, "Majority still supports single-payer option, poll finds," *The Hill* (Jan. 19, 2015).

56   E.g. Monica Crowley, "Socialist red is the new black: Obama's leftist policies are changing the very nature of America," *The Washington Times* (June 24, 2015).

57   Ishaan Tharoor, "Trump's outrageous 'pig blood' comment a reminded or an often forgotten history," *The Washington Post* (Feb. 22, 2016).

58   Steve Mollman, "Hillary Clinton's new ads use Republican leaders—and Donald Trump himself—to bash Trump," *Quartz* (May 5, 2016).

59   Lisette Mejia, "Hillary Clinton's New Anti-Trump Ad Is Straight-Up Savae," *Popsugar* (May 4, 2016).

60   "Clinton releases devastating anti-Trump ad," *Vancouver Sun* (May 4, 2016).

61   Greg Sargent, "This brutal new ad shows the shredding machine that awaits Trump," *The Washington Post* (May 5, 2016).

62   Josh Voorhees, "Hillary Lets Republicans Do All The Talking In Her New Trump Attack Ads," *Slate* (May 5, 2016).

63   "Sen. Clinton Calls Iran a Danger to U.S., Israel," *Associated Press* (Feb. 2, 2007).

64   Danielle Allen, "Hillary Clinton in walking into Donald Trump's trap," *The Washington Post* (May 4, 2016).

65   Glenn Greenwald and Zaid Jilani, "Beyond Schadenfreude, the Spectacular Pundit Failure on Trump Is Worth Remembering," *The Intercept* (May 4, 2016).

66   Joshua Green, "The Front-Runner's Fall," *The Atlantic* (Sept. 2008).

67   Stephen Collinson, "Why Trump is dredging up 1990 attacks against the Clintons," *CNN* (May 25, 2016).

68   Rebecca Savransky, "Trump Overtakes Clinton In Poll Average For First Time," *The Hill* (May 22, 2016).

69   Jamelle Bouie, "Donald Trump Isn't Going to be President," *Slate* (May 4, 2016).

70   See Nathan J. Robinson, "Nominating a Presidential Candidate Under Active FBI Investigation Is An Incredibly Risky Gamble," *Current Affairs* (Mar. 5, 2016). In this article I pointed out what seems obvious but was apparently controversial, namely that whatever one's position of the legitimacy of the investigation, it was a considerable political *risk* to run a candidate being investigated, because one was *assuming* that the investigation wouldn't lead to anything or cause any hiccups. That meant that we were putting the fate of the election in the hands of the FBI, something that turned out to be (in light of the Comey letter) a poor idea.

71   Steven Lee Myers and Eric Lichblau, "Hillary Clinton Is Criticized for Private Emails in State Dept. Review," *The New York Times* (May 25, 2016).

72   Margaret Sullivan, "Were Changes to Sanders Article 'Stealth Editing'?" *The New York Times* (Mar. 17, 2016).

73   Mark Landler, "Hillary Clinton's Campaign Rebuffs Report's Criticism of Email Use," *The New York Times* (May 25, 2016).

74   Undated CBS report, available on YouTube: https://www.youtube.com/watch?v=8BfNqhV5hg4

75   "Exclusive: Clinton acknowledges a 'misstatement' on Bosnia sniper fire," *Philadelphia Daily News* (Mar. 25, 2008).

76   "Hillary Clinton: 'I've Always Tried' To Tell The Truth," *CBS News* (Feb. 18, 2016).

77   C. Eugene Emery Jr., "Hillary Clinton says she didn't endorse the TPP trade deal until it was actually negotiated," *PolitiFact* (Feb. 5, 2016).

78   Amy Chozick, "Emails Add to Hillary Clinton's Central Problem: Voters Just Don't Trust Her," *The New York Times* (May 25, 2016).

79   Michael A. Cohen, "Still panicked about Trump? Don't be." *The Boston Globe* (May 23, 2016).

80   Philip Bump, "Why Donald Trump's polling advantage may be a bit misleading," *The Washington Post* (May 22, 2016).

81   Doyle McManus, "Polls show Hillary Clinton and Donald Trump in a virtual tie. Should Democrats be worried?" *The Los Angeles Times* (May 25, 2016).

82   Darby Saxe, "A Letter to a Bernie-or-Bust Voter," *Slate* (May 24, 2016).

83   See "Unless Democrats Nominate Sanders…"

84   Mark Z. Barabak and Noah Bierman, "Trump paints a grim portrait of the U.S. and casts himself as its only savior in GOP acceptance speech," *The Los Angeles Times* (July 21, 2016).

85   Joan Walsh, "Donald Trump's Angry, Dark Speech Caps Off a Disastrous RNC," *The Nation* (July 22, 2016).

86   John Cassidy, "Donald Trump's Dark, Dark Convention Speech," *The New Yorker* (July 22, 2016).

87   Tim Hains, "Van Jones: Donald Trump Was Describing A 'Mad Max America' – It Was Terrifying," *RealClearPolitics* (July 21, 2016).

88   German Lopez, "Eric Holder is right: Trump's description of a dangerous American hellscape is wrong," *Vox* (July 26, 2016).

89   Inimai Chettiar and Ames Grawert, "Why Donald Trump Is Wrong About Crime," *U.S. News & World Report* (July 22, 2016); Neil Howe, "What's Behind The Decline In Crime?" *Forbes* (May 28, 2015).

90   Ezra Klein, "Donald Trump doesn't want to make America great. He wants to make it afraid." *Vox* (July 21, 2016).

91   Eliza Collins, "Clinton: America is already great," *Politico* (Mar. 1, 2016).

92   Peter Sullivan, "17 million gained coverage under ObamaCare, study finds," *The Hill* (May 6, 2015).

93   "Labor Force Statistics from the Current Population Survey," Bureau of Labor Statistics (2016).

94   Mark Hensch, "Dems selling 'America is already great' hat," *The Hill* (Oct. 9, 2015).

95   Kaitlyn Schallhorn, "DNC 'America Is Already Great' Parody Hats Offend College Students," *The Blaze* (Oct. 31, 2015).

96   "Full text: Donald Trump 2016 RNC draft speech transcript," *Politico* (July 21, 2016).

97   Glenn Kessler and Michelle Ye Hee Lee, "Fact Checking Donald Trump's convention speech: A dark vision based on specious stats," *The Washington Post* (July 21, 2016).

98   Ben Casselman, "The Economy Will Probably Be Pretty Good On Election Day," *FiveThirtyEight* (July 22, 2016).

99   Janell Ross, "Donald Trump's favorite black pastor may not be best source on black unemployment," *The Washington Post* (July 20, 2016); Tessa Dixon Murray, "Donald Trump misstates unemployment among black youths," *The Cleveland Plain-Dealer* (July 22, 2016).

100   Rakesh Kochhar and Richard Fry, "Wealth inequality has widened along racial, ethnic lines since end of Great Recession," *Pew Research Center* (Dec. 12, 2014).

101   Sonari Glinton, "Unemployment May Be Dropping, But It's Still Twice As High For Blacks," *NPR* (Feb. 5, 2016).

102   Annamaria Andriotis and Robin Sidel, "Balance Due: Credit-Card Debt Nears $1 Trillion as Banks Push Plastic," *The Wall Street Journal* (May 20, 2016).

103   Chris Arnold, "Millions of Americans' Wages Seized Over Credit Card And Medical Debt," *NPR* (Sept. 15, 2014).

104   Matthew Desmond, "Forced Out," *The New Yorker* (Feb. 8, 2016).

105   Olga Khazan, "Middle-Aged White Americans Are Dying of Despair," *The Atlantic* (Nov. 4, 2015).

106   Trip Gabriel, "50 Years Into the War on Poverty, Hardship Hits Back," *The New York Times* (Apr. 20, 2014).

107   Betsy McKay, "Life Expectancy for White Americans Declines," *The Wall Street Journal* (Apr. 20, 2016). There is some controversy over these statistics. See Andrew Gelman, "Is The Death Rate Really Increasing For Middle-Aged White Americans?" *Slate* (Nov. 11, 2015).

108   Maggie Fox, "Americans Are Drinking More – A Lot More," *NBC News* (Aug. 22, 2014).

109   Christopher Ingraham, "The incredible crushing despair of the white working class," *The Washington Post* (June 7, 2016).

110   "Matt Ferner, "Chomsky: Donald Trump Is Winning Because White America Is Dying," *The Huffington Post* (Feb. 26, 2016).

111   Quoted in Rod Dreher, "Trump: Tribune of Poor White People," *The American Conservative* (July 22, 2016).

112   Hillary Clinton on Twitter (July 22, 2016), https://twitter.com/HillaryClinton/status/756612369070055425

113   "American Deaths in Terrorist Attacks," National Consortium for the Study of Terrorism and Responses to Terrorism (2014).

114   See Ford Fessenden and Haeyoun Park, "Chicago's Murder Problem," *The New York Times* (May 26, 2016).

115   Trump RNC speech, *supra.*

116   Zack Beauchamp, "Brexit was fueled by irrational xenophobia, not real economic grievances," *Vox* (Jun. 27, 2016).

117   Adam Taylor, "The uncomfortable question: Was the Brexit vote based on racism?" *The Washington Post* (June 25, 2016).

118   Bob Davis, "Immigrants Push Down Wages for Low-Income Workers—But How Much?" *The Wall Street Journal* (Feb. 9, 2016). See also Brianna Rennix, "Some Troublesome Questions for Liberals On Borders," *Current Affairs* (Oct. 23, 2016).

119   Fredrik deBoer, "When Will Pro-Trade Journalists Begin Outsourcing Themselves?" *Current Affairs* (May/June 2016).

120   Tim Worstall, "2020 AD: By Now, Half The World's Wealth Is Controlled by Millionaires," *Forbes* (June 8, 2016); Larry Elliott, "World's eight richest people have same wealth as poorest 50%," *The Guardian* (Jan. 15, 2017).

121   Rich Yeselson, "The Decline of Labor, the Increase of Inequality," *Talking Points Memo* (Nov. 2015).

122   Emmett Rensin, "The Smug Style in American Liberalism," *Vox* (Apr. 21, 2016).

123   Maya Rhodan, "President Obama on Donald Trump: America Is Already Great," *TIME* (June 1, 2016).

124   Barack H. Obama, "United States Health Care Reform: Progress to Date and Next Steps," *Journal of the American Medical Association,* Vol. 316, No. 5 (2016), pp. 525-532. Then, in January, after Clinton had lost the election, and at the very time when it would have when it would have been useful to be Trump-proofing the White House and finding some more people to pardon (and immediately before his retirement would liberate him to spend his days producing as much academic writing as he pleased), Obama would release *two more* journal articles. See Barack H. Obama, "The Irreversible Momentum of Clean Energy," *Science* (2017) and Barack H. Obama, "The President's Role in Advancing Criminal Justice Reform," *Harv. L. Rev.* 811 (2017).

125   Andrew Sullivan, "America Has Never Been So Ripe For Tyranny," *New York* (May 1, 2016).

126   Andrew Sullivan, "Andrew Sullivan Liveblogs the RNC, Night 4," *New York* (July 21, 2016).

127   Anna Maria Barry-Jester and Ben Casselman, "33 Million

Americans Still Don't Have Health Insurance," *FiveThirtyEight* (Sept. 28, 2015).

128   Jonathan Easley, "Woman at Sanders rally tearfully details life in poverty," *The Hill* (Jan. 25, 2016).

129   "New Media Guru Clay Shirky Drops 'Stop Trump Tweetstorm On White Liberals," *Talking Points Memo* (July 22, 2016).

130   Amy Chozick, Alan Rappeport, and Jonathan Martin, "Hillary Clinton Selects Tim Kaine, a Popular Senator from a Swing State, as Running Mate," *The New York Times* (July 22, 2016).

131   Jenna Johnson, "Donald Trump's vision of doom and despair in America," *The Washington Post* (July 21, 2016).

132   Nicholas Fitz, "Economic Inequality: It's Far Worse Than You Think," *Scientific American* (Mar. 31, 2015).

133   Emily Cuddy, Joanna Venator, and Richard V. Reeves, "In a land of dollars: Deep poverty and its consequences," The Brookings Institution (May 7, 2015).

134   Christine Rushton, "Liberals rip into Tim Kaine over letter that they see as pro-banking," *The Los Angeles Times* (July 22, 2016).

135   Matthew Yglesias, "4 Winners and 3 Losers in Hillary Clinton's vice presidential pick," *Vox* (July 22, 2016). Yglesias cites Kaine's pick as a rebuke to the left and a gift to centrists, writing: *"Progressive activists have been enjoying a rising tide of intra-party political power ever since the 2014 midterms… It even looked for a brief, shining moment like they might be able to install Warren as the vice president. But nope! You get boring, centrist Tim Kaine! What are you going to do — vote for Donald Trump?"* The answer to that question turned out, quite predictably, to be "No, stay home."

INDEX

ACKNOWLEDGMENTS

I AM INDEBTED TO MY MANY EXTRAORDINARY FRIENDS FOR helping me through the exhausting production of this book. I could not possibly thank all of them by name here, but I would like to give special mention to Amber Phelps, Paul Waters-Smith, Sarah Hailey, Sparky Abraham, Fiona Heckscher, Zach Wehrwein, Robert Manduca, and Matt Kaliner. Bart Bonikowski has been extremely kind in tolerating my ineptitude. Oren Nimni has, as usual, been a stalwart friend and colleague without whom this could not have happened. This project was also made possible by the great editorial staff of *Current Affairs*: Amber Frost, Yasmin Nair, Alex Nichols, Tyler Rosebush, and Brianna Rennix. Thanks to Greg Valen for exceptional and diligent copyediting. Finally, my parents continue to be endlessly supportive and indulgent, and I cannot possibly thank them enough.

As can be seen from the copious endnotes, this work was entirely made possible by the work of the diligent journalists who have made it their business to unearth the facts about Trump over the past thirty years. I am indebted to all of those who came before me and on whose work I draw.

About the Author

NATHAN J. ROBINSON IS A POLITICAL COMMENTATOR and attorney based in Louisiana. He is the editor of *Current Affairs* magazine, and has written about politics for numerous publications including *The Nation, The New Republic, Salon, The Washington Post, Al Jazeera America,* and *Jacobin.* He is a graduate of Yale Law School and a PhD student in Sociology and Social Policy at Harvard University. He is also the author of *Superpredator: Bill Clinton's Use and Abuse of Black America, Blueprints for a Sparkling Tomorrow* (with Oren Nimni), and *The Mayor of New Orleans Gets Her Way: A Child's Municipal Policy Adventure.*

About *Current Affairs*

CURRENT AFFAIRS IS A BIMONTHLY PRINT MAGAZINE OF political commentary, journalism, and satire. It's a fresh, fearless, and independent antidote to contemporary political media. We focus on challenging preconceptions and undermining orthodoxies. *Current Affairs* showcases some of the country's best contemporary writers, and is edited by a highly experienced team of professionals with backgrounds in law, literature, design, technology, and politics. We bring a sharp critical eye to the absurdities of modern American life, and provide a new and unique set of perspectives on major political issues.

currentaffairs.org

Printed in Great Britain
by Amazon